Offshore Fishing
From Virginia to Texas

OFFSHORE FISHING FROM VIRGINIA TO TEXAS

Robert J. Goldstein

John F. Blair, Publisher
Winston-Salem, North Carolina

Designed by Debra L. Hampton
Cover photograph by Joel Arrington

Black and white photographs
by the author unless otherwise noted

Composition by Superior Typesetters
Manufactured by Port City Press

On the opposite page—

*Three days in April of 1987 saw some
of the best fishing ever off Oregon Inlet,
North Carolina. Captains and mates of* Best Revenge,
Billfisher, *and* Fight-N-Lady *pose
with four whopping blue marlin.*
Photo by Vanessa Foreman, Dare County Tourist Bureau

Library of Congress Cataloging in Publication Data

Goldstein, Robert J. (Robert Jay), 1937-
Offshore fishing from Virginia to Texas.

Includes index.
1. Saltwater fishing—Southern States.   2. Saltwater
fishing—Mexico, Gulf of.   I. Title.
SH464.S68G65 1988   799.1'66148   88-2893
ISBN 0-89587-058-4 (pbk.)

To
the Oregon Inlet
Fishing Center
charter boat fleet
and the
Raleigh Salt Water Sportfishing Club,
with gratitude for all you've taught me.

Contents

Foreword

Fishing books reflect the author's attempt to be inspirational, boastful, or helpful. Whatever the intent, the reader will find the book good, bad, or indifferent. Like everyone else, I'd rather read a good book than a bad one, but, if it's helpful enough, I'll doggedly plow through a treatise. Maybe it's because my fishing skills are eternally in need of help, but I've always been partial to helpful books, especially good ones.

Bob Goldstein has written a good, helpful book. If I'd had this book years ago when I first started fishing the southeast coast, it would have saved me a lot of time and confusion. As I read the manuscript, I found myself taking notes of things I want to remember for that Florida fishing trip I hope to take this winter: good, practical stuff that will make the trip more fun.

I've already had a lot of fun chuckling over the author's testy impatience with the "adolescent silliness" indulged in by "the TV clowns with silly hats." I don't so much mind their using fly rods in salt water for "gimmicky stories" as I do the monotony of their plots. Sometimes I think that panel discussions of global monetary trends are more entertaining than bass being caught one after the other, supported by such erudite commentary as, "Son, I b'lieve that's a better fish."

As I sit here, deskbound and facing a northern winter, I itch to get out there and try what I have learned from this book. I own a lot of fishing books, and I often have two copies of the most useful ones: an archival copy for the book shelf and another that can travel with me semiprotected in a Zip-lock bag. I'll need two copies of this one.

Gary Soucie
New York City

Offshore fishing in the southern states is not the same as it is elsewhere. The fishing grounds and the fish are different, the boats are different, and the methods vary from state to state. That's important.

Some states are better than all the rest for certain kinds of fishing, and the people who fish there are the best. Nobody knows black drum like the small boaters who fish Delaware Bay. Nobody knows sailfishing better than the regulars in south Florida.

That's why a group of hotshots from Wilmington, North Carolina can trailer their center-consoles down to Florida year after year and truck on back home with an outrageous share of the prizes from the Jacksonville Open King Mackerel Tournament, smirking all the way. When it comes to kings, they're tops and they know it. But they'll stay home rather than compete against the Floridians for sailfish.

In this book, you'll learn the methods practiced today by the hard-fishing regulars who catch 90% of the fish. Not the TV clowns with silly hats who use fly rods in salt water for gimmicky stories. If you're interested in that adolescent silliness, go watch television. If you want to learn about real fishing as it's done by the best fishermen around, then read on.

You may wonder why I'd go to the trouble of spending years researching and writing a book like this, finding and then giving away some of the best-kept secret methods and secret places, and laying it all open for anyone to see. Hell, I did it for the money.

Acknowledgments

I am very grateful to the following individuals for providing data or suggestions:

Henry Ansley, Georgia Department of Natural Resources, Brunswick; Bud Cannon, Dare County Tourist Bureau, Manteo, N.C.; Kent Cullen, R & R Systems, New Smyrna Beach, Fl.; Gary Graham, Texas A & M University Sea Grant, College Station; Elmer J. Gutherz, National Marine Fisheries Service, Pascagoula, Ms.; Bill Hosking, Alabama Sea Grant Cooperative Extension Service, Mobile; Bill Hogarth, North Carolina Division of Marine Fisheries, Morehead City; Tom Leahy, Florida Sea Grant Cooperative Extension Service, Gainesville; Jon Lucy, Virginia Sea Grant Advisory Service, Gloucester Point; Gary Matlock, Texas Parks and Wildlife Department, Austin; Michael H. Meier, Virginia Marine Resources Commission, Newport News; Charles J. Moore, South Carolina Wildlife and Marine Resources Department, Charleston; Fentress H. (Red) Munden, North Carolina Division of Marine Fisheries, Morehead City; Liz Noble, North Carolina Division of Marine Fisheries, Morehead City; Mac V. Rawson, Georgia Sea Grant Marine Extension Service, Brunswick; James H. Rhodes, National Marine Electronics Association, Norfolk, Va.; Keith Richmond, United Nations Food and Agriculture Organization, Rome, Italy; Norma Stoppelbein, Florida League of Anglers, Sanibel Island; C. David Veal, Mississippi Sea Grant Advisory Service, Biloxi; and Susan Wright, BOAT/U.S. Foundation for Boating Safety, Alexandria, Va.

I want to particularly express my thanks to George Reiger, Conservation Editor of *Field and Stream*, Gary Soucie, Executive Editor of *Audubon Magazine*, and Claude M. Bain, III, Director of the Virginia Fishing Tournament, for reading the entire raw manuscript and making an enormous (and often embarrassing) number of corrections. There is no editor like a tough editor, and I appreciate their no-nonsense approach to what is usually a thankless job. I've incorporated virtually all their advice, and hope the patient wasn't too far gone. Gentlemen, thank you!

INTRODUCTION

The serious fisherman doesn't need any advice on his own turf. He knows the best methods, best tackle, best rigs, the best time to go, and the best fishing grounds. But he's an expert only in his home area, and sometimes only at one kind of fishing.

In the pages that follow, we'll go over the skills that every serious fisherman should have before venturing offshore, whether for cobia or marlin. We'll review the newer types of saltwater fishing equipment and techniques used for each kind of game fish. We'll discuss the facts about each kind of fish, and learn what they really eat, and when they're really in our waters. We'll find out if it's safe to take all we can catch, and if not, then why not.

Perhaps you're planning a charter trip for tuna or billfish. Maybe you want to get on a headboat to fish the deep reefs of the Gulf Stream for groupers. Or maybe your own boat is capable of offshore fishing, but you need to know the Loran coordinates of hot spots away from home.

This is a guidebook for the serious southern saltwater fisherman who wants to be as good away from home as he is on his own turf. If you follow every bit of advice in this book, you still might not be as successful away from home as one of the regulars. But you'll be pretty damned good.

Offshore Fishing
From Virginia to Texas

Heading Offshore

Basic Training
and Equipment

Navigation

T he United States has always been a maritime nation, and love of seamanship is a part of our national heritage. Perhaps that's why we have such a strong nationwide system of training in boat safety and navigation. You don't have to live on Cape Cod to learn seamanship; you can live in St. Louis and get the same training. We have opportunities everywhere for learning seamanship. To determine the location of the nearest U.S. Coast Guard Auxiliary or U.S. Power Squadron boating course, telephone 1-800-336-BOAT.

Boating has changed as improvements in power plants, expanded construction of artificial reefs, and advances in navigation have made more hot spots and a wider range available to fishermen from virtually every port in the southeast. The greater opportunities require more knowledge of navigation. You can now go far offshore, precisely to specific wrecks and outcrops, and have great confidence in getting back, even in dense fog. In an emergency, you can call for help over much greater distances, and with the assurance that you can provide a precise location to your rescuer.

That's all the more reason that a solid course in boating is essential to every boat owner.

A good boating course will use a top-notch textbook like Bowditch's *Piloting*, Saunders' *Small Craft Piloting & Coastal Navigation*, Markell's *Coastal Navigation for the Small Boat Sailor*, or *Chapman's Piloting*. An excellent publication is the U.S. Coast Guard Auxiliary's *Coastal Piloting*. The Power Squadrons and the Coast Guard also offer advanced courses leading to the possibility of earning a captain's license.

What can you learn in a basic boating course? Basic navigation begins with an understanding of magnetic vs. geographic north, local magnetic disturbances, the calculation of distances and directions over water, and use of the compass rose, course plotter, or parallel rulers to "lay a course" using appropriate nautical charts. You'll also learn about alternative tools, such as paired triangles, a course protractor, or a "courser."

COMPASS NAVIGATION   Because compass navigation is in nautical miles, latitude and longitude, you need to know that latitude and longitude are in distance (not time) units of minutes and seconds, where a nautical mile equals one minute of latitude and one-tenth of a nautical mile equals six seconds of latitude. You'll learn to calculate distance, speed, and time from the relationship of $D = SxT/60$, $S = Dx60/T$, and $T = Dx60/S$. You'll learn to read channel markers and charts (sea maps), hazards to navigation (such as shoals), and the location of channels. You'll learn to account for the effects of wind and currents in your calculations, and tides where rocks are close to the surface. You'll learn about dead reckoning, and how to get a fix on a point offshore by learning to spot the intersections of pairs of landmarks. You'll learn about required boat equipment, who enforces the laws, safety, rules of the road, and the consequences of failure to abide by every detail you're taught. Perhaps your most important lesson will be the seriousness with which expert boaters take and teach these courses. And if you still have questions, you can call the U.S. Coast Guard Hotline at 1-800-368-5647.

LORAN C NAVIGATION   Loran C navigation is used to locate artificial and natural reefs, rocky outcrops, wrecks, and other structures, to navigate through several changes in distance and direction, and to get home in fog or at night. How does it work?

Loran (LOng Range Aid to Navigation) is a system of 100 kiloHertz radio signals sent at microsecond intervals from Coast Guard transmitting stations around the country. For each area, there's a master transmitting station and at least two secondary or slave stations. The combination of a master and its slaves is known as a chain. For each master and each slave, there is a distinct time difference in receipt of the radio pulses, known as the Group Repetition Interval or GRI. In our region, we utilize the southeastern chain, with a GRI of 7980 microseconds between the transmission of the master and the firing of its secondaries. The master is located in Malone, Florida, and the secondaries or slaves in Grangeville, Louisiana; Jupiter, Florida; Carolina Beach, North Carolina; and Raymondville, Texas. The boat-mounted Loran C receiver records the time differences (TDs) between the radio pulses it receives from the master and the preferred (closest to a right angle) secondary, and sometimes two secondaries. These time differences give you not points, but lines of position or LOPS. The LOPS from two or more TDs intersect at your Loran coordinates, equivalent to a specific latitude and longitude, but far more precise. An added advantage is the high repeatability, often (close to shore) within 50 feet of a previous plotting. Loran can be slightly off due to interference (which can be controlled with notch filters), partial overland transmission (this can be corrected), extreme weather, or regional problems in areas such as the western portion of the Gulf of Mexico.

Navigation with Loran C is similar to compass navigation in the use of overprinted charts and dividers or card plotters to plot positions. It should be used with, and not as a substitute for, compass navigation.

Articles in current sportfishing magazines will keep you updated on features, costs, and uses of Loran C units. The National Marine Electronics Association sells an excellent booklet, *Guide to Loran C*, available from NMEA, 1216 Granby Street, Suite 18, Norfolk, Va. 23510 (804-622-9639). The Coast Guard publishes the *Loran C Users Handbook* (M16562.3) available from the Superintendant of Documents, U.S. Government Printing Office, Washington, D.C. 20402 as stock number 726-183/1295 (telephone 202-783-3283 for orders, 202-275-3054 for problems). Instructional videotapes are available from Bennett Video (730 Washington Street, Marina del Rey, Ca. 90292) or SiTex (P.O. Box 6700, Clearwater, Fl. 33518).

In the rear half of this book, you'll find Loran C coordinates for wrecks, artificial and natural reefs, and other structures listed by state. These stations are all within reach of recreational fishing boats. Commercial fishing boats often work much farther offshore, where the water depths exceed a hundred fathoms and canyons and other complex structures break up the bottom. Long range fishing boats interested in significant hard bottom information are referred to :

1. *Bottom Obstructions in the Southwestern North Atlantic, Gulf of Mexico, and Caribbean Sea*, by G.M. Russell and coworkers, 1977, NOAA Tech. Report NMFS SSRF-715 (Supt. of Documents, Washington, D.C. 20402, Stock No. 003-020-00140-8. Data in Loran A coordinates).

2. *Hangs and Obstructions to Trawl Fishing, Atlantic Coast of the United States*, by J.A. McGee and R.H. Tillett, 1983, UNC Sea Grant Program, UNC-SG-83-01 (UNC Sea Grant, 105 1911 Building, North Carolina State University, Raleigh 27650).

3. *Hangs and Bottom Obstructions of the Texas/Louisiana Coast, Loran C*, by G.L. Graham, 1983, Texas A & M University Sea Grant Program, TAMU-SG-81-501 (Texas A & M University, Sea Grant College Program, College Station 77843).

Of particular interest to Gulf of Mexico offshore fishermen are the 4,000 blue water oil and gas drilling rigs from Florida to Texas. The U.S. Coast Guard Eighth District keeps the public apprised of their locations through weekly notices to mariners. To get on the mailing list, call the Aids to Navigation Branch in New Orleans at 504-589-6234. You can purchase the most recent *"Listing of Offshore Oil, Gas, Mineral and Related Structures Including Sub-sea Installations in the Eighth Coast Guard District"* for $90 postpaid from Corporate Search International, P.O. Box 50519, Dallas, Tx. 75250 (214-742-9624). The listings are all in latitude and longitude.

A twenty-year-old navigational system (SATNAV), based on TRANSIT satellites, is in use for military and commercial ships, but is too expensive for private boats. It depends on the satellites being in line-of-sight with the receiver for an accurate fix. In the next few years, expect the Global Positioning System (GPS) to replace Loran. GPS will be based on a large number of satellites, with four at a time giving a fix down to a few yards anywhere in the world. The technology is here, but the satellites are not yet in orbit, and costs of the receiver units are unknown.

Purchasing Electronics

Today's electronics have brought advanced features, previously seen only on naval and commercial ships, into the price range of the average owner of a small boat. However, not all brands are equal, and price is not a reliable indicator of quality. Ask other boaters (not salesmen) what brands they've been happy with over the years, and which ones have given them problems. Read product reviews in fishing magazines. Stick with established marine electronics companies like SiTex, Furuno, Lowrance, Humminbird, Datamarine, Genetron, Ray Jefferson, Standard Communications, International Marine, Northstar, and Raytheon, and then go for their latest, full-featured units. Avoid consumer electronics companies that also make telephones. Buy your unit from somebody qualified to service it. With these warnings in mind, let's look at basic electronics for the modern sportfishing machine.

Radio   You can take your citizens' band (CB) radio out to the lake, but its limited range (not much more than line-of-sight) makes it inadequate and unsafe for offshore communications. You need a marine radio. Today's VHF (very high frequency) marine radios cost about $250 to $350, and offer waterproof construction, quick disconnect for removal from the boat, multiple weather channels, programmable private channels, scanning and monitoring of Channel 16 (which the Coast Guard also monitors) and of any other channels you wish. VHF radios have a range of less than about 25 miles, and you still need to remain within radio range of other boats for safety. You can get radio-telephone hookups for very little additional cost. Single side band (SSB) radios have a far greater range, but are expensive.

Radar When fog covers a group of boats in a channel, radar can be a lifesaver. But fog isn't common enough to warrant buying an expensive ($1,300 to $6,000) radar. Its value is to the skipper who navigates in the dark, perhaps because he leaves very early to catch menhaden in the Intracoastal Waterway or night-fishes for swordfish. If that's your activity, then radar is worth the money for your boat.

Modern radars are digitized, with variably illuminated screens bright enough to view in full daylight. They all have essentially the same features, including six or more ranges from 1/4 to 16, 24, or 48 miles, rain and snow clutter eliminators, interference rejectors, electronic bearing lines, range markers, visual and audible alarms, and three or five kilowatt transmitters. Some have Loran interfaces.

Loran C Today's Lorans start at about $500 and run to four times that amount. But the optional (and often standard) features are staggering, including automatic interconversion with latitude/longitude coordinates (enabling you to punch in either parameter and get a readout in both), quick-disconnect, rechargeable battery packs (in case of failure of the boat's electrical system), remote control, liquid crystal map display, automatic pilot, up to a hundred programmable waypoints, memory, filters for improved reception, and highly accurate estimated time of arrival. If you already own an older unit that doesn't read latitude and longitude, or you have lots of latitude/longitude data for hot spots in your area, you can get a computer program that interconverts these parameters from R & R Systems of New Smyrna Beach, Fl. (904-427-5476).

Depth Sounders Depth sounders or "fish finders" are underwater radars or sonars. They go hand-in-hand with Loran C, enabling you to precisely locate and then "see" ledges, dropoffs, pinnacles, sunken barges and Liberty ships, and other underwater features, all with very high repeatability and accuracy. By using your Loran unit to locate these features and your depth sounder to verify (or correct) the coordinates, you can generate a virtual three-dimensional map of the sea floor in the range of your boat.

These units are also called "fish finders" because they reflect not only hard structures like rocks, but soft materials like vegetation and schools or individual fish above the bottom. You can examine an entire reef with your depth sounder and locate sites (perhaps upcurrent) where large fish are concentrated at the moment. You can also tell if a structure is barren of fish large enough to produce big, distinct echos.

The basic types of depth sounders are video, chart, liquid-crystal display (LCD), and cathode ray tube (CRT) telescan video sonars. Color video units are very fast and sensitive. Chart recorders are slower because it takes time to print the rather expensive paper, but you get a permanent record to examine and keep; the additional moving parts make repair costs likely. LCDs are inexpensive and don't have the resolution of either video or chart recorders, but can retain images in memory for recall. CRT telescan video sonars convert the sonar signal into a two-dimensional image of the bottom on a television screen, and are priced from about $300 to $600.

Modern units combine two or more types with additional features. A typical, modern "fish finder" combines LCD or video with an optional chart switch. Other features are digital depth displays on-screen, concurrent pH or temperature measurement at the water surface (which is your transducer depth), Loran (and latitude/longitude) interface, image zoom, speed log, bottom lock, and image recall. Prices for these combination, full-featured units run from about $350 to $800.

Underwater acoustic technology is the fastest-changing area of marine electronics. Scientific units in use today are able to acoustically determine the biomass of plankton in an area, the size of a school of fish and the average size of fish in the school, and even estimate the total size of the stock when integrated with other data.

Sandbar Shark

Fishing Tackle

T ackle today is more than rods, reels, and rigs. It includes live wells, downriggers, and all the gadgets a fisherman uses to enhance chances for a hookup. The choice of tackle is more a matter of fishing conditions, familiarity, and personal taste than it is cost. For every high-priced item, there is a reasonable alternative.

Because conventional, revolving-spool tackle is standard offshore, and because this tackle varies greatly in features and quality, it is the only gear we'll discuss in detail. Spinning tackle is mechanically and operationally simple, reliable when well-built, limited in what it can handle, and very useful for small-game bottomfishing and light tackle casting. You probably already know all about it and don't need to read anything further on the subject. Fly-fishing is a specialty of a small group of (mostly TV) fishermen, but for the rest of us saltwater fishermen it is neither the way we fish nor care to fish, and it won't be covered.

How do we fish? Some people prefer high-speed trolling with artificial lures off flatlines and outriggers, while others prefer a slow, deliberate pull of live menhaden off a pair of downriggers. In Florida, many skippers swear by kites bouncing live bait on the surface, and some Carolina skippers won't go out without a daisy chain of plastic squid. Are these items useful? Do they pay for themselves? If they work for you, then the answer is yes. We'll take a brief look at the principal gear used by today's saltwater fishermen.

Daiwa Sealine [R]
Lever Drag Series

Photo courtesy of the Daiwa Corporation

Reels

I f you're an old hand at saltwater fishing, you probably own a Penn Squidder or Jigmaster for surf, pier, jetty, and bottomfishing and perhaps a 6/0 Senator for grouper or shark fishing. Penn reels are virtually unbreakable, and you have to drop one on concrete to bend the spool or crack the side plate. You could also take one apart for cleaning and become more sympathetic to all the king's horses and all the king's men. These older reels are excellent for bottomfishing and going after both small and very large game, as well as passing on to your descendants.

But today's fishermen are live bait aficionados and require high-speed, precision reels with features like centrifugal or magnetic anti-backlash devices, and lightweight, single-piece construction. Penn and several other companies have responded to that need.

The most popular offshore reels are the 20-, 30- and 50-pound-class models, with 80- and 130-pound-class reels used exclusively for giant bluefin tuna, blue marlin, and sharks. For bigeye and yellowfin tuna and most billfish, the standard charter boat reels are the lever drag Penn International 50 and 80 models, but they cost $300 and up, and are outside the price range of the average sportfisherman. In the same class are the Daiwa SLT series reels, giving you some choice.

Spinning Tackle

A big notch down in price are the Daiwa LD series and the Shimano TLD series, which feature a lever drag that operates much like the Penn Internationals. For casting or high-speed fishing, Penn's newer models are its HS (high speed) and GTi (graphite and titanium) casting and trolling reels in the 20- to 30-pound-class size range. In the same category is the Daiwa Sealine H series, which features a quick no-tool takedown for replacing the spool, and the Shimano Triton trolling (TT) and Speedmaster (TSM) series of reels. There are other acceptable reels for high-speed fishing, such as the Newells and the Garcia Ambassadeur 9,000 and 10,000 CA, preferred by many king mackerel fishermen. Mitchell's model 782, which looks like a big saltwater fly-fishing reel, is being advertised as a downrigger fishing reel. As with electronics, check out various brands and models with other fishermen before settling on a particular reel.

Rods

Boat rods are usually stiff, six- to seven-foot sticks (except for downrigger rods), that vary in heaviness, operation, construction, and (especially) in price. Big-game, sit-down trolling rods cost about $350. Other high-quality, saltwater conventional rods range in price from $50 to $125.

You can make your own rod from components, but I've never seen a homemade rod that was cheaper to build than its ready-made equivalent. Very good rods can be purchased from a coastal tackle shop or major mail-order house. It's a good idea to go through catalogs to learn what features the major manufacturers are offering in this year's models. It's better to wait for the rod you want than take what's on the shelf at the moment.

Big-game trolling rods made to work with fighting chairs (80- or 130-pound-class tackle) have a bent aluminum butt with a notched base and a fiberglass or graphite composite tip above the reel seat. The notch fits into a gimbal on the chair, and the bend allows the angler to more easily stay within arm's length of the reel while pumping. To pump a straight rod from a chair, the fisherman must reach far forward to keep the butt in the gimbal. The chair rod has chromed roller guides throughout, including the guide at the outer (tip-top) position.

New, medium-weight rods are available for stand-up big-game fishing with 30- to 50-pound-class tackle. The butt is usually straight, with the notch fitting into a belt- or apron-mounted gimbal. The rod blank is a single piece of graphite or composite, from tip-top through the slip-over reel seat, all the way to the base of the butt. The guides are fixed and constructed of ceramic or silicon carbide. In some models, the outermost (tip-top) guide or the first base (stripper) guide is a metal roller.

For slow-trolling with big live baits, lighter, 20- or 30-pound-class tackle is preferred. A typical slow-trolling rod is fiberglass, graphite, or composite; there are seven or eight fixed (non-roller) ceramic or silicon carbide guides along the tip; and the reel seat is made of composite material rather than metal. There may or may not be a notched base. The taper is slow, meaning that the rod bends evenly throughout the tip, rather than increasingly toward the top. This enables the whole rod to be used in hauling the bait, as well as putting pressure on a hooked fish the size of a king mackerel.

For stand-up drift-fishing with smaller live baits, similar 20- to 30-pound-class tackle is used, but many anglers prefer a fast-tip rod, which helps keep small live baits from being wrenched from the hook with the tossing of the boat.

Examples of the big sit-down rods are the Penn IGFA Internationals, Fenwick IGFA Trolling, and Daiwa IGFA Special Tournament series. Comparable are the less well-known Sabre Custom Stroker series and the Kunnan IGFA series. Penn's Special Senator and Senator II rods are lower priced, comparable to the Daiwa Beefsticks. The stand-up "tuna sticks" are in between. The Shimano Speedmaster series runs the gamut from big-game trolling to live-bait rods. Daiwa, Penn, Fenwick, Shimano, Eagle Claw, Berkeley, and several other major companies make "live-bait" rods characterized by a lot of guides, a slow taper, and composite materials for the guides and reel seat, giving the entire rod an extremely light total weight.

Downrigger rods are different. The typical rod is a one-piece eight- or nine-foot stick, very light and limber, with about ten reinforced ceramic bridge guides. Look for steelhead salmon rods or popping rods. If you can't locate exactly what you need, you can take a heavy spinning rod and replace the big metal guides with ceramic conventional rings or use a live-bait rod.

You can get a rod at a discount department store for $5 or $10, but you get what you pay for. Cheap rods are heavy, made with brittle blanks or corrosion-prone metals, and have fragile guides that frequently pop apart. Because rods should not wear out, you should own and fish with the best you can afford, even for small game. The best way to learn the difference in rod quality is to use a cheap big rod on big inshore fish like sharks and amberjack. They'll teach you a lot about rods in a hurry.

Outriggers

A pair of outriggers marks the professional 30-to 50-foot offshore charter boat, but more and more private small boat owners are finding them easy to operate on 24-foot craft. Outriggers let you troll two lines in addition to your two or four flatlines, and more if you're experienced. Outriggers are intended to fish surface baits at any speed well away from the boat's wake. They take pressure off the rod tip during trolling and can be adjusted to fish the bait various distances back and slightly below the surface, but mostly away from all your other baits. They can also be used to pull baits for light tackle, tackle incapable of directly trolling a big bait at high speed.

An outrigger is just a rotating flagpole with an extra-heavy monofilament line as a lanyard with which to hoist the "flag" or clip. When not in use, the outrigger is either removed from the boat or locked in the straight up or straight down position. To troll, you swing it about 45 degrees outboard. The important part of an outrigger is its clip, because that's the part that must hold your line during high-speed trolling and must let it go on a strike. Clips come with flat plate grips or grips made of opposing rounded heads, like pencil erasers. The grip tension must be set carefully by an experienced hand; if you're new at it, then use a spring scale to set the preferred number of pounds of pressure. Note that the clip holds the fishing line itself—not the leader, not a tag, and not a piece of terminal tackle. The clip must grip the line without its fraying or abrading, and that requires a strong hold and a smooth surface. Even so, there is a tendency for the line to slip under the strain of the dragging bait. Twisting the line and inserting a loop will prevent the line from slipping through the clip's jaws. The standard clips on the market are Black's, Trip-Eze Single and Double, Aftco rollers, Nok-Out, and Snapper. Try several on other boats, and then decide which type you prefer. Outriggers and clips are not expensive (about $100 for a complete set).

Wire Line, Drails, and Planers

You can troll below the surface for bluefish or mackerel using wire line, which is expensive and difficult to handle, since it readily forms coils which seek out reel handles and rod guides. When it's not wrapping around your tackle or fingers, single-strand wire kinks and braided wire frays. Wire doesn't weigh enough to get you down very far anyway. You can add a drail, an elongated sinker with a ring eye at each end, and this will pull your leader down a little deeper, but not much. Wire line also requires special narrow spool reels like the Penn Sailfisher, and heavy rollers to avoid eating notches in your guides. I don't like wire and don't know anyone who still uses it. There are more effective ways to get down.

The most popular planer in our area is a flat piece of stainless steel, either chrome or flat black, with a ring at the back end and a weighted metal slide at the front. Clip your line's snap-swivel to the back side of the metal slide so that the planer, when pulled, dives downward. When strong pressure is exerted from a strike at the rear and the planer is momentarily jerked to a virtual standstill, the line rides up the slide to the front and the planer is jerked into a near-horizontal position so that it rides back upward until it is running straight through the water.

Sea Striker makes planers in several sizes to match your tackle. The SSP1 is the smallest and is ideal for Spanish or Boston mackerel fishing. For medium tackle fishing, the SSP3 or SSP4BR is appropriate. Many charter boat skippers use a big OS24 planer off a line tied directly to the boat's transom for wahoo offshore and king mackerel inshore. Commercial king mackerel fishermen use them on hand lines.

There are several efficient and easy-to-use plastic planers. A couple of recommended types are the Doel-Fin (Valencia, Ca.) Fish Seeker, and Penco Tackle's (Destin, Fl.) Command-Trol tubular planer.

Downriggers

F ish are often down deep and just won't come up to a surface lure. If the mountain won't come to Mohammad.... Downriggers are easy to use, and permit you to troll deeply, near the bottom if you prefer. No offshore sportfisherman should be without them. Often, fish follow a particular subsurface isotherm or concentration of food, prefer a particular distance above structure, or are averse to coming to the surface because of the light, traffic, or just because they're ornery. Downriggers take your terminal tackle where the fish are with minimum bow in the line and allow you to use reasonably light tackle encumbered with a minimum of hardware.

The downrigger is a big winch that is bolted to a stern transom plate and is readily removed (by you or anyone else) when the boat is unattended. Get one that swivels and locks in position, an electric model if you can afford it. The oversize, narrow reel holds up to 200 feet of 135-pound-test stainless steel cable attached to one of two eyes, one on top and the other slightly in front, on a 6- or 10-pound round or elongated "cannonball" with a release clip on the back side. Round balls are for normal slow running, and elongated weights are for medium speed running. Slim Darters are deep-diving elongated cannonballs that plane more vertically the faster you go, rather than the other way around. On all weights, the top eye is for normal running with ordinary tackle. For shallow running, use the front eye, which rotates the ball backward and tips the release clip and its following line down a little bit lower in the water. The release clip has a tension adjustment screw that allows you to use this equipment for everything from trout to tuna. Cannonballs and cable can hang up and be lost, and if your downrigger doesn't have a ratchet and free-spool setting, it can be wrenched out of the transom, plate and all, and fly overboard.

How do you use a downrigger? Typically, the release clip on the downrigger doesn't grip your fishing line. Instead, it has a pin that runs through the hole of a tab attached to the line and pushes against a plate. Because you need the tab pre-attached to the line, a particular rod-and-reel is reserved for downrigger fishing. For king and Spanish mackerel or bluefish, that rod will be about eight feet long and limber enough to set a good bend. The reel can be a Penn 920, Newell, or 20- or 30-pound-class Daiwa, Shimano, or Ambassadeur, loaded with reasonably light line. For bigger game, heavier tackle is necessary, as a long, limber rod would sacrifice necessary backbone.

Rig the lure as you normally would and, with the boat running at trolling speed, let it out the distance at which you want to fish. Put on the ratchet and set the reel in free-spool. Twist the line about the tab, insert the tab in the downrigger clip and, finger on the reel spool, let the cannon-ball down to preferred depth, watching it on your depth recorder if possible. A limber rod will get a good bend in it, and will snap to attention when the fish hits and the release gives way. On the strike, bring the ball up immediately, as the fish is liable to wrap the line around your cable.

Some downriggers can be rigged for multiple lures by stacking additional release clips on the cable above the weight. If you get several hits at once, you'll have a real mess on your hands.

The most popular downriggers are the Cannons and Penn Fathom-Masters. Prices range from about $100 for a small mechanical outfit without options to over $500 for an electric, full-featured, big-water outfit.

You will lose some cannonballs and, at $30 each, you might want to mold your own. A mold costs about $20.

TEASERS

Teasers churn up the water and are supposed to excite tuna and other fish by resembling fleeing bait fish. They may be single, big bubble-makers like a 12-inch plastic squid tied to the transom, close to the boat, or they may consist of a series (daisy chain) of smaller, bubble-making objects. A single teaser can also be placed on a fishing line between the reel and the lure. Offshore charter boat skippers generally use a daisy chain made of anything from old beer cans (when fishing alone) to small plastic squids (when carrying paying passengers). When a billfish comes up to examine the teaser, it is brought slowly inboard while one of the rigged lures is brought into position in its place.

For fishing a single teaser in the fighting line, you can use a piece of broomstick with an eyelet at each end, flattening the front end to throw up a bigger spray or inserting a horizontal wing in the sides to throw up a wide wake. The latter types are called "birds" and are becoming very popular. They are shaped much like flying fish. You can make your own from wood or buy a plastic bird for a few bucks.

LIVE-BAIT FISHING

So far, we've covered a number of kinds of tackle that are largely geared for trolling with lures or rigged, dead baits. The sole exception is the use of downriggers, which can also be used to slowly troll a live menhaden.

Slow-trolling and float fishing with big baits, such as menhaden or bluefish, are very productive on king mackerel around structures, but they also produce well offshore in the Gulf Stream. Whether you slow-troll, kite, or balloon fish, your first problem is live bait. If you think you'll find all you need offshore, think again. The smart fisherman is out before dawn hunting live menhaden in the Intracoastal Waterway with a cast net, or bluefish and pinfish with rod-and-reel around the dock. Catching your live bait is always your first problem. Your second problem is keeping those big baits alive.

Live-Bait Wells   Along the eastern seaboard and Gulf Coast, king mackerel fishermen have discovered that slow-trolled live menhaden selectively induce strikes from giant "smoker" kings. Fishing with big live baits requires keeping plenty of them on board and alive for many hours.

Standard built-in live wells are fine for minnows, but are inadequate for a couple of dozen 10-inch menhaden. Built-in wells are usually small, square-shaped, and have a single drain hole near the bottom. They just won't work. Menhaden need continuous water changes to wash away their copious waste products, or they may die in minutes. They must swim constantly to get oxygen across their gills, and can only do that in a round container.

For most boaters, fishing with big live baits is a once-in-a-while affair, so the live well should be inexpensive, readily removed when not needed, and simple to handle. It should be built so that new water is pumped in at the bottom, pushing the overflow waste water out through a discharge port near the top, providing a continuous water change. The components of a good live well are a large rounded barrel, a stern bracket, a bilge pump and associated fittings and hoses, and proper wiring.

Commercial live-well barrels are available from the Caddy Company, 57 Bayonne Avenue, Central Islip, N.Y. 11722 (516-234-0144) or from Universal Plastics, 739 NW Second Street, Hallandale, Fl. 33009 (305-456-0661).

You can also construct your own from readily available materials. The well should have a capacity of 24 gallons or more and should be rounded to prevent the fish from jamming in a corner. A four-inch rim at the top will prevent sloshing. The cheapest approach is to use a trash barrel with the lid fastened on, and a hole cut in the lid for reaching inside.

A plastic chemical drum will cost about $25 from an agricultural supply store. The standard drum is 32 gallons in capacity, and comes with both ends sealed, but no separate lid. Cut a lid out of one end with a jigsaw, leaving a four-inch rim to the drum, and fit the lid with brass hinges, a hasp, and a knob. Using flared wood-boring bits on your electric drill, cut holes on one side of the drum to accommodate the lower intake and upper outflow. Insert standard marine thru-hull fittings (about $4 each) with marine sealant. A three-fourths inch intake fitting will match the discharge from the average bilge pump, and a one and one-eighth inch outflow fitting will easily handle the overflow.

There are other sources of large plastic barrels. Check your telephone directory yellow pages under BARRELS for steam-cleaned, recycled plastic drums from many sources. A 55-gallon recycled plastic drum can be purchased for about $10.

The stern bilge pump bracket should be one-eighth inch aluminum, shaped, painted, and then mounted onto the outboard motor bracket. If your boat has an inboard motor, you can bolt the bracket to the transom. Bolt the base plate of the pump low on the bracket so that it is submerged when you are slow-trolling or at rest.

A good bilge pump should have a capacity of 360 to 500 gallons per hour (gph). Rule and Attwood pumps retail for about $15. Carry a prewired spare bilge pump that you can substitute in case of pump failure by snapping off the top portion from the bolted lower portion (which has no moving parts to fail). Since the leads that come with bilge pumps are short, you will have to add wire. Make your connections waterproof, using shrinking tape and marine sealant. The addition of some wire, a switch, and an in-line fuse will cost about $5. The switch should be located near your battery or on the console. Put your switch and in-line fuse on the positive lead.

The six-dollar hoses normally used with bilge pumps are suitable for your live well. The hose diameter for the lower inlet fitting to the live well should match the nozzle diameter of the pump. Locate the barrel inlet fitting about three inches from the bottom. The outlet or passive overflow hose should be larger to prevent the water from backing up. Locate the outlet about three inches from the top of the barrel. You can direct the discharge overboard or into the motor well.

When racing to or from the fishing grounds, the bilge pump will be dry, unable to push water into the barrel. You can rig an intake scoop to supply fresh water while planing. A hard, three-inch funnel feeding into one and one-half inch PVC intake hose will create a Venturi effect to force water up over the transom and (here is where the work really comes into play) into the bottom of the barrel. The funnel will require a strong bracket to withstand water pressure while running. A garden hose cutoff valve should be mounted close to the barrel so that the well doesn't drain when you stop the boat. You can simply locate the passive scoop inlet above the water line on the top of the barrel. This causes water to pour in and doesn't allow the hose to siphon the barrel.

Kite and Balloon Fishing   Kite fishing while drifting or anchored is popular in south Florida for sailfish. The kite line carries the fishing line aloft on a release clip, such as a plastic clothespin, which grips a snap-swivel or paper clip through which the fishing line passes, dangling a live blue-fish or menhaden below, some distance away from the boat. As the kite rises and falls in the breeze, your line can run freely through the loop in the paper clip or snap-swivel, keeping your bait where it belongs. You can rig more than one live-bait outfit to a kite. Commercial kites cost about $20.

King mackerel float fishermen use balloons, which have several advantages over kites besides being cheaper and more quickly rigged. They can keep the bait at a specific depth from the surface as many feet down as you want, and you can fish half a dozen at different distances from the boat (matching rods with different balloon colors so you always know which to grab). An important difference is that a bait fish frightened by a predator below will drag the balloon around, preparing you for the hit, while a kite-rigged fish's action is not easily seen from water level.

Slow-trolling is a specialty of king mackerel tournament fishermen, but has many other applications. It will be covered in detail in the section on king mackerel fishing.

62-pound Black Drum
Caught by Dale Reddish, pictured with mate Ralph Walls,
aboard *Buccaneer* out of Cape Charles, Virginia

Photo by Walton F. Reddish

THE BROWN WATER ZONE

The south Atlantic coast is awash in vast amounts of runoff from rivers that race down the rocky slopes of the Appalachians, slow slightly while draining the urbanized piedmont, and meander almost imperceptibly through the flat, agricultural coastal plain. Some rivers empty into enclosed bays or estuaries, where they drop much of their sediment before continuing seaward; others pour directly into the ocean. At the shore, this water is mixed into the prevailing ocean currents and churned by two strong daily tidal cycles. Its salinity is low and its color is translucent brown for a distance of perhaps a half-mile off the beach, where stronger tides and currents push against it, keeping the mixing zone close to the beach.

On the Gulf Coast, it's not the same. Freshwater runoff is dominated by the massive Mississippi River, yet other rivers contribute also. Currents are weak, driven by a slowly rotating internal wave that produces one tidal cycle each day. Silt loads accumulate at river mouths, creating vast grass flats and muddy near shore bottoms. The opaque brown water mass is pushed seaward by more water coming in from behind, and eastward by the weak internal circulation. Silt is deposited over vast areas, and brown water extends perhaps twenty miles or more into the Gulf of Mexico before it is blocked by blue or green ocean water.

There are also differences in the bottom. On the Atlantic coast, sandy bottoms with other kinds of grasses predominate near shore, and the bottom rapidly drops to deep, rocky outcrops offshore, interrupted by occasional undersea granite mountains and deeply cut ancient river valleys (canyons). Silt and mud accumulate in isolated pockets, but the shelf zone is otherwise sand with rocks.

On the Gulf Coast, silt from the Mississippi and other rivers blankets the bottom for great distances offshore, creating the Gulf's unusual "blue mud bottoms." The slope is extremely gradual and undersea canyons are rare.

There are exceptions. A principal canyon occurs off western Florida. Quirks in the circulation have preserved rare coral reefs offshore in the western Gulf of Mexico off Louisiana and Texas, and tongues of blue ocean water lap the beaches between Destin and Panama City, Florida.

Water color is a marker for dissolved organic materials and suspended sediments. Chemicals and silt can clog or irritate the gills of certain fish, which then asphyxiate on their own mucus. The dissolved organic materials, in moderation, support phytoplankton and grasses, larval fish, and other animals. A shift in water conditions causes a shift in the different kinds of marine life. That's why local conditions can appear similar, yet differ in fishing quality.

Silt provides a base for certain coastal grasses, while sand supports other kinds. Many fishes and invertebrates require grass beds at some stage in their lives, for hiding places or food. But coastal grasses can be killed mechanically by boat traffic or chemically by petroleum products from marinas, wastewater from industrial facilities, or agricultural runoff. Sewage contains household and yard chemicals unaltered by treatment plants and toxic to some marine life. Phosphates from farms or from detergents, when out of balance with nitrates, promote noxious blue-green cyanobacteria that use up oxygen and add cyanotoxins to the water, which in turn appear to kill fish outright or make them susceptible to red-sore and other diseases.

The distribution of clean, clear, and opaque water, silty and rocky bottoms, grass beds, and the frequency and strength of currents all influence the distribution of fishes. Offshore, different conditions control the movement and activities of fishes. In the brown water zone of estuaries, river mouths, and beachfront areas, freshwater runoff, silt, grass flats, and mud determine the kinds and numbers of fishes that can exist in each area.

SUMMER ANd SOUTHERN FLOUNdERS

There are fifty-five species of flounders on the Atlantic and Gulf coasts of the United States, divided into four fish families. These are the righteye flounders, lefteye flounders, soles, and tonguefish. Most of them are very small species, and some have distinctive shapes or patterns. Most righteye flounders are northern species, like the halibut and the blackback or winter flounder. Tonguefish are common in shrimp trawls and beach seines. American species of soles are very small, sometimes pretty fish, whereas their European relatives are large and important food fish.

Our most important flounders are the lefteyes, which include the southern and summer flounders, and the smaller and less common Gulf and broad flounders. All have large mouths and toothy jaws.

Summer flounders are usually solid brown or gray on top, with many "eyespots" or ocelli, including a group of three in the rear that form a triangle with its apex pointing forward.

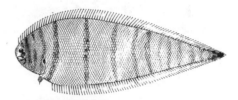

Tonguefish
Symphurus urospilus

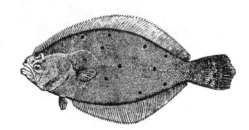

Summer Flounder (Fluke)
Paralichthys dentatus

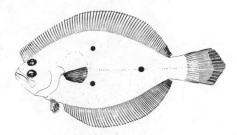

Gulf Flounder
Paralichthys albigutta

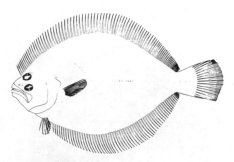

Broad Flounder
Paralichthys squamilentis

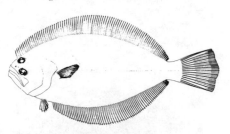

Southern Flounder
Paralichthys lethostigma

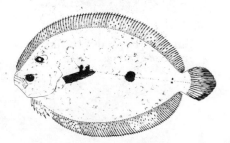

Peacock (Bluering) Flounder
Bothus lunatus

The closely related Gulf flounder and some other species have triangular arrangements of ocelli, but none has the summer flounders' pattern. Southern flounders are usually mottled dark and light. Broad flounders are very wide. Most fishermen don't realize that we have several species of flounders, and believe that the fish camouflage themselves with different colors and patterns according to bottom type.

Summer flounders (called "fluke" in the Northeast) are abundant from Cape Fear to Cape Cod. The southern flounder is the major species in the Gulf of Mexico.

Southern, Gulf, and broad flounders range from Cape Hatteras to Texas. All four overlap on the south Atlantic coast and are rare on the Florida east coast, perhaps because there are no big rivers below Jacksonville.

All can run a pound or two. Only the summer and southern flounders get large, with eight- and ten-pound "doormats" possible anywhere.

The only other commonly hooked flounder is the windowpane. It's a pretty fish, generally about 10 inches long and weighing a quarter-pound, and usually much too thin to eat. There are many other kinds of flounders, varying in shape, markings, patterns, and distribution. Many occur only in deep water in our area.

Summer and southern flounders are not fussy about where they live and what they eat. They forage on mud, sand, or rocky bottoms, in swift, deep channels, and on shallow, quiet beaches. In the summer they feed in the sounds, and in winter range a few miles offshore to breed. On rocky bottoms and around pilings, they lie in wait for passing prey, and on bare sandy bottoms they'll rise up, chasing bait fish all the way to the surface. They eat worms, shrimp, small crabs, killifishes, silversides, anchovies, sand launces, pinfishes, pigfishes, spots, croakers, little bluefishes, and young mullets. They're sight feeders with keen vision even in murky water, and will hit anything that moves.

A live shrimp suspended from a float is effective in quiet water at the edge of grass beds, while a live mummichog killifish, hooked through the lips, back, or tail and fished on the bottom, is excellent around structure. Sand fleas and declawed fiddler crabs are effective on bare sand and on rocky bottoms. A three-inch live pinfish will often entice the big flounders associated with structure.

The preferred cut bait is a three- by half-inch strip of squid, or of belly skin from a shark, ray, flounder, puffer, or any other tough-skinned fish. If you're out of belly skin, use the dark top side. They both work. A cluster of squid tentacles is also effective. Change baits after every fish or every five minutes in order to keep juicy meat on the hook. With flounder, fresh baits catch fish, and big fresh baits catch big fish.

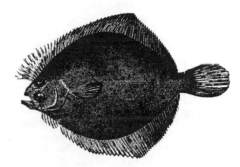

Sundial
Scophthalmus aquosus

Basic Summer Flounder Rig

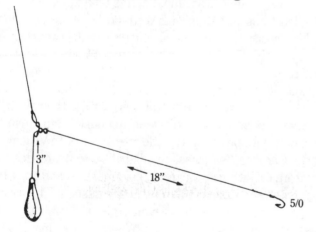

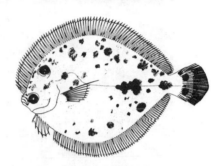

Eyed Flounder
Bothus ocellatus

The usual cut bait rig is a single 5/0 hook snelled to an 18-inch leader tied 3 inches above a smooth sinker that will slide easily over sand; but any rig will do. Some commercial rigs have the leader tied below the sinker, but that makes

Hogchoker Sole
Trinectes maculatus

**Commercial Two-Hook
Bottom Rig with Clips
for Bare Hooks and Sinker**

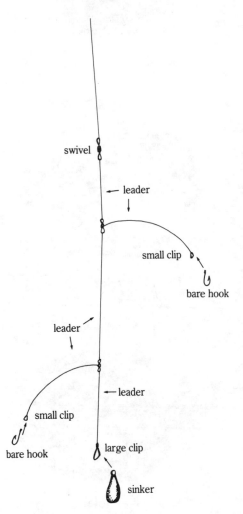

swivel

← leader
↓

small clip

bare hook

leader
↓

← leader

small clip

bare hook

large clip

sinker

the hit harder to feel. There are commercial one- and two-hook rigs with spinner blades, red floats, and beads that attract fishermen and don't seem to bother flounders. Drift with the wind or current, or troll at slow speed in slack water. The bait should slide over the bottom, slower in murky water and a little faster in clear water.

Flounders also hit jigs, plugs, spoons, and feathers worked slowly on the bottom. If abundant on a beach or sandbar, they can be snagged by jerking a weighted treble hook through the bottom.

When a flounder hits (it can feel like a strong strike or simply being stuck), slack off to let him take it deep down, away from the delicate skin behind the jaws. Then set the hook with a short, sharp jab and maintain pressure, allowing not a moment's slack, until he's on top of the water. Always net big flounders, even those that swallowed the bait, as their weight pushing against their teeth can cut very strong line.

Inshore, flounders are most active on a moving tide. The best locations are drop-offs, channels, rips, the ends of jetties, or other areas of swift current. Offshore, they feed anytime, with the largest fish occuring on wrecks and other structure.

Flounders are not averse to entering polluted water, where they'll accumulate petroleum odors in their flesh, but otherwise pollution doesn't seem to hurt them. Fish that are partly dark on the white side are not rare. In Virginia and North Carolina estuaries, swollen fish that are dead and dying are found during severely cold months, suffering from a parasitic protozoan in their blood and tissues. The parasite is transmitted by leeches, which get it from hogchoker soles. Hogchokers don't show any symptoms and don't get sick.

Winter Flounder

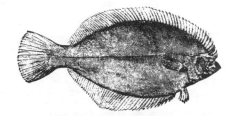

Winter (Blackback) Flounder
Pseudopleuronectes americanus

Virginia (to the surprise of most Virginians) is the usual southern limit of the blackback or winter flounder, a small fish with a small mouth that feeds on tiny sea worms and other animals. Winter flounder range up into Maine during the summer and might occur as far south as Georgia in cold years. The best months in our region are February and March. The best locations are the middle drainages of shallow (under 25 feet deep), mud-bottomed estuaries with little local current, and away from dead grass.

Anchor and set out a chum pot. You can make a chum pot of PVC pipe (not ABS, which floats), drilling small holes in the sides, gluing an end cap on the bottom, and slipping an end cap on the top for a removable lid. You can also chum without a pot. Good chums are corn kernels, crushed crabs, crushed mussels, or dry rabbit food.

Spreader rigs are commonly used in northern states, but aren't common in our region. You can order them from a catalog or make them from coat hangers. Use two small, long-shanked number eight or nine hooks on the spreader rig, and add a couple of yellow beads. Paint some small sinkers yellow, as this seems to attract the fish. Recently, Massachusetts fishermen have been sliding yellow Mr. Twister grubs onto the bottom of the leaders just above the hooks, and claim that this really attracts the fish.

Bait up with pieces of bloodworms, sandworms (earthworms in a pinch), clam, or fresh mussel meat small enough that the fish will engulf it all, and not merely nibble it. Winter flounder tap the bait, which feels really good when your hands are frozen stiff. Their lips are thick, so set the hook right away. If you miss, leave the rig where it is for at least a minute before checking the bait.

Winter flounder average a half to three-fourths of a pound, and are the tastiest kind of flounder in American waters.

Basic Rig for Winter Flounder

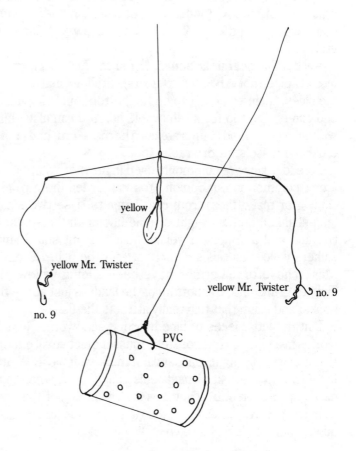

yellow

yellow Mr. Twister

no. 9

yellow Mr. Twister

no. 9

PVC

Seatrout

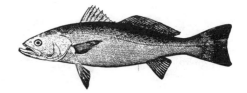

Gray Seatrout
Cynoscion regalis

eatrout are not really trout (members of the salmon family), but members of the drum family. Their relatives include red drum (redfish), black drum, spot, croaker (hardhead), whiting (sea mullet), the freshwater drum, and several other species in our waters. There are over 160 species of drums around the world.

Four species of seatrout occur in our area. The gray trout (squeateague, weakfish, summer trout) is the most northerly, ranging from Cape Cod to Cape Canaveral, but uncommon below the Carolinas. The spotted seatrout (speckled trout, speck, winter trout) ranges from Virginia to Texas, and is the most sought after of all the seatrout. Grays and specks are both big seatrout, averaging one to two feet, one to five pounds, and reaching more than ten pounds. The silver seatrout is a smaller fish, seldom over a foot long. It ranges from South Carolina to Texas, preferring beachfront and offshore waters, and is commonly caught in shrimp and squid trawl nets. Because it often occurs with gray seatrout, it has been confused with that fish. The larger sand seatrout (white trout) is confined to the Gulf Coast, where it frequents the bays and shallow inshore waters and is regarded a good sport fish. It can be distinguished from the silver trout easily; the scales of silver trout rub off in your fingers.

There are differences among the species of seatrout. Grays prefer, and spawn in, deep bays like Chesapeake and Delaware bays and Long Island Sound, or occupy the deepest parts of more shallow bays. They cannot stand cold temperatures, and move offshore for the winter. Fish north of Cape Hatteras grow more slowly, reach larger size, migrate separately, and are essentially isolated from southern fish. Southern fish below Cape Hatteras mature in about a year, and don't reach a large average size.

Spotted Seatrout
Cynoscion nebulosus

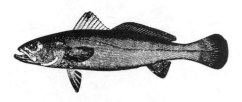

Silver Seatrout
Cynoscion nothus

In the northern part of our range, grays and specks are as often found together as they are found separately. In the southern part of our area, silver seatrout commonly occur with gray seatrout, but usually stay further from shore.

Spotted seatrout are pretty much shallow water, grass bed, estuarine fishes, inside the bays year-round and seeking deep holes inside the estuaries for the winter. They may leave the bays during the cold months, but don't move far from the beaches.

The Gulf Coast sand seatrout is often found with the speck, preferring the bays, but it spawns in the near shore Gulf waters in late spring and late summer and moves offshore for the winter.

Seatrout fishing is year-round for those who know where to find them. For the average fisherman, the peak season is October through December. Grays and specks mass along the beaches and in the inlets, taking advantage of the annual shrimp migration out of the estuaries.

There are several ways to catch seatrout. Popular baits are live shrimp, live pinfish, or a big chunk of fresh soft-shelled crab suspended from a float over a deep hole. They sometimes take live killies, small mullet or herring, or strip baits like slivers of squid or flounder belly.

Seatrout are fussy, and failure to get a hit doesn't mean the fish are elsewhere; they could be there but not feeding, or not feeding on what you have to offer, no matter how scrumptious. The trick to trout fishing is being in the right place at the right time, carrying everything anybody has ever caught them on, trying it all, and varying your technique from still-fishing with live bait to fast surface retrieves and slow drags of lures on the bottom. It's not unusual for some people to get doubles with every cast, and other people not a single hit. The difference may be in what they're using or how they're working it, but it won't be luck.

Work the deep holes, inlets, and cuts between barrier islands with small, hammered metal jigs like the Conner

Z1H and Hopkins No = EQL lures. Work the sides of jetties and deep channels of big bridges with blue- or yellow-headed, white-bodied lead jigs like the Gotcha and Jerk Jigger. Other heavy, small, silver, blue, or green lures are effective, with green and silver the favored colors. Mr. Twister green curly tailed jigs are engulfed by all types of trout, while a deep-running MirrOlure (often with a red head) pulled over the bottom at a snail's pace is frequently the only lure a speck will take. A fly on a one-foot dropper behind any kind of lure will frequently yield a bonus trout.

Tie the monofilament line directly to the lure. If bluefish are around, add a dark-colored wire leader and avoid lures with red on them. The biggest fish seem to be caught after dark, but the best time to go after trout is when everybody else is hauling them in.

Red Drum

Red drum (redfish, channel bass, spottail bass, puppy drum) stocks are associated with specific estuaries from Chesapeake Bay to Yucatan, and different populations have different mixes of big, old fish and young, small fish.

Reds mature at two to four years of age, when they reach a length of about two feet. A 20-pound female may produce 2 to 60 million eggs in a season, and some states protect the large (32-inch and up) fish.

Peak breeding takes place in September, October, and November, when the water temperature drops to about 72-76 degrees Fahrenheit and the days are shortened to about nine hours. Just before dark, the fish begin spawning on the ocean side of barrier island beaches and inlets (passes).

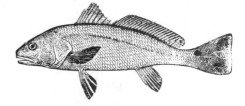

Red Drum
Sciaenops ocellatus

The eggs float and develop in seawater, but sink and die if they're swept into the bays too soon. In most fish eggs, glycogen (animal starch) is the main energy store. In red drum, the embryo relies equally on fats (triglycerides and wax esters) and glycogen during development. Some eggs develop and hatch in less than 20 hours, and just about all of them are hatched by 30 hours post-spawning. Because the red drum egg metabolizes very fast, it is highly susceptible to pollutants from petroleum drilling.

Red drum are well adapted to living around estuaries and beaches. Chloride cells in the gill epithelium contain the enzyme ATPase (adenosine triphosphatase), which assists transfer of sodium and potassium ions into and out of the blood, so the fish can rapidly adjust to virtually any salinity.

Baby drum feed on zooplankton for the first month until they are about a half-inch long, then switch to small invertebrates and baby fishes. At three inches, they feed on shrimp, crabs, and larger fishes. At adult sizes, they feed mostly on blue crabs and shrimp.

Gulf Coast reds differ from the reds of the middle Atlantic states. Mid-Atlantic fish leave the sounds in the fall for warmer offshore waters, after one year of age. At winter's end, the big fish come back to forage in the sounds for the summer, leaving again in late fall. On the Texas coast, red drum remain in the sounds or the inlets throughout their entire juvenile period, perhaps two to three years. Only then do they leave for the open Gulf, where they remain for the rest of their lives, coming to the passes for spawning.

If the water is flat calm, you can sight-cast hammered metal lures, plastic plugs, or a live finger mullet to schools of the bronze-backed giants as they cruise shallow estuaries, roaming along the edges of grass beds and oyster flats close to channels. They eventually spook, running into deeper waters out of sight. Narrow, deep channels also attract reds, where you can blind-cast using yellow or white lead-head jigs, spoons, or just about anything else. Small reds will take almost anything.

The best places for big reds in the fall are the sides of the deepest channel toward the outside of the inlet, or other steep slopes around bars or the edges of passes. Use whatever weight you need and a short, stiff rod. The standard method is to still-fish on the bottom with cut bait (mullet or herring) or a whole finger mullet. Other good baits are spot, croaker, or whiting heads. Whatever meat you use, it should be juicy with blood and slime, only a few hours old at most, never frozen, and changed every 10 minutes. Live baits, for some reason, don't seem to produce as well as juicy dead baits.

A standard two-hook bottom rig is fine for small reds, but single hook rigs are better for big fish. Fish-finder (slider, leger) rigs are, in my opinion, less effective than standard three-way bottom rigs. I prefer a brass swivel, less than a foot of 80-pound-test monofilament leader, and a short-shanked 9/0 hook. A drum with a mouthful of bait will as soon run toward you as away, so don't rely on a loud ratchet or a tightening line; a slackening line is also a drum alarm.

Big drum should be netted or lip-gaffed, enjoyed with a photograph, and then released. Sportsmanship and conservation considerations aside, they're very difficult to dress and not worth eating. The little ones are fine in the pan, better than gray seatrout, but not nearly as flavorful as spotted seatrout or flounder. If you want to try a New Orleans-style blackened fish, keep in mind that almost any fish fillets more neatly, cooks easier, and tastes better than a red drum.

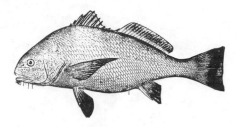

Black Drum
Pogonias cromis

Black Drum

Black drum are as large and widely distributed as red drum, and can be copper-colored at large sizes, but that's where all similarity ends. Black drum have barbels on the chin for sensing food on the bottom, and their young have broad, dark bands like sheepshead. Black drum prefer rocky bottoms or oyster bars in deep water, and tend to be dispersed except at breeding time. Just as the best time to catch big red drum is during the November spawning run, the best time for big black drum is the May spawning run. Don't bother casting lures or hooking up with cut fish for bait. Black drum browse reefs and structures for clams, oysters, crabs, and other shellfish, and won't take a lure. The best baits are clams, crabs, squid, and shrimp, and the best rig is a one- or two-hook bottom rig still-fished on the bottom. Chumming with crushed clams helps keep the fish near the boat.

The best drum fishing is in Delaware Bay and Chesapeake Bay at the northern edge of our range, and the rocky bottoms off the coasts of South Carolina and Texas. Black drum can be anywhere that structure dominates the bottom, and are more likely than redfish to occur on rocky bottoms. The young are often found with spadefish and sheepshead.

If you're just fishing for black drum, nothing stays on the hook better than clam, but crab is also excellent for its tasty juices. Peeler (shedder) crabs are favored on Virginia's eastern shore. Where people fish for black and red drum at the same time in the same place, the favored bait is a "clamwich" of clam combined with either fish or crab.

Tackle should be matched to the fish, and heavyweight gear is necessary for big drum. Small black drum are delicious, but the big ones have almost impregnable scales and tough meat.

To clean a big black drum, remove the dinner-plate-sized scales with a garden hoe or shovel, and cut fillets from the flanks. Don't worry about those white, stringy things that look like worms (and really are). They're harmless larval tapeworms that only mature in requiem sharks, so you can fork them into your mouth with supreme confidence. These so-called "spaghetti worms" also occur in the meat of red drum and seatrout and are undoubtedly nutritious.

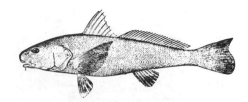

Gulf Kingfish
Menticirrhus littoralis

Kingfish, Croaker, Spot, and Silver Perch

Other common, small, schooling members of the drum family are associated with beaches, shallow bays, and inlets, and can be taken on cut bait using a two-hook bottom rig and small hooks. Kingfish (sea mullet, king whiting) are powerful fighters, attaining a couple of pounds. Croaker can be as large or larger, and hordes of three-pound "yellowbellies" are common in some years, especially above Cape Hatteras. Spot are small, seldom attaining a pound, but occur in vast numbers. Silver perch are not as common as the others, and are the poorest food and sport fish in the group.

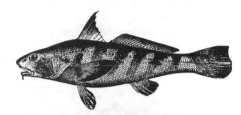

Southern Kingfish
Menticirrhus americanus

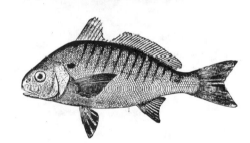

Spot
Leiostomus xanthurus

Bluefish

Bluefish range from the coast of Maine southward, across the Atlantic to Portugal and southern Africa, around the Cape to Mozambique in the Indian Ocean and Australia in the Pacific Ocean. There is just the one species, and it has no close relatives.

Bluefish fight hard at any size. Small ones are called "snappers," 2- to 4-pounders are called "tailors," and the big ones (10 pounds and up) are called "choppers." Chopper bluefish are abundant from Cape Cod to North Carolina, but

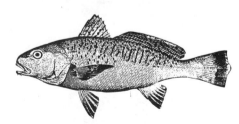

Croaker
Micropogonias undulatus

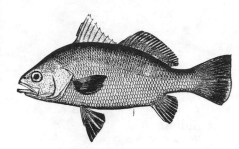

Silver Perch
Bairdiella chrysura

Bluefish
Pomatomus saltatrix

big fish sometimes work south to Florida in pursuit of menhaden hordes, where they've cut swimmers on the beaches during feeding frenzies.

There are two or three separate spawning stocks on the Atlantic and Gulf coasts, and they make separate migrations. Bluefish also travel in groups of same-sized fish, so that many groups (size and stock) are cruising parts of the coastline all the time. That gives us a long bluefish season.

All the stocks move offshore in the winter and back to the beaches in spring, spreading along the coast for the duration of warm weather. Little snappers are abundant in estuaries and tidal rivers, and swarm on ocean beaches and around jetties in pursuit of anchovies, silversides, and young menhaden. Choppers tend to remain offshore at steady temperatures and ocean salinities, coming inshore after fleeing bait fish only where the water is of very high quality.

It doesn't take a genius to catch bluefish. They can be caught on anything, always matching the tackle to the size of the fish.

Trolling with big, silver, wobbling spoons is effective, but you can use virtually any kind of silver, white, or red trolling lure, a three-foot dark wire leader, and a black snap-swivel; blues will slash anything that shines. I once lost $20 worth of shark hooks, chain, and cable to a slashing bluefish that found a chrome swivel to its liking, and Gary Soucie has seen bluefish cut away a hundred bucks worth of bluefin tuna lures in an instant.

Free-line fishing with cut bait in a chum slick is exciting. Use 9/0 hooks with three feet of black or brown wire, a dark swivel, and no weight other than the wire and bait. Chum should be ladled overboard slowly but steadily to bring the fish to the boat. Keep the slick thin enough to keep the fish at the stern so you can watch for sharks and the deep flash of an albacore (in the northern part of our area) or little tunny (everywhere else). With the drag off and ratchet on, slowly strip up to 40 yards of line into the slick, but no more or your bait will bounce to the bottom while your chum keeps going. Standard baits are inch-thick slabs of cut menhaden, herring, or mackerel. When the line starts zipping out under its own power, wait ten seconds for the fish to swallow the bait, engage the drag, and disengage the ratchet. As soon as the line becomes really taut, hit him hard.

When blues are on top, you can try a casting outfit. Use metal lures like the Hopkins, Conner, Gotcha, and Jerk Jigger, in chrome, green, or red-headed white. A one-foot wire leader is sufficient.

Okay, he's at the boat. Don't stick your hand in the water! Use a gaff to bring the fish aboard. Because blues have razor-sharp teeth, powerful bodies, clamping jaws, and a nasty disposition, it's easy to get cut to the bone or have the hook buried in your hand. Grip the fish firmly by the back of the neck, squeezing the gill plates together, and work out the hook, but only if the shank is outside the jaws. If he's taken the hook deeply, use long-nosed pliers to reach inside for the hook, or cut the wire and get the hook later. If you don't intend to eat them, choppers should be released immediately. They don't tolerate being out of the water while they're passed around for admiring comments.

Little blues have delicious white meat. Big choppers should be released, but can be smoked. Some guys grill them outdoors on a barbecue with lots of lemon juice. I'd rather eat the lemons. Gary Soucie eats these things (ugh!), and offers the following recipe, for which I disclaim all responsibility:

"Kill and ice the fish quickly. Skin the bluefish, fillet it, and remove the strip of dark, myoglobin-rich meat along the midline. Liberally sprinkle the fillets with onion salt a half-hour before cooking. Heat an equal amount of butter in olive oil, then add lemon juice, fresh black pepper, and stir in a single type of green herb to taste. I prefer fresh, chopped coriander or cilantro, but I also like (for a change) dried dill weed (not seed), dried or fresh parsley, thyme, lovage, or basil. Don't use a combination of herbs, as they cancel each other out and leave you with the muddy flavor of badly prepared bluefish. Baste the fish with this herby, oily mix and place it on a grill or under a broiler. Turn once during cooking, basting again. Cook the fish no more than 10 minutes per inch of thickness and it will be just right."

Cobia
Rachycentron canadum

Cobia

Spring is the time to tangle with as rugged a fish as any you've ever fought, the cobia (ling, lemonfish, crabeater, cabio). Cobia are inshore everywhere around Memorial Day, and remain for most of the summer.

Where they come from is anybody's guess. Commercial fishermen tell of large schools moving northward along the Atlantic coast during late March or early April. According to modern-day biologists with the U.S. Fish & Wildlife Service, those fish are returning from their overwintering grounds "presumably (in the) West Indies," a presumption based on an off-the-wall comment made in 1877, and never verified. One modern Caribbean specialist says that cobia are "rare in the West Indies," while another states that he's never seen or collected any in the Bahamas, although he's heard of them caught at Bimini. Many big cobia are caught in the northern Gulf of Mexico in early spring, but nobody has traced their source. Is it possible that cobia overwinter in the southern or central Gulf of Mexico?

In the Chesapeake Bay area, the cobia's numbers and average size declined during the 1970s, perhaps due to overfishing by sportfishermen and commercial fishermen. The Feds have placed a 33-inch minimum size limit on cobia taken more than three miles offshore, and many states have

70-pound, 61-inch Cobia
Caught by Michael Grover off Nags Head, North Carolina

Photo by Kirk Wilson, Dare County Tourist Bureau

identical or even stricter regulations for fish taken in inshore waters. In recent years, there is evidence of some recovery in numbers of fish.

The annual arrival of cobia begins in early spring when the water usually reaches the low 70s. However, it may not be water temperature that is important. Cobia always seem to arrive on schedule and leave on schedule, which suggests that their migrations are tied to day length rather than temperature. The fish remain in coastal waters until cold weather sets in in the fall, and then disappear.

The first cobia are usually taken in mid-April. Landings reach a peak around the last week of May. About a week or two later, the larger fish move offshore for spawning over the entire shelf, from right outside the bays all the way to the Gulf Stream. The 50- to 70-pounders begin returning to the beaches and inshore waters in July, and remain throughout the summer and into early fall, moving all through the low-salinity sounds and well up into the rivers.

Cobia have the curious habit of following rays feeding on the bottom, apparently picking up prey the rays have missed or chased out of hiding. The behavioral and color-pattern similarity to remoras, their only relatives, is obvious.

They're big fish. Biologists regularly report their maximum size at five or six feet, and quite a few fish over 100 pounds have been landed. The current world record is a 110-5 fish from Mombasa, Kenya. An even larger fish was taken in Florida in 1982, but disqualified from the record on a technicality. A 108-pounder was caught in Kenya in 1980. Near Destin, Florida, two monster cobia of 103-12 and 100-8 were landed in late April of 1980, and the Virginia record of 103-8 was set the same year. Most state records are in the 80- and 90-pound ranges. Fishermen regularly see, sometimes hook, and most often lose huge cobia, and nobody knows for certain how big they get.

They average 10 to 60 pounds, and most of the larger ones are females. Scientists think cobia are loners, but sportfishermen usually see groups of them that appear to be a big female and several smaller males.

Cobia often associate with holes inside channels and estuaries, and with structures (buoys, bridge stanchions, pier pilings, floating debris) outside. Any small boat is big enough for a cobia; if the boat is too small to take outside the inlet, then find the deep holes inside on the rising and high tides, and you'll also find the cobia. They tend to leave the estuaries when the tide is close to low, and that's the time to search around outside channel buoys.

Cobia eat anything slow, no matter how ugly, from crabs, dogfish sharks, pipefish, squid, and shrimp to pieces of dead fish. Cut bait, live bait, and lures all work at times. For surface fishing around structures, live eels are best of all. You can catch your own with baited minnow traps, fishing in narrow, deep (even polluted) canals. Dead eels hooked through the lip for casting and retrieving work just as well as live eels. While a dead eel won't sink toward the bottom, neither will it intentionally wrap your line around a buoy cable!

For bottomfishing, use large chunks of cut menhaden or mullet. When fishing in the sounds, bring a cooler full of bait, because you'll have to feed the crabs.

Cobia are powerful fish well matched to heavy tackle. A good outfit is a medium-sized conventional reel loaded with 20- to 30-pound-test monofilament line, a casting rod with plenty of backbone, and a sharp gaff. For sight-casting, anti-backlash reels are excellent choices. Many cobia are taken on heavy spinning gear, but a good, stiff, conventional rod is more effective.

To rig up for sight-casting, tie a 9/0 short-shanked hook directly to 10 feet of 80-pound-test monofilament leader. The leader is thick enough to resist a cobia's crunching jaws and tiny teeth, and scrapes from buoy anchor chains, pilings, stanchions, and other structures.

Fish-Finder Rig for Cobia

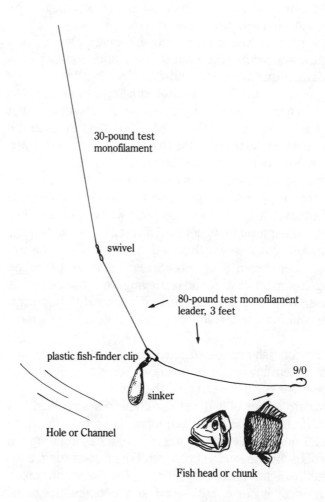

30-pound test
monofilament

swivel

80-pound test monofilament
leader, 3 feet

plastic fish-finder clip

9/0

sinker

Hole or Channel

Fish head or chunk

Cut the engine to slow speed as you approach a buoy or
bridge piling, and inch up to it slowly, watching for brown
backs just under the surface, but be careful not to spook
them. If you don't see fish, they may be down deep. Cast to
the structure, let the bait sink, and then retrieve slowly.
Sometimes cobia will feed down deep, but usually they rise
to the surface. If the fish are on top, cast beyond and slightly

to the side and work the bait back slowly. If the cobia start to move away, don't panic and cast on top of them. Cobia tend to remain near their home structures. The fish are just cruising around and won't go away. Be patient and keep your bait where it is, or come back later.

If you're anchored at a deep hole or in the dredged channel inside the sound, use a fish-finder rig with as little weight as possible and a 9/0 hook on three feet of 60- to 80-pound-test monofilament leader. You'll still lose some cobia, since they know all the submerged structures. Use a fresh fish head or a palm-sized chunk of fresh, oily menhaden or mullet for bait, and change it every 10 minutes, more often if the crabs are thick. Live baits work well, but are not necessary in fishing depressions where cobia lie in wait for dead and dying fish swept in by the current.

Cobia rarely miss a bait. Even a small one has a grin 8 to 10 inches wide, and the bigger ones have a square foot of maw that could engulf your motor's lower unit. If you fail to stick a cobia, it's because the hook was too small or the rod too light to sink it. Because the mouth of a cobia is bonier than the throat, let the fish run with the bait before striking.

A cobia might respond several ways to being stabbed with the hook, but rarely will it jump. If the fish runs, it will head for structure to cut you off. Usually it will back off and refuse to be budged, sitting well off on top or down on the bottom. You might fool one into coming toward the boat early on, but a cobia is a two-edged sword. A "green" fish should not be brought aboard a small boat, for it can wreck the cockpit. If you can wear it down in 20 minutes to an hour, that's the time to sink the gaff, and not before.

Cobia meat is rich, wet, yellowish white, and chunky. The pièce de résistance is smoked cobia, and I've known gourmets who would kill for it. Even the head can feed two to four people. Prepare a simple vegetable broth and simmer the entire head for about an hour, add some white potatoes, carrots, and a stalk of celery. Early female cobia will have enormous roes, and they are delicious sprinkled with orange juice, wrapped in bacon, and broiled.

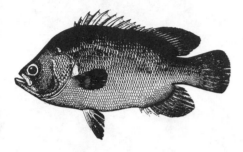

Tripletail
Lobotes surinamensis

Tripletail

The tripletail is a bulky fish, not built for pursuit, but too smart to go hungry. Drifting on its side at the surface of open coastal waters or near a seawall or piling, the tripletail mimics floating debris, which attracts passing shrimp, crabs, and squid. It can ease up to schooling herrings, anchovies, or small fishes seeking shelter without scaring them. A quick gulp and the tripletail resumes its leisurely float. Look for tripletails inshore near structures and at sea near patches of seaweed or debris. They're most common in Gulf of Mexico waters, but range throughout our area.

Tripletails are the only members of a small family (four species) that occurs in all the warm seas of the world. They breed in late spring and summer at a year of age, when they weigh about 7 pounds. They grow fast, live 7 to 10 years, and get up to about 45 pounds.

They're so easy to catch, it's embarrassing. Use light casting tackle and toss a live or dead shrimp, a small piece of meat, or even a fly or small plug just past its head, and work it toward the fish's nose. Jiggle the bait until the fish gets curious, rolls its eyes around, and, like an overweight person, slowly angles its body into position to yawn it into its maw. Set the hook immediately.

If it runs, you've got an exceptional tripletail. Most just stubbornly refuse to budge, turning their flat bodies at right angles to the pull. You can take big fish on light gear. Tripletails are excellent on the table.

TARPON

Tarpon
Megalops atlanticus

Tarpon are the ultimate inshore game fish, attaining eight feet and 300 pounds or more. A big one close to the boat can scare the hell out of you and make you doubt your own and your tackle's competence. It might approach your bait many times, perhaps never to strike (but giving you a huge adrenaline rush), then unexpectedly rip into your bait and sometimes tear your rod out of your hands, running, leaping, and head-shaking like no other fish. A tarpon looks like the herring that ate Tokyo, fights like a billfish restrained by shallow water, and is catchable by anyone with a strong heart, lots of skill, and considerable luck. But it isn't easy.

Tarpon are primitive fish, occurring round the world in warm seas. In our area, they're common north to Cape Fear, North Carolina, but overwinter and breed from Georgia to Texas. Top northern locations are off Bald Head Island, North Carolina, off Hilton Head, the inlets of the Santee rivers, the mouth of Andersonville Creek in South Carolina, and the Altamaha River east of the U.S. 17 bridge in Georgia. In Florida, they're common from Jacksonville to Key West Harbor but a bit trickier to find on the Gulf Coast.

Tarpon are inshore fish their entire lives, going offshore only to spawn. The flat, leaflike, clear, glassy young fish (leptocephalus larvae) come inshore to metamorphose into fishlike juveniles. Then they grow, and grow, and grow. Fifty-pounders are abundant, and 100-pounders ordinary.

Tarpon can be found on the seaward side of big ocean sandbars, in ports and ship channels, at river mouths, near jetties, or anywhere with a strong current and locally deeper water.

They aggregate during the winter at the hot water discharge canals of electric power plants on the Intracoastal Waterway. When you see a lot of small boats working close to shore or at the mouth of one particular canal, it's a good bet they're fishing for tarpon.

Tarpon tend to occur in big groups, probably with at least one big female and several smaller males. They eat crabs, herring, pinfish, spot, croaker, or anything else. You can troll a big red-and-white plug or wobbling spoon or sight-fish while anchored. In crowded, urban waters, the usual gear is high-quality conventional tackle. The bait is a live pinfish free-lined out to the group or drifted under a float, with a big treble hook and five feet or more of 60- to 80-pound-test monofilament leader.

Tarpon Rig

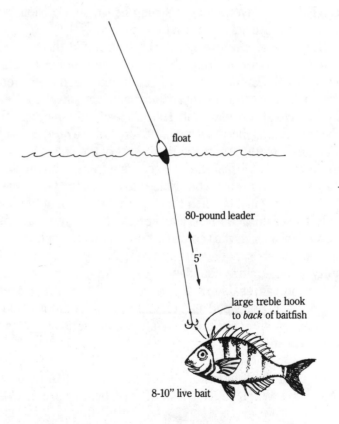

float

80-pound leader

5'

large treble hook to *back* of baitfish

8-10" live bait

139-pound Tarpon
Caught by Wendy Mead off Gould's Inlet, Georgia
Photo courtesy of the Georgia Department of Natural Resources

Out on open, shallow flats, light, 12- to 15-pound-test tackle is preferred. Light tackle fishermen sometimes use chum (shrimp gleanings are preferred in the Florida Keys), and cast small lures such as quarter-ounce, yellow lead-head jigs, often tipped with shrimp.

The tarpon is the ultimate fly-rod fish, but getting one on a fly rod or any other type of light gear requires someone else to run the boat after the fish before your line runs out. Fly-fishing tackle should be big and heavy, and any light tackle setup should include a reliable buddy to run the boat, chasing the fish before your line runs out.

About half of all tarpon jump, and all of them run. In the ICW they can't go far, and remain within the confines of locally deep water, so smaller reels may be sufficient. On ocean beaches, they'll head for Portugal or Mexico, sometimes greyhounding spectacularly, and bigger reels are better. Some people have been badly hurt by tarpon jumping into the boat, or getting jerked into the boat while in the air. Telling you to be calm and to control the fish is a waste of time; you'll be too excited to think.

Virtually all tarpon are lip-gaffed for a picture and released alive at the boat. They're bony and inedible. Anyway, how could you kill a gladiator like that?

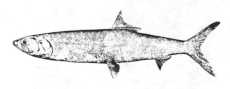

Ladyfish
Elops saurus

leptocephalus larva

Ladyfish

The ladyfish is no lady. It's badly named, and should have been called the "what-the-heck-was-that" fish. You usually realize you've been hit by a ladyfish after it's gone. Seldom is it on more than a second, which is all it takes to run a hundred feet and throw the hook.

A close relative of the tarpon, ladyfish occur round the world in warm coastal waters, and tend to be more southerly than tarpon, uncommon north of Florida. These primitive fish remain in coastal waters their entire lives, except for an offshore migration for spawning. They have the tailed leptocephalus larvae, in common with tarpon and bonefish. (Eels also have leptocephalus larvae, but without tails.)

Ladyfish are sometimes taken on cut bait, but more often on lures, especially fast-moving jigs. They frequent the same waters as snook, but are smaller (less than two feet), more common, and much faster.

Bonefish

Bonefish are common on shallow, clear-water grass flats of south Florida and south Texas, but not anywhere else in our region. Here they pick on the bottom, rooting out snapping shrimp and mud crabs and rushing off, laughing like hell, when a northern tourist who watched too many TV shows starts to flay the water with a ropelike fly line.

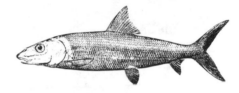

Bonefish
Albula vulpes

leptocephalus larva

The favored tackle is spinning or light conventional casting gear. The best baits are a live shrimp or a small bonefish lure like the Phillips Wiggle Jig, operated quietly.

Run the boat quietly, cast quietly, and let the bait hit the water quietly. Like mountain trout, they spook very easily, and you can spend a lot of time going after one, compared to the short period you actually have one on to talk about later.

Bonefish don't jump, but they run hard, fast, and far. You might think that fishing on open grass flats gives you the advantage, but marine grasses are hard-edged, often support tiny barnacles or other calcareous animals, and hold lots of obstacles that can foul and cut a line. You don't have a bonefish until it's in the net. Take a picture, and turn it loose.

Related to tarpon and ladyfish, the bonefish breeds far offshore and has a leptocephalus larva. Bonefish live up to 12 years and attain about 20 pounds, but half that weight is a good fish. The average bonefish is 2 to 6 pounds, two feet long, and 8 or 9 years old.

Jacks

There are about 200 species of jacks around the world, with 27 species in our region. The best known game fish is the amberjack. The most important inshore jack is properly called the crevalle jack (not "jack crevalle").

Occurring throughout our area, the crevalle jack is a schooling fish common in shallow, inshore waters from South Carolina to Texas. It is attracted to thermal discharges of power plants, and massive fish kills have resulted when the discharge of waste heat was suddenly increased (in summer) or abruptly stopped (in winter). The average size is 5 to 15 pounds, and the largest on record is 55 pounds. An unidentified 70-pounder is suspected of being a crevalle jack. Crevalle jacks eat all kinds of fish and shellfish. They'll take cut bait on the bottom or a fast-moving lure. They're among the most common fish caught trolling small, silvery lures inshore. Voracious feeders, they're also powerful fish and give a strong fight on any tackle. Edible but not great, most are released alive.

Blue runners or "hardtails" occur throughout our area. Smaller than crevalle jacks, the average fish is under a foot long and less than a pound, but they get twice as long and four times this weight. They're schooling fish that breed offshore throughout the summer and range inshore constantly. They're not bad on the table. They make excellent live baits for king mackerel, slow-trolled or on float rigs.

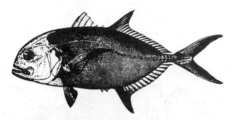

Crevalle Jack
Caranx hippos

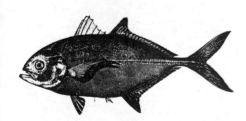

Blue Runner
Caranx crysos

Lookdowns are thin, virtually meatless fish with high foreheads that frequent structures inshore in Florida and Gulf Coast waters, but occur elsewhere as well. They are common under lights at night, where they dart up to the surface and down again in wide arcs, feeding on shrimp and small fish. They may take tiny jigs, small silvery spoons, live shrimp, or even flies, but are not easy to fool. They feed day and night, offer a sporty but short fight on ultralight tackle, and should be released alive.

Pompano are small (usually under a pound) inshore fish, common from the Carolinas to Texas, and more abundant at present in the northern part of our area than on the Gulf Coast. They'll take live shrimp, sand fleas (mole crabs), small blue crabs, cut bait, or small jigs. They usually have a yellow flush on the anal fin.

Permit look like overgrown pompano with misshapen heads and red-flushed anal fins. They're much larger, commonly in the 5- to 10-pound range, and get bigger than this. Although the small ones range widely through our area, just about all the big ones are taken in south Florida and the Keys. Here, they frequent wrecks offshore, and sand flats with nearby deep channels inshore. Many are taken by casting jigs, but the best bait is a live crab. Permit are powerful fighters, taking second place to no other fish in their size class.

Bumpers, moonfish, and lookdowns are also common jacks in southern waters, taken on live shrimp or small jigs. They all fight hard, but are usually considered too thin and bony to bother cleaning.

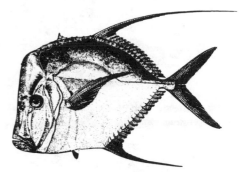

Lookdown
Selene vomer

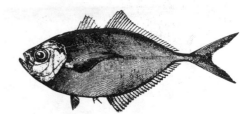

Bumper
Chloroscombrus chrysurus

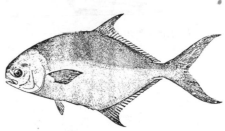

Pompano
Trachinotus carolinus

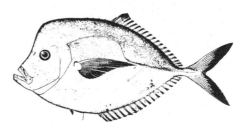

Moonfish
Selene setapinnis

American Eel
Anguilla rostrata

leptocephalus larva

Conger Eel
Conger oceanicus

Eels

While eels are not sport fish, they're commonly hooked, and few people can tell one from another. That's understandable, because there are many kinds. They will all, at times, take cut bait on a bottom rig. All of them have leptocephalus (glass ribbon) larvae, but without tails.

The best-eating eel is the common American eel that we find up rivers, inside estuaries, and in coastal waters. It's about two or three feet long, solid yellow-brown to brown above and white below. American eels don't bite, and can be handled safely. This is excellent cobia bait, and even better in the frying pan.

Eels are gourmet fare the world over, but are little used in this country out of ignorance. To handle any eel, set it in your cooler until it becomes dormant and then grip it with a fishing towel. If you intend to use it for a live bait, be aware that remaining too long on ice will kill it.

Big (up to six feet long), gray, and nasty is the conger eel, common in the north of our area. They're caught mostly inshore on big, bottom baits, but might occur anywhere. Congers will bite, squirm, and shed slime profusely, which instantly hardens, making a blister-pak out of you and your boat. Although congers are edible and widely used in Europe, they are fishy-tasting by American standards.

Pale-spotted eels are small, thin, reddish brown with white, fuzzy blotches, and very pretty. They occur throughout our area. They'll bite, and are too small to eat. Release them alive by cutting the leader at the hook.

Morays come in various sizes, patterns, and temperaments, but are only common in rocky bottom areas from South Carolina through south Florida. They're shy fish, and should be released alive.

Puffers

There is a large group of fishes, consisting of hundreds of species in several families, that are known as puffers (blowtoads, swellfish), porcupinefish (burrfish), boxfish (trunkfish, cowfish), triggerfish, and filefish. They're all poor swimmers that feed on shellfish, with enlarged front teeth that have, in many cases, evolved into a beak.

Most of them are not eaten by other fishes, as their skin contains substances called crinotoxins, which are usually offensive but not deadly, and not restricted to this group. Many fish, including some moray eels and soles, also have crinotoxins in their skin. Several of the better-known crinotoxins appear to work the same way, interfering with the so-called sodium channel of nerve cells.

In puffers, many species have a particularly powerful crinotoxin, called tetrodotoxin or TXX after the family name of puffers (Tetraodontidae). Severe neurological damage may accompany recovery, and this has been regarded as the basis of the mythical (I think!) zombie of Haitian folklore. Tetrodotoxin is produced in skin glands, and can be forced into the water for analysis by giving the live fish an electric shock. It also occurs in the meat, ovaries, and liver of some species.

While TXX was once thought unique to puffers, it has now been found in certain species of frogs, salamanders, starfish, blue-ringed octopus, goby fish, sea snails, and flatworms. Since we don't eat those things, our interest is in puffers.

The highest concentrations of toxin are in some kinds of Japanese puffers (species of the genus *Fugu*), which have killed many people who ate the raw fish. South African farmers dry whole puffers and use them as rat poison.

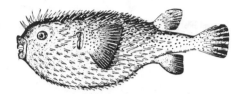

Porcupinefish
Diodon hystrix

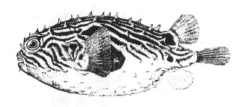

Striped Burrfish
Chilomycterus schoepfi

Northern Puffer
Sphoeroides maculatus

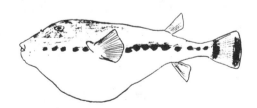

Bandtail Puffer
Sphoeroides spengleri

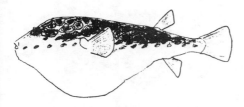

Checkered Puffer
Sphoeroides testudineus

Tetrodotoxin has been claimed to be the active ingredient in Haitian zombie potions, but recent laboratory analyses of potions supplied by so-called witch doctors have found nothing harmful. It might be worth a chuckle, but we can't rule out the possibilities that the scientists got bad batches, that the "witch doctors" were just local good-old boys jiving them, or that the material has to be fresh to work. It's noteworthy that the Japanese, with a long history of neurological victims of fugu poisoning, have never described anything like the zombie of the movies.

We have several puffers in our region. The marbled puffer occurs only in very deep water, and is easily recognized by a couple of black, fleshy tabs on its upper sides, just above the rear of the pectoral fins. It is a small fish, only getting up to seven inches long.

Far more common are the big, one-foot-long northern and southern puffers. Both are big enough to eat, have clear tail fins, and are, for the most part, identical. Some northern puffers have rich orange color on the side, and many southern puffers are heavily sprinkled with orange dots. The northern puffer will have some oblique, dark streaks on the side, while the southern puffer either has a very few fuzzy blotches or none at all. The northern puffer occurs in deep bays and near shore waters from Canada to the mouth of the St. Johns River at Jacksonville, Florida. The southern puffer is a shallow-water fish that occurs along the beaches and in estuaries from the St. Johns to the Mississippi River Delta.

We have other puffers, more common the farther south you go. The checkered puffer has a beautiful, yellow-gold network on a dark back. The bandtail puffer is a small fish, up to about six inches long, with a prominent row of sharply defined, dark marks along the side and two dark bands on the tail fin, one at the base and one at the edge.

In general, if a puffer is 10 to 12 inches long and doesn't have black, fleshy tabs on its body, the meat is probably safe to eat. (I still wouldn't trust the roe or liver.) Puffer poisoning is rare in our waters, with the very small bandtail our only frequently toxic puffer. Some marbled puffers contain tetrodotoxin, but they're distinctive and usually too small to clean.

Cleaning the large, common puffers is different from cleaning other fishes. The skin has no scales, but rather is very prickly, like a skate's back, and loose and elastic. Cut down to the bone all around the body about halfway back, and peel the rear skin off to the tail. Then cut free the meaty tail section, which will look like a small, white drumstick, and discard the remainder.

King Mackerel

THE GREEN WATER ZONE

Beyond the silt and suspended muds of the coast, clean offshore ocean water glints with sunlight, reflecting tiny particles of minerals, marine larvae, and flotsam. Foam churned by the waves quickly dissipates for lack of dissolved organic substances to hold the bubbles together. The salinity is high, about thirty-five parts of dissolved solids per thousand parts of water, twice as salty as beach water and seven times as salty as the water in the upper estuaries.

On the Atlantic side, this ocean water sweeps northward or southward over the sea bottom, driven by seasonal prevailing winds. In the Gulf of Mexico, it slowly rotates clockwise, the massive Mississippi outflow blocking the western Gulf from the eastern mass. The moving ocean rolls over uneven bottoms, swirling fine silts and minerals up from the sea floor in unseen, undersea dust storms. Some of the fine particles are engulfed by tiny sea creatures, broken up, and dissolved. They break down and become part of the seawater, to be absorbed by tiny green diatoms in glassy silicon shells multiplying in the sunlight, turning the water cloudy with their numbers and green with their chlorophyll.

Vast schools of game fish migrate through the green mists, sport and commercial boats hot on their tails. Submerged armies of Boston mackerel and silver hake migrate inexorably between Cape Cod and offshore Virginia waters, while Spanish and king mackerel move inshore, offshore, north, and south according to their age, breeding stock, and residence on the Atlantic slope or Gulf of Mexico.

The seasons are marked by subtle differences in day length and seawater temperature, and the fish respond massively. The spring ocean is different from the winter ocean, and the summer ocean different as well. In Virginia waters, spring brings bluefin tuna from offshore and bluefish from the south, and chases Boston mackerel back to the air-conditioned Gulf of Maine. In the Gulf of Mexico and on the south Atlantic coast, the empty seas begin once more to teem with the hunters and the hunted.

Down below, there are no grass beds. Vast empty stretches of barren sandy bottom mask silver- and sand-colored fish as they erratically dart and freeze on the monotonous landscape. Suddenly, rocks erupt from the bottom, teeming with boldly marked fish and shellfish hurriedly scurrying around and over, always close to shelter, while predators cruise far above like hawks.

In the north, the outcrops are so overgrown with sponges, soft corals, brown algae, red algae, worms, hydroids, and tunicates that you can't see the rocks for the encrusting marine life. Southward, a shallow shelf and intense sunlight nurture symbiotic green algae inside the tissues of sea anemones and hard corals. Calcium carbonate secreted by worms and corals rapidly builds upon rocks, shells, and skeletons. What was a stone or shell ten thousand years ago is a car-sized reef today, a living skin of hydroids, corals, and algae on its surface, archaeological layers of past civilizations below.

The hard bottoms are cities—large, complex, all different—roamed by a vast assortment of native, immigrant, and transient marine life. Schools of anchovies, herrings, jacks, tiny grunts, and porgies pick plankton in the shade of the rocks, ready to hide at the sudden appearance of a shadow. Sheepshead in strongly striped polo shirts and tautog in dull black overcoats unconcernedly crush securely cemented barnacles and tube worms, while aggressive little gobies and blennies roam through inch-high forests of hydroids courageously attacking inch-long shrimp. Giant groupers lie still among the rocks, bodies blending with the bottom, emerald eyes constantly searching in different directions, slowly breathing gill plates no more than drifting fronds of seaweed.

There's more live bottom today than ever before. With man came ships at the mercy of storms and wars; those ships became the skeletons of new reefs. Today, state agencies and fishing clubs are creating artificial reefs by sinking old ships and railroad cars, waste concrete rubble from culverts, buildings, bridges, and other massive materials clean enough to meet federal environmental standards. These reef materials are barged to appropriate bottoms where they won't sink in mud, wash away, or silt over, and then sunk in precise alignments to create or enlarge reefs of predesigned length, width, and height.

The wrecks, rocks, natural and artificial reefs, and other structure-laden bottoms are the hot spots for offshore fishermen. Most of them are too far from shore to locate by taking a range on coastal features, and many are too small to hit by compass navigation. Loran C navigation, however, can guide you to these sites with pinpoint accuracy. You'll find Loran coordinates of hard bottom features in the back of this book by state and, where appropriate, by portion of coastline.

Tautog
Tautoga onitis

TAUTOG

T he tautog ('tog, blackfish) is a thick-skinned heavyweight that lives among rocks and crushes crabs and barnacles for a living. The average fish is a pound or two, with fish in the five- to ten-pound range real armbusters.

Tautog are important from Virginia to Cape Cod, where headboats (party boats) specialize in fishing for them on rocky bottoms from spring to fall. They occur year-round in Virginia and North Carolina, but the best time to find them in our area is when the black sea bass have moved offshore and the northern populations of tautog have migrated south to spend the winter on warmer rocky bottoms.

Common Tautog Rig

(Modified Two-Hook Bottom Rig)

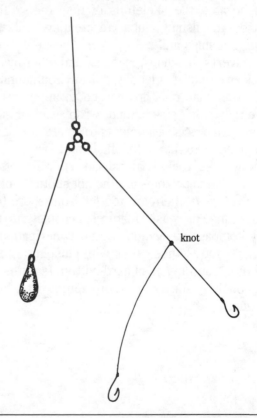

knot

Tackle is medium weight (30-pound-class), with a two-hook bottom rig. In your grandpa's day, the hook was snelled with tarred, linen codfish line. Today's anglers use short wire or heavy monofilament leaders. The standard bait is green crab, but any juicy shellfish, especially clam, will do in a pinch. Green crabs are usually caught around the dock or among rock jetties with a fish head on a string. Packed in wet newspaper and ice, they'll stay alive and dormant all day. Cut the crab in halves or quarters, and remove the claws and legs. Insert the hook through a leg joint and out the cut edge of the body, with the point exposed.

Tautog usually hit hard and fight to stay in the rocks, where they can cut your line on the ubiquitous barnacles. Strong rods are needed to convince a 'tog to give up.

Scales and skin are thick and slimy, and 'togs are best skinned. The meat is white and exceptionally light and tasty, even uncooked. I recommend it highly for sashimi.

Black Sea Bass

The black sea bass is an abundant rocky-bottom fish. There are three groups. The population that ranges from Cape Cod to Cape Hatteras is composed of larger fish than the separate group that ranges from Cape Hatteras to Cape Canaveral. The Gulf of Mexico population, generally small fish, has been isolated so long that it is now a separate subspecies. The average black sea bass is under a pound, and a three-pounder is a very large fish. Like groupers, their big heads make them look heavier than they are.

The black sea bass is not related to striped bass, but is a cousin of the groupers. Its nearest relatives are the less

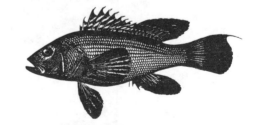

Black Sea Bass
Centropristis striatus

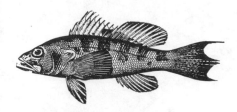

Rock Sea Bass
Centropristis philadelphica

Hand-Tied Two-Hook Bottom Rig

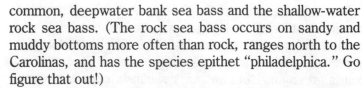

common, deepwater bank sea bass and the shallow-water rock sea bass. (The rock sea bass occurs on sandy and muddy bottoms more often than rock, ranges north to the Carolinas, and has the species epithet "philadelphica." Go figure that out!)

From New York to South Carolina, black sea bass support an important near shore headboat fishery. In the north, about a quarter of the fish caught by headboats on near shore rocky bottoms are black sea bass, about 5 percent are tautog, and most of the rest are scup (porgy). In Carolina waters, probably 95 percent of the fish caught by near shore headboats are black sea bass, scup are only seen in the winter, and the likely non-sea bass are small gag grouper and red snapper.

Northern fish move inshore in the spring for spawning from their deepwater wintering grounds far out on the continental shelf, often down to 500 feet. Southern sea bass are not migratory, but year-round residents on rocky bottoms. They also spawn in the spring.

Large fish are all hump-headed males with iridescent blue napes and white-tipped filaments on their fins. Smaller fish are all females. In common with their grouper relatives, sea bass begin life as females, most of them changing to males when they're about 10 to 12 inches long and three years old.

Sea bass eat everything and anything, with size not an issue. They often load their bellies with sand launces, anchovies, squid, or crabs. A four-inch fish will engulf a five-inch bait without a second thought. Standard tackle is a light conventional rod with a two- or three-hook bottom rig and 5/0 hooks, although hook size makes little difference. Any bait will do, from cut squid or clam to lead-head jigs.

Drop your rig to the bottom, wait for the hit, then retrieve, and you're as likely to have a double as a single. People stop catching black sea bass when they're tired of hauling them in.

The black sea bass has sweet, white, wet meat, but requires fast handling. It is recommended in many Chinese cookbooks, an honor for any fish! Sea bass should be iced, scaled, and gutted as soon as possible, not tomorrow. After death, the gallbladder (a green or yellow tube and sac on the liver) leaks, staining the meat and making it bitter. The skin weakens after death, so that scaling is apt to tear it unless the fish is very fresh, not merely iced.

Spadefish

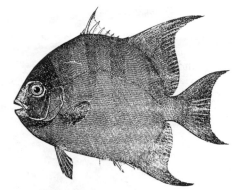

Spadefish
Chatodipterus faber

The Atlantic spadefish is strikingly similar to the South American angelfish kept in home aquariums. Occurring throughout our area, the spadefish is the only member of its worldwide family in the western North Atlantic. An almost identical fish in a related family occurs off southern Africa, where it is also called the "spadefish."

You've probably seen the half-inch-long post larvae drifting with the waves in sandy shoreline shallows on southern beaches during the summer. The tiny fish resemble small pieces of dead, black leaves, detritus, or seeds, and swim away when you attempt to catch them by cupping your hands.

Big spadefish aggregate around structures. They occur in small groups or huge schools of over a thousand fish around bridge stanchions and above jetties, artificial reefs, and wrecks at depths of 20 to more than 100 feet. They feed on worms, soft corals, algae, jellyfish, and swimming types of tunicates (sea squirts).

Although reputed to attain 20 pounds, a 5- or 6-pounder is average, and a 9-pounder is an exceptional fish. Spadefish fight hard, and are hard to catch unless you know the trick of using jellyfish for bait.

There are many kinds of jellyfish, and the one called the jellyball is preferred. Jellyballs are practically all head and almost no tentacles (for jellyfish). Other jellyfish are also effective, and most of them don't sting. Those that can sting the heck out of you are the Portugese man-of-war (recognized by its blue float shaped like a sail or a wonton pinched along the top margin) and the sea wasp (a square-bodied jellyfish). All other jellyfish are round-bodied, and either don't sting at all or not enough to bother you.

Where do you get them? You can scoop jellyfish out of the water or look for them washed up on the beach. Keep them iced and they'll last for hours. Any jellyfish that falls apart is probably old and rotten, and shouldn't be used. Strips, about a half-inch wide by two to three inches long are preferred, but small, whole, one- to three-inch long jellyballs work fine.

Tackle should be one-handed and light, about 20-pound-class or less. Bury a short-shanked, 1/0 or number one hook in the jellyfish meat and free-line the baited hook down into the water column over the wreck or reef, perhaps assisted by a split-shot. Spadefish are nibblers, so wait until the fish moves off rapidly with your bait before setting the hook. Like other flat-bodied fishes, spadefish put up a very strong fight for their size, and there's always the chance of a monster.

If you don't get action right away, tease or chum the school up to the boat. Drop pieces of jellyfish into the water to entice them up, or skewer a group of jellyballs on a wire and drop it to just above the bottom. When you feel nibbles, work the teaser upward to within sight of the boat and keep it in the water to hold the school nearby.

Spadefish should be skinned first, the meat filleted from the bones and the red strip removed. The white meat is similar in quality to that of sea bass, and should be iced immediately.

Sheepshead

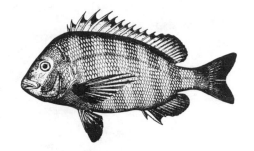

Sheepshead
Archosargus probatocephalus

T he sheepshead (sheephead, convict fish) is a banded member of the porgy family that occurs wherever hard bottoms are washed by a strong flow of clear water. Using its sharp eyes and equally sharp incisor teeth, it picks off barnacles, tube worms, crabs, and shrimp from rocky bottoms, jetties, and reefs, crushing the prey's shells with heavy molars on the sides of the jaws and roof of the mouth. There isn't much that can withstand a sheepshead's dentition.

Sheepshead migrate slightly offshore in cold weather, but otherwise are common, year-round residents of rocky bottoms from North Carolina to Texas. At one time they were abundant in New York and common as far north as Cape Cod, but may have been eliminated in northern waters by competition from northern porgy or scup, which undergo great cycles of abundance.

Sheepshead breed offshore in the spring. The babies make their way to estuaries and bays, where they seek out low-salinity grassy areas, feeding on soft foods until their adult teeth form. They then move outside to hard bottoms, where they take up adult food habits.

As adults, sheepshead graze over rocks, feeding on small, mostly attached shellfish such as tube worms, barnacles, and mussels, which probably account for their tasty meat. They get much larger than tautog, probably up to 30 pounds, with 5-pound fish common, and 10- to 15-pound fish not rare.

Sheepshead fight hard and are hard to catch. The light tap of even a big sheepshead is difficult to feel, and specialists prefer short, heavy graphite rods for their sensitivity and backbone.

A single number one hook, snelled with a six-inch-long, 50-pound-test monofilament leader, is baited with a whole sand flea (mole crab) or fiddler crab, alive and roe-laden if possible. The hook is tied above the sinker for fishing on the bottom or below it for fishing just off the bottom. Live or dead shrimp, clam, and squid also work, but attract too many other fish.

The bait is fished right at the top of the rocks. If you feel anything at all, set the hook in a short, sharp jab, and if he's on, hang on.

People who don't change bait because they didn't get a bite don't catch sheepshead. The bait should be changed at least every 10 minutes, tapped or not. One of the tricks is to forget about feeling the bite, but to simply jerk the rod upward at frequent intervals. The old saw about "hooking him just before the bite" has more than a kernel of truth.

Scup

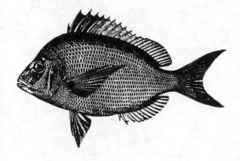

Scup
Stenotomus chrysops

Millions of silvery scup (scuppaug, porgy, silver snapper) cover the sandy or rocky, shallow, near shore ocean floor from New Jersey to Cape Cod all summer long like iridescent locusts, eating all manner of invertebrates from amphipods to sand dollars and crabs to worms, and even taking squid and an occasional small fish. As the waters chill with the onset of fall, they migrate south and offshore to the warm, dark waters of the continental shelf off North Carolina and Virginia, where commercial fishermen haul them up from depths of 20 to 50 fathoms (120 to 300 feet). Winter sportfishing for scup out of North Carolina (where they're indiscriminantly lumped with all other porgies as "silver snapper") is just beginning.

Breeding occurs near shore during the spring and summer, with the young getting up to 4 or 5 inches the first year. Breeding begins at two years of age, when the fish are 7 inches long. A good fish is 12 to 14 inches long, one or two pounds, and five or six years old. Top size is about a foot and a half and three or four pounds.

The standard tackle is light to medium weight (20- to 30-pound-class), armed with a two-hook bottom rig baited with clam or squid and still-fished on a hard bottom, or wherever the other boats are grouped. Doubles are common.

Scup, scuppaug, and porgy are corruptions of the Narraganset Indian name "mishcuppauog." Silver snapper is a name invented by headboat skippers to make offshore porgies more attractive to people who pay $45 in the oversold expectation that they'll catch red snappers.

There are other common porgies in our area. The largest are the red, jolthead, and whitebone porgies. Somewhat smaller (but not much) are the pinfish and spottail pinfish. Much smaller is the longspine.

Longspine porgies are only common in southern waters. Pinfish and spottail pinfish are abundant on southern rocky bottoms, where they commonly attain a size of well over a pound and make fine eating. The red, whitebone, and jolthead porgies, considerably larger, are usually taken offshore on the snapper and grouper banks, where they make up most of the summertime "silver snapper" fishery.

All porgies are excellent food fish which should never be filleted, as the bones give much of the flavor to the meat. Little ones are usually fried, while larger fish should be poached or steamed like red snappers to bring out their quality.

Pinfish
Lagodon rhomboides

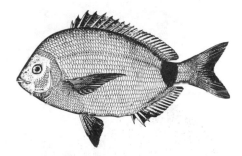

Spottail Pinfish
Diplodus holbrooki

Amberjack

At six feet and 170 pounds, the greater amberjack is our largest jack. Longer than a crevalle jack, and with a dark, oblique band through the eye, its eight dorsal-fin spines distinguish it from the smaller (up to

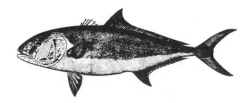

Amberjack
Seriola dumerili

three feet), similar, and less common almaco jack, which also occurs in our waters. Ranging from Cape Cod to Brazil, amberjack are on virtually every reef, rocky bottom, and offshore rig. Big ones aggregate on offshore structures in blue or green water, and amberjack of all sizes school when they enter clear or green (but not brown) murky beaches for feeding. Amberjack average 20 to 70 pounds, and often get larger. They'll take any live bait, most dead ones, a surface plug, or a deep jig. It's hard not to hook an amberjack, but it will put an ache in your back before it comes to the boat.

Big ones are considered a nuisance by king mackerel tournament fishermen, bait by sharkers, trip-savers by charter boat captains, and useless by eaters because of the unsightly larval tapeworms in their tail meat. The small ones (10 to 20 pounds) are considered edible by people who have no taste; amberjack at larger sizes have a unique flavor, comparable to wet ashes from burned garbage.

Now, as to making good shark bait...

Sharks and Sawfish

The sharks and their derivatives, the rays, skates, and sawfishes, number less than a thousand species. They have distinctive kinds of parasites found in no other animals, digestive organs unique in the animal kingdom, and their own set of diseases. They don't have a swim bladder or scales, but sharks have rock-hard dermal denticles. The skin of shark jaws produces a never-ending supply of teeth to replace those lost. Shark livers may be a fourth the body weight and rich in vitamin A or almost devoid of it.

Commercial shark fisheries have been established often in the United States. They all fail after a few years because

Mako Shark
Photo by Bob Benway, National Marine Fisheries Service

Shark Rig

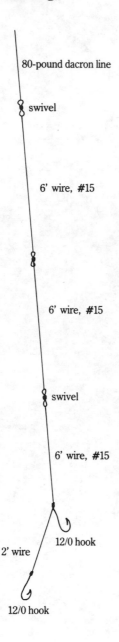

80-pound dacron line

swivel

6' wire, #15

6' wire, #15

swivel

6' wire, #15

12/0 hook

2' wire

12/0 hook

sharks are not equally valuable and because they cannot take the fishing pressure. It may take a shark a decade or more to reach sexual maturity, but they may reach harvest size first, so they are rapidly wiped out wherever commercial fishing starts.

Many sharks are migratory, from the east-west trans-Atlantic blue shark to the far-ranging tiger. If you'd like to participate in a shark-tagging program, write to John G. (Jack) Casey, NOAA-NMFS, Narragansett, R.I. 02882.

The IGFA recognizes the white, mako, porbeagle, tiger (but not the sand tiger), blue, thresher, and hammerhead sharks as game fish. Today, there are shark clubs and tournaments all along the Atlantic coast.

Many of our sharks range from inshore estuarine waters to the Gulf Stream, while others typically occur only in blue water. In general, the techniques are the same.

Stand-up sharking from a boat requires a big reel loaded with heavy line, a heavy shark rod, gimbal rod belt, and a Florida shoulder harness. Sharks are better fought sitting down with your feet propped against the transom.

Anything over 4/0 will provide some sport, and novices begin with a 6/0. Serious sharkers use 9/0 to 12/0 reels loaded with 80- to 130-pound-test dacron line.

Terminal tackle varies in different locations. Most depend on a two-hook rig in series or parallel, both hooks imbedded in the same bait. A typical rig is a wishbone arrangement of 600-pound-test cable with 10/0 to 16/0 fixed hooks and 20 feet of number 15 wire leader. Other rigs depend on 6-foot segments of wire separated by swivels to counter twists. The weight of the bait and tackle holds the rig in place. Gary Seay, the "Virginia Beach Sharkman" (who only fishes for half-tonners), starts with a barrel swivel crimped to 29 feet of heavy cable. The cable is crimped to 10 feet of light chain, and the end of the chain holds two 16/0 O'Shaughnessy hooks in series, about 18 inches apart, and filed on four sides for easier penetration. Big rubber bands are wrapped around chain and hook to keep the hook points out of the links. Gary fishes several 9/0 to 12/0 outfits at different depths, using plastic milk jugs as floats.

I use a 10/0 reel and heavy rod. My terminal rig begins with two 12/0 hooks bolted in series to a 5-foot length of light chain, the chain crimped to a 15-foot length of 600-pound-test trailer cable, and the cable crimped to a swivel that connects to my 80-pound-test dacron line. Cable withstands being wrapped around a twisting, struggling shark, and chain withstands the teeth, which cable may not.

It's dangerous to fish alone, as sharks can be awfully big, and just as unpredictable as they are powerful. You will need help holding the fish at the boat for tail-roping if you want to keep it.

The best baits for sharking on the surface are a live bluefish or menhaden. For bottom or mid-depth fishing, use half a stingray or skate or a fillet of shark. Other favored baits are big tuna or mackerel heads from a charter boat marina, or a two-foot-long fillet of amberjack, split to look like an Uncle Josh pork rind. Using baits this big and bloody makes the value of chumming questionable. If you want to chum, frozen mink food from a commercial fish house (processing scraps of flounder, trout, and bluefish) is a good buy at $20 for a 50-pound sack.

Most sharkers don't use flying gaffs on these bruisers, preferring a long-handled gaff to manipulate the fish for tail-roping. The tail rope is a big sliding loop that goes over the tail as the shark comes alongside, then is tightened up, the tail lifted out of the water, and the line lashed to something that won't rip out, like the entire center console. If that tail should get back into the water, you're in trouble.

Several shark identification guides are available, including *Angler's Guide to Sharks of the Northeastern United States* (U.S. Fish & Wildlife Service Circular 179, Superintendent of Documents, Washington, D.C. 20402); *Sharks, Sawfish, Skates, and Rays of the Carolinas* (F. J. Schwartz, 3407

Shark Rig

80-pound dacron line

swivel

cable clamp

15' trailer cable, 600 lb. test

cable clamp

light chain

bolt

12/0 hook

bolt

12/0 hook

Shortfin Mako Shark

Photo by Harold Wes Pratt, National Oceanic and Atmospheric Administration-National Marine Fisheries Service

Arendell Street, Morehead City, N.C. 28577); *An Angler's Guide to South Carolina Sharks* (Marine Resources Department, Box 12559, Charleston, S.C. 29412); and *The Sharks of North American Waters* (Drawer C, Texas A&M University Press, College Station, Tx. 77843).

Blue Shark   Blue sharks are cobalt-colored fish with distinctive, enormous pectoral fins. They're very common from Virginia northward, occasionally ranging south to the Carolinas. They occur offshore in both green and blue water, feeding on bluefish, small tuna, herring, and other ocean fishes which they easily pursue at high speed. Blue sharks are sporting fish on light tackle (30-pound-class), but will put an ache in your back even with 50-pound-class gear. They're bright blue with a white belly, and most regular sharkers tag and release them.

Mako Shark   Spectacular leapers and runners, reaching enormous size, makos are the blue marlins of sharks. Unfortunately, they're uncommon south of Virginia during the bulk of the season, but might be in offshore Carolina waters during the winter. Look for blue water offshore at 65-69 degrees Fahrenheit and use a bluefish for bait; bluefish are the mako's favorite food. Mako fishing generally requires a fighting chair and billfish tackle. They're too big, fast, and strong for stand-up fishing for most of us. In our region, few anglers are likely to see a mako, and that's too bad.

Bigeye Thresher Shark   Bigeye threshers are our only common thresher shark. They occur throughout our area, but are more common offshore and to the north. Threshers feed on schooling fish, which they herd with their elongated tail into a compact mass before rushing in to feed. Powerful and aggressive, threshers have been known to attack small

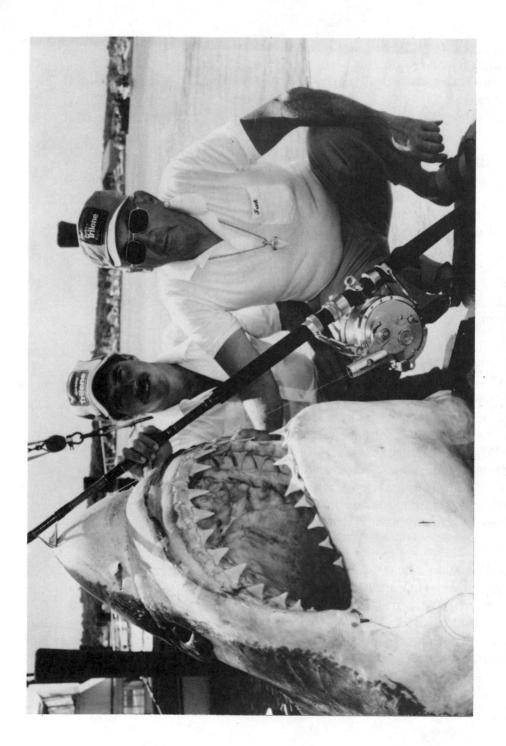

3,427-pound Great White Shark
Largest fish ever taken on rod and reel
Caught by Donnie Braddick and Frank Mundus

Photo courtesy of Berkley

boats. Fifteen-footers are common (half is tail). A 740-pounder was taken off New Zealand, but they probably reach 1,000 pounds. Threshers are readily identified by the enormous upper lobe of the tail fin.

WHITE SHARK   Years ago, before the Endangered Species Act was in effect, Captain Frank Mundus (the model for the irrational shark-hating skipper in the movie, *Jaws*) used to carry a gun offshore and shoot small black whales, porpoises, and sea turtles for shark chum. He was not very popular with other skippers, for obvious reasons. Fortunately, that kind of behavior is illegal today.

Curiously, on August 6, 1986, Donnie Braddick and Frank Mundus brought a 16 + -foot white shark, weighing 3,450 pounds to dock at Montauk, New York. It was, according to the proud fishermen, feeding on a dead whale floating offshore. That must have been a stroke of luck. Of the hundred or so skippers I've interviewed, not one has ever seen a dead whale floating offshore.

The largest white ever measured was a 20-footer landed off Cuba many years ago; it was not weighed. Whites (known as white pointers in Australian waters) are the smallest of a prehistoric group of similar sharks that, to our knowledge, no longer exists.

The white is a cold-water shark that migrates between Canadian waters and Cape Hatteras. In the Bay of Fundy, it comes right up against the rocky shoreline after seals, and pursues tuna into nets, destroying both. It winters off Cape Hatteras.

Resembling the mako and porbeagle, the white is distinguished by its perfectly triangular teeth serrated on both sides, heavy body, sharply delineated white belly, and a well-developed keel on the base of the tail. It seldom occurs where people swim, and feeds on large fish, dead whales, live porpoises, sea turtles, swordfish, marlin, and live seals. It is the only truly dangerous shark in American waters, but it's wrong to call it a "man-eater." It is a seal-eater, and the people most often attacked today are divers wearing black wet suits and swimming where seals feed. Whites were probably the sharks that attacked merchant seamen from torpedoed Liberty ships in the North Atlantic during World War II, and also ravaged victims of the *Andrea Doria* tragedy. There are a few cases of whites attacking swimmers on northeast beaches of the United States.

The white is unusual in other ways. Most sharks are cold-blooded, having no system for regulating body temperature. You've heard that giant bluefin tuna are heat conservers, able to hold their body temperatures several degrees above the surrounding seawater. Warm-bloodedness has also been determined in white, mako, thresher, and porbeagle sharks.

Whites are slow growers, and there aren't many of them. There is no way they could support a sustained commercial or recreational fishery. If any shark species needs federal protection, it's this magnificent animal. For more information, you can order *Biology of the White Shark* (Memoirs of the Southern California Academy of Sciences, vol. 9, 1985, 150 pp., $22.50) by writing SCAS, 900 Exposition Boulevard, Los Angeles, Ca. 90007.

Tiger Shark The tiger shark is our largest common southern shark, with half-ton fish caught from just about every coastal state in the South. The world record was a 1,780-pounder caught from a pier in South Carolina by the amazing Walter Maxwell, who lost a bigger one the day before. Maxwell also holds the North Carolina state record for a fish almost as big. Several half-tonners have been caught in Virginia, South Carolina, and Florida. Tigers are abundant wherever they occur, extend from New England to South America, and range from the beach to the Gulf Stream. One tiger tagged off New York was recovered off Costa Rica, a distance of 1,850 miles. It is the ideal shark for fishermen, and plenty of sharkers in shark clubs fish only for big tigers, starting the season when the water temperature gets above 64 degrees Fahrenheit. Big tackle is recommended (although a 900-pounder was taken by a Virginia Beach sharker in 1986 on 30-pound-test line), and the favorite bait is a whole, big seatrout, but they're not particular.

It may be the most indiscriminate feeder of all; its stomach commonly contains tiny birds, whelk operculums, dogs, pigs, sea turtles, fish, crabs, and tin cans. Tiger sharks have been blamed for numerous attacks, and are listed second only to whites in the Shark Attack File. But there's only one report of confirmed human remains in a tiger, and that corresponded with a seaman who fell off a ship and drowned. A recent mass attack by sharks in the Caribbean killed a large number of people from a sinking boat, but the sharks, observed from the air, were not identified.

Tigers are not so much aggressive predators as they are indiscriminate scavengers. They're also very powerful fish that fight hard.

Tiger sharks have triangular teeth serrated on both slopes but notched on the back side, normal gums that can hide the teeth, and (usually) mottled flanks.

Lemon and Bull Sharks   Lemon and bull sharks eat sting-rays, sea catfish, other sharks, crabs, and anything else that comes their way. Averaging 150 pounds, 300- and 400-pounders are not rare, and they get much larger. Both are common throughout our area, but most common on the Gulf Coast.

Bull sharks are aggressive, and they're dangerous because they come into very shallow water and range well up rivers into virtually fresh water. The largest, in the 800-pound range, were taken well up in Chesapeake Bay. In South America's freshwater Lake Nicaragua, in Asia, and on the coast of Africa, bull sharks occasionally attack people. In mid-April of 1987, a young girl's arm was severed by a shark while she was in chest-deep water at Port Aransas, Texas. That was probably a bull shark attack.

Lemon sharks, which usually occupy the same habitat (murky, low-salinity water close to shore), are readily identified by having two dorsal fins of equal size, regular shark teeth that can be hidden by the gums, and no markings. Lemons are not aggressive, and are favored laboratory animals by Eugenie Clark and other shark behaviorists.

Sand Tiger Shark   Sand tigers are big, inshore sharks that come right up to the beaches. Weak swimmers, large sand tigers can be caught on moderate tackle. That's a nice feat for a fish that averages 150 to 200 pounds, but gets much bigger. The jaws make spectacular trophies, and the meat is delicious even among sharks. Sand tigers look like gangly mouthed catfish. They're easily identified by having prominent, long, curved teeth that go in all directions, two dorsal fins of equal height, and usually some mottled markings on the sides.

Hammerheads   We have several species of hammerhead sharks in our area. The smalleye hammerhead only occurs in the Gulf of Mexico. The smooth hammerhead is a northern fish ranging south to the middle Atlantic coast. The great hammerhead is a southern form ranging northward to the Carolinas. The scalloped hammerhead is common throughout our area.

Hammerheads are big fish with small but dangerous jaws, and are powerful swimmers. They feed on live fish of all kinds, especially love to eat stingrays, and seldom take a dead bait. They're exciting fish to watch, as they make sudden, quick movements when close to their prey. Very active and quick to encircle a structure when hooked, they give the impression of being intelligent sharks.

Sandbar Shark   The sandbar shark (New York ground shark, brown shark) is common both inshore and offshore in the Gulf Stream. One individual tagged off New England was recovered off Mexico. Sandbars live at least 20 to 30 years but attain a length of only about eight feet. The 213-pound world record was set off Virginia in 1986, but most fish are under 100 pounds.

Blacktip and Spinner Sharks   Blacktip and spinner sharks are relatively small sharks, usually in the 100-pound range or smaller, and are common inshore off sandy beaches throughout our area during the warm months. The blacktip has a white anal fin. Both species leap out of the water and spin, and you might see ten or more in the air at the same time, if you're lucky. They're also quite good on the table.

Sawfish   The sawfishes are sharklike rays that get up to 18 or 20 feet and 1,000 pounds or more. The smalltooth sawfish ranges north to Chespeake Bay, while the largetooth is more common on the Gulf Coast. Sawfishes usually feed in shallow water, and may penetrate up rivers. They slash schools of fish with their toothed bills, then pick up the pieces and chase down the wounded. Powerful fighters, they're seldom landed.

King Mackerel
Scomberomorus cavalla

King Mackerel

King mackerel occur from Cape Cod to Brazil, but because the South Atlantic Ocean fish may actually be a different species, we'll discuss data from North American waters only. Kings occur throughout our range, but are most abundant from Cape Lookout, North Carolina, south to Jacksonville, Florida. On the Gulf Coast, they're no longer common. Decreased commercial landings in recent years have prompted the National Marine Fisheries Service, the South Atlantic and Gulf Fishery Management councils, and various states to place two- or three-fish possession limits on king mackerel. Check the current regulations at your marina before any trip.

King mackerel are seasonally abundant on the Atlantic coast in the spring and fall, and are most likely to be found in the northeast and northwest Gulf of Mexico in summer and fall. Smaller fish are strongly migratory, while larger fish tend to be year-round offshore residents off North Carolina, south Florida, and Louisiana.

There are several groups. The smaller fish making up most Gulf Coast stocks have virtually disappeared from overfishing, and it may be a few years until management measures can bring them back. Kings spawn when they're only two-and-a-half feet long, so a few years of strong management may do the job.

They grow rapidly for the first three years, and then slow down considerably, but growth rates vary in different parts of the country and may be related to food supplies or competition.

Female king mackerel get to be at least fourteen years old and nearly six feet long, and males are known which were nine years old and three feet long. Maximum size and age are unknown, and it's not certain that there's a sex difference in this regard. Stocks seem to differ in average size. The largest fish, as a group, all came from the offshore Louisiana stock. Maximum size is 100 pounds, and the largest taken on rod-and-reel (so far) was 90 pounds.

The little 5- to 15-pound "snakes" make up the charter boat and commercial fishery. The "smoker" kings in the 30-pound-and-up class are the ones sought by serious king fishermen. To learn about those fish, you need to ask the tournament fishermen who catch them with the selective techniques that snake fishermen don't use. The most important of those techniques is slow-trolling with live bait.

Most anglers are uninformed, which is excusable, or lazy, which is not. They troll at normal speeds with Drone spoons, Japanese feathers, or strip baits. They catch small fish, but don't win tournaments. Instead, they build up the kitties for the benefit of the guys who know how to win. There are no finer experts than the tournament fishermen of Wilmington, North Carolina, and this is how they do it.

You can find big fish inshore, but you'll find more of them offshore. The top spots are offshore structures, freighter and tanker wrecks, and high-profile reefs. The best places also hold amberjack, and signify that there's plenty of food around.

Smokers aggregate at offshore structures and seldom take fast-moving baits. Free-lining a big, live bait to them usually brings an amberjack, and there goes the next hour. The trick is to get the bait to the smokers, but to keep it away from amberjack and snakes.

You need to know four things to catch smokers: what to use, how to get it, how to keep it, and how to rig it.

Kings have different food preferences in different waters. In the Carolinas, menhaden and "grass shad" (thread herring) are the most important food item and the top bait fish. From Georgia to north Florida, small jacks called scads or "cigar minnows" are the most important food item in the diet. Blue runners or "hardtails" are a good substitute. Spanish sardines (actually small, rounded herrings) are best on the middle east Florida coast, ballyhoo in south Florida, seatrout

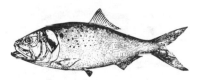

Menhaden
Brevoortia tyrannus

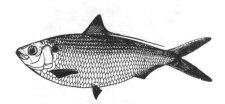

Thread Herring
Opisthonema oglinum

Spanish Sardine
Sardinella aurita

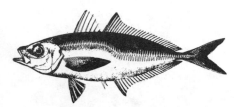

Rough Scad
Trachurus lathami

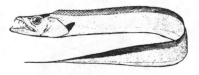

Cutlassfish
Trichiurus lepturus

Ballyhoo
Hemirhamphus brasiliensis

in Louisiana, and cutlass fish off Texas. Try to use what's most important in your area, if you can get it.

In general, the bait fish should be frisky and at least 10 inches long. Menhaden and small bluefish (with the tails lopped off) work everywhere and are readily caught.

Most tournament fishermen use menhaden, which they catch early the morning of tournament day, as the baits seem to lose scent after a few hours. Look for menhaden in backwaters and at intersections of the Intracoastal Waterway, near marinas, or close to the beach outside, behind jetties, or near piers or breakwaters. Watch for blips, rings, and flashes. Outside, you may have to rely on diving pelicans. Ignore gulls; they don't eat 10-inch menhaden.

Use a 7- to 12-foot, very wide mesh, nylon monofilament cast net, or the largest you can throw. Cast net sizes refer to the radius, so even a 7-footer will cover an area of 154 square feet. Let it sink to the bottom, or nearly so, before drawing it up through the center hole and bringing in the purse. Sometimes a single cast will load the net with a day's supply; other times, you can't find bait or they're too small and too few. If a menhaden boat or a shrimper is working nearby, you might be able to buy all the live bait you want.

Menhaden require lots of oxygen and room, and need to keep swimming. If they get into a corner, they burn up lots of energy pushing straight ahead and produce excess slime that covers their gills and kills them. A circular live-bait well will let them swim in circles without expending lots of energy or producing too much slime.

Rigging a live menhaden for slow-trolling requires hooking it with minimal damage. If you hook it through the jaws, it can't breathe and will die. If you hook it high on the back, it will drag unnaturally. The fish can be hooked through the eye sockets (not the eyes). However, nostril hookups give the most natural pull with the least damage.

The pulling hook should be a single, short-shanked, 1/0 to 3/0 bronze hook on a three-foot black or coffee-colored wire leader, number 2 (27-pound-test) to number 5 (45-pound-test). Knot the braided wire or twist or crimp the single-strand wire.

To the bend of the pulling hook (not the eye; it might pull out), crimp or tie a six-inch wire dropper ending in an extra-strong, bronze number 1 to 2/0 treble hook. Insert one prong lightly through the skin of the fish's back. A second dropper, rigged in parallel or in series, dangles freely.

King Mackerel Slow Trolling Rig

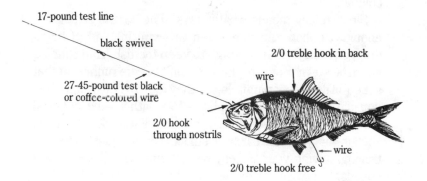

17-pound test line

black swivel

27-45-pound test black or coffee-colored wire

2/0 hook through nostrils

wire

2/0 treble hook in back

wire

2/0 treble hook free

Use a 20-pound-class live-bait rod and high quality conventional reel. Ignore advice to set the drag at a quarter the breaking strength of the line. Tournament fishermen set the drag tension to just above free spool, so the fish runs under minimal pressure. Small hooks tear out easily; don't let that happen.

In the past, a secret weapon of tournament winners was jury-rigged chum. They would take fish dying in the live-bait well or worn out and removed from the hooks, and crank them through a hand-operated meat grinder clamped to the transom. It didn't take much chum to put out a big slick and, since trolling was done very slowly anyway, the slick would hold together. Sometimes the slick would bring bluefish or sharks, and then it was time to break the chum line and move somewhere else.

A few years ago, the Wilmington guys started buying fish meal and oil from the local menhaden processors and mixing them for chum, eliminating the need for the old meat grinder. Today, oil alone is used, and can be purchased at some tackle shops for about six dollars a gallon. Dip a sponge in the oil and drag the sponge behind the boat to produce a surface chum slick. Although devoid of sinking particles, it works; apparently, the smelly molecules work down into the water column.

Slow-trolling means what it says. The boat is run slowly enough to allow the menhaden to swim instead of being dragged, and just fast enough to keep the fish from running up to the stern. Some big motors can't handle running at that speed all day; their plugs clog or they die. To get around this, you can run at a slightly higher RPM with a vertical board mounted on the lower unit, you can pull a bucket as a sea anchor, or you can carry a smaller motor just for slow-trolling, saving your big engine for running at its intended speeds.

Big kings hit from the back or side, or erupt from below like a submarine-launched missile and cut the bait in half. With luck, he'll take the half with hooks. If he's on, don't jerk the rod. If he's not, don't reel in to change bait for a full minute; if the fish hasn't hooked itself, it may come back for the other piece.

On a good hit, the king hooks itself inside the mouth or in the skin of the face. Because the small treble hooks have a shallow bite, and because mackerel skin is very delicate, just let the fish run. Seldom will a king run more than a hundred yards, and it will never run out all your line. If the drag is set very lightly, the fish won't get away.

Kings usually make one high-speed run, let you bring them to the boat, and then make a second run. After that they bulldog, and should be eased in with slow, gentle pumping and absolutely no slack at any time. You can increase pulling pressure on the fish by lightly thumbing the spool on the lift, but don't tighten the drag. The only link between you and the fish may be one prong of a tiny treble hook slowly tearing through paper-thin skin.

There are big bucks in king mackerel tournaments, and some guys will do anything to win. In the 1986 Wrightsville Beach (North Carolina) tournament, a keypuncher accidentally recorded a 49-pound amberjack as a king mackerel, awarding it second place. Before the error was discovered, the guys with the jack had already accepted the $10,000 prize money and had to be sued to give it back.

There's also the possibility of crooked fishermen entering previously caught smokers in tournaments. This problem is combatted by using a biochemical method to measure freshness of fish meat, known as the K value. First, inosine and hypoxanthine are extracted from the suspect fish meat. Then, the total amount is compared with the total adenosine triphosphate (ATP) and breakdown products by treating the mix with specific enzymes. The red color change in the final stage tells you whether the fish was recently caught or not. Another method for determining freshness is to look at ionic changes in the muscle cells of fish. This is done with an electronic K meter.

Atlantic Mackerel
Scomber scombrus

Atlantic Mackerel

Atlantic (Boston) mackerel range from the Gulf of Maine to Cape Hatteras. The larger, older fish occur near shore in late March and early April for spawning. The fish then slowly move northward and offshore, and enter the Gulf of Maine about mid-June. Headboats operating out of Virginia ports pursue them in early spring, but this is the southernmost point of traditional recreational fishing.

The average mackerel caught is 16 inches long, one to one-and-a-quarter pounds, and 5 or 6 years old. Atlantic mackerel are long-lived, but even a 10-year-old fish weighs less than two pounds. Maximum size is about four pounds (age unknown) and 22 inches.

Mackerel eat plankton, small squid, pelagic crustaceans, small fish, and fish eggs. Catches are very variable from year to year.

Prodigious spawners, a single female may produce a quarter-million to two million eggs. Although a large stock would seem to favor maximum reproduction and a large year class, it doesn't work that way. Instead, good year classes occur when adult stocks are down, suggesting that either the big fish are major predators of their own eggs and young, or that ocean water quality and food supplies determine egg and larval survival.

Mackerel schools are massive, ranging from just under the surface to about mid-depth.

Jigging with small (about two-inch) silvery lures is the easiest way to catch mackerel, but they'll hit anything that moves, especially if it's silver or white. Some guys tie on a heavy chromed jig for weight, and add a series of small white jigs or bare hooks covered with tubing at one-foot intervals above, with or without short droppers. They can also be taken on a fly rod with a sinking line and a white streamer, and may even jump. It's no trick to catch a mackerel; the trick is to catch several at a time, and meat fishermen use a "mackerel tree"—a cluster of lures on a spreader—or a long series of short-leadered lures on a long dropper, ending in a heavy jig.

Most of the commercial catch is brined and pickled. Split and grilled with lemon and salt over an outdoor barbeque, fresh mackerel are pleasantly flavored rather than strong-tasting.

The related chub mackerel occurs worldwide, is smaller, seldom attaining more than 12 inches, and has a bigger eye (very noticeable when both kinds are side by side) and a different pattern on the back. The chub mackerel is an irregular visitor to our northern waters and is equally good to eat.

Chub Mackerel
Scomber japonicus

Spanish Mackerel

S panish mackerel migrate all along the east coast from Maine to the Caribbean, over-wintering off northern South America, then coming north in April or May, and splitting into Gulf and Atlantic groups.

As the water warms above 72 degrees Fahrenheit, small groups of Spanish begin spawning at night at the mouths of estuaries. Spawning activity peaks in May, but continues all summer. The floating eggs hatch the next night, the tiny larvae only a tenth of an inch long, but already impressive with big heads and sharp teeth. They grow quickly, and by two months are an inch and three-quarters long. Spanish mackerel move north and south with the seasons, mature at three years of age, when they're fourteen inches long, and may get up to thirty inches long, 6 pounds in weight, and nine years of age. The IGFA world record is a 13-pound fish caught off North Carolina in 1987. Females grow faster and larger than males. They school at mid-depth or near the

Spanish Mackerel
Scomberomorus maculatus

surface, close to shore wherever the water is of high quality, feeding on anchovies, silversides, and small herrings.

In recent years, Spanish mackerel landings have plummeted, and the South Atlantic and Gulf of Mexico Fishery Management councils have restricted the commercial and recreational catches. At this writing, there was a ten-fish-per-person limit in effect, and the recreational fishery in the federal zone was just closed with six months to go in the season. The regulations will probably change at least once a year, so check with your state agency or marina.

The ideal outfit is a light, short, stiff rod with 17-pound-test clear monofilament line. They spook in clear water, so don't use snap-swivels to connect the lure to the leader; use a knot. The small silvery lure should be tied to 20 feet of 25-pound-test monofilament leader, and the leader connected to your line with a small black swivel to take care of line twist.

The best lures are small Clark spoons, #1 Hopkins jigs, and other long, silvery, wobbly lures. Troll at moderate speed well back from the prop wash to avoid bluefish. Work the outer edges of inlets, deep waters of bights, slack areas behind jetties, or along the drop-offs off the beaches. Most Spanish will be under three pounds, but four-pounders are taken on occasion.

There are several kinds of mackerel in the Atlantic, and it is possible that some large "Spanish" mackerel were cases of misidentification, based on the presence of yellow spots. That's not a reliable characteristic. You should identify mackerel primarily by the shape of the lateral line, and secondarily by the shape and arrangement of orange or yellow spots plus the presence of a black smudge on the dorsal fin. King mackerel have a lateral line that drops steeply at about the middle of the body; small ones may have scattered dark or brassy yellow spots on the side. Spanish mackerel have brassy yellow round spots on the side, a gently falling lateral line, and a black smudge on the front of the dorsal fin. The rare cero mackerel resembles the Spanish but is larger, and its more elongated yellow spots are arranged into one or two broken rows. The IGFA record book states that the Spanish mackerel is "considered large at 10 pounds . . . (but) . . . some record specimens will grow to more than twice that size."

Twice that size? What "record" specimens? Can Spanish mackerel really get into the 20-pound range? Every "record" of Spanish mackerel attaining giant size can be traced back to a single hearsay report of a field identification in Hugh Smith's *Fishes of North Carolina* (1907). Smith remarked:

> The fish attains a large size, 9 or 10 pounds being the normal maximum. Very exceptionally, however, it becomes larger; and a few years ago one was found in the Washington, D.C. market from Chesapeake Bay which was 41 inches long and weighed 25 pounds; it was seen and identified by Professor B.W. Evermann and others from the United States Bureau of Fisheries.

If the lateral line was not examined (and we have no way of knowing), then Evermann's 25-pound "Spanish" was probably a king or cero mackerel.

CERO

C ero are normally found from the Florida Keys northward to Dade County. They are abundant in the Bahamas, Cuba, and the West Indies, and have been reported (with varying degrees of reliability) from northern states. See the section on Spanish mackerel for identifying characteristics.

Cero
Scomberomorus regalis

Males mature at 14 inches, females at 15 inches. They spawn inshore of the continental shelf throughout the year, with peaks in May and September. The average fish is 3 to 5 pounds, but they get up to four feet long and 26 pounds. Reports of fish to six feet and 35 pounds are unreliable.

Great Barracuda
Sphyraena barracuda

Barracuda

Barracuda occur in all the warm seas of the world. There are some twenty species worldwide, with three of them (the great barracuda and two minnow-sized relatives) occurring throughout our area. The great barracuda occurs inshore when small, and most individuals move offshore with increasing size. It is very common on reefs from Virginia to Texas.

Great barracuda get up to 6 feet and 103 pounds (reports of 10-footers are unverified), rarely exceed 4 feet or 50 pounds, and are generally harmless. There are only about thirty documented cases of "attacks," some in murky coastal water, some from fish attacking jewelry that probably looked like small bait fish, and some resulting when skin divers speared fish which then panicked and darted about wildly. Of far greater importance is the frequency of ciguatera toxin in large offshore fish. Usually associated with fish caught in Florida and the Caribbean, ciguatera poisoning from a North Carolina barracuda was reported in 1987.

Small ones are usually edible, but large ones could be toxic. The toxin is more often in the guts than the meat. Large ones smell like rotten fish at the time they're brought aboard alive, and I don't know why anyone would want to eat them.

Barracuda sometimes form great aggregations over reefs, but also occur as loners. They breed offshore all during the warm season throughout their range. Males mature at two years of age, and females at age three or four. Because barracuda are not exploited, they are in no danger of being overfished.

Big barracuda are not selective feeders, and will hit any live or trolled bait on top or down deep. On shallow flats, they'll chase down rapidly retrieved, green, surgical-tube lures, and are terrific on ultralight tackle and small metal jigs, zipping back and forth like greased lightning. Offshore on deep reefs, they'll take cut bait fished near the bottom or rapidly trolled surface baits. They're powerful fighters on any tackle.

Little Tunny

Three species of small tuna are called "bonito" in southeastern waters. They are the little tunny (false albacore, fat albert), the skipjack, and the Atlantic bonito. They differ in range, habitat, and food quality, and should not be confused. The little tunny has wavy lines on top. The Atlantic bonito has straight lines on top, and the skipjack has straight lines on the bottom.

Little tunny occur throughout the Atlantic Ocean, Gulf of Mexico, and Mediterranean Sea. They range from 35 degrees north to 35 degrees south latitude, and are seldom far from land. Little tunny are continental, not ocean, fishes, common in our waters from just off the beach to well out to sea. Frequently associated with schools of large bluefish or roaming in small packs during the colder months, they're known as "albacore" by New Jersey headboat fishermen, "fat alberts" or "false albacore" on the middle Atlantic

Little Tunny
Euthynnus alletteratus

seaboard, and "bonito" or "bonita" in Florida and on the Gulf Coast.

Little tunny mature their first year, when they're less than two pounds and only 15 inches long. They spawn year-round, with larvae recovered off North Carolina, Florida, Cuba, Mississippi, the Lesser Antilles, western Yucatan, the coast of South America, the eastern Mediterranean Sea, and the Black Sea.

On the middle Atlantic seaboard, the average fish landed is 2 years old and weighs 6 pounds. The average Florida-caught fish is smaller. A 7-year-old fish would be 32 inches long and weigh 20 pounds. Little tunny may attain 40 inches and live to 10 years of age.

Foods are mostly small fishes and invertebrates, principally herring, Spanish sardines, anchovies, scads (small jacks), ballyhoos, small members of the drum family, other little tunny, and mackerel. When feeding on small fish, they herd their prey into tightly packed schools, then pick stragglers or crash into the pack, mouth agape, filter-feeding rather than picking individuals. In turn, little tunny are eaten by sharks, yellowfin tuna, and sailfish.

They'll take fast-moving, small, silvery lures tied directly to monofilament line or a black wire leader and trolled or retrieved at high speed across their noses, but are more easily caught on small live baits drifted under a float. Light tackle is sufficient, as they run fast but not far.

Little tunny have red meat that is acceptable in the West Indies but not on the mainland of the United States. The meat is flavorful raw but mediocre cooked. Most fishermen cut them up into strip baits for sailfish or cube baits for dolphin, or release them alive.

Atlantic Bonito

Atlantic Bonito
Sarda sarda

Atlantic bonito are small tuna that occur both inshore and offshore, often in mixed schools with other tuna, bluefish, or Spanish mackerel. They occur on both sides of the Atlantic, including the Gulf of Mexico, Mediterranean Sea, and Black Sea, and are locally known as "bonito," "piramida," "palamida," or phonetically similar names. They're most common in the middle Atlantic states, range northward to New England, and are uncommon off south Florida.

Atlantic bonito mature at two years of age and less than two feet in length. In our waters, they appear to spawn in the summer off New England and in the winter off the southern states.

Foods consist of locally abundant fishes (not always small) and invertebrates, including sand launces, mullet, bluefish, scad, anchovies, mackerel, alewives, menhaden, silversides, squid, shrimp, spot, other Atlantic bonito, and sea robins. One 25-inch bonito had a 15-inch bonito in its stomach.

The average fish is 1 or 2 pounds. Top size is about three feet and 12 pounds.

Atlantic bonito are taken by trolling or casting small to medium-sized baits, but are often discarded by sportfishermen who are unaware of their excellent white meat. A related species in California waters is heavily exploited by the headboat fishery and managed with a creel limit.

Skipjack

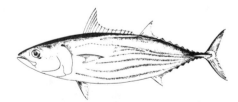

Skipjack
Euthynnus pelamis

Skipjack (oceanic bonito) are offshore fish that occur worldwide in large or small schools, often mixed with other species of tuna. In the Atlantic, they're commonly found in the Gulf Stream crashing bait on the surface, but they also enter green coastal waters. They're taken everywhere on fast-moving trolled lures or by casting with live anchovies, feathers, jigs, and anything else that moves or suddenly falls in the water nearby. They'll hit Japanese feathers in the first wave of the prop wash about 15 to 20 feet behind the transom.

Skipjack are warm water fish that average two feet and 5 pounds, but may attain three-and-a-half feet and up to 50 pounds. The meat is red, tasty raw and edible cooked.

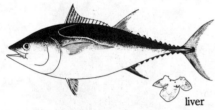

liver

Bluefin Tuna
Thunnus thynnus

Bluefin Tuna

No North American game fish is as familiar and as poorly understood as the bluefin tuna. The reasons for error range from nonsense in old fishing books to inadequate techniques for evaluating stocks. With years of tagging and landing data under our belts, we still are not certain where the fish go and how they get there.

At the turn of the century, "horse mackerels" were not highly valued. A few down-easterners harpooned them for the abundant oil in their heads, but most considered them pests that bulldozed circular holes in their herring and salmon weirs. Today, giant bluefin tuna are rare. We have younger fish coming along to replace them, if we manage them properly.

Bluefin tuna occur off the eastern United States and Canada, the west coast of Europe, and in the northern Pacific Ocean. Since 1982, the International Commission for the Conservation of Atlantic Tunas (ICCAT) has managed bluefin tuna by outlawing commercial fishing on their

Bluefin Tuna

Photo courtesy of the Nova Scotia Department of Government Services

breeding grounds and by severely curtailing catches by cooperating nations.

Identifying smaller bluefins can be difficult. This is especially true from Cape Hatteras southward, where the fish is less common than yellowfin or bigeye. Sportfishermen can use a key to identify tuna.

Quick Key to the Identification of Tunas From the Atlantic & Gulf coasts of the United States

You must begin at 1a.

1a. Prominent stripes on body 2
1b. No prominent stripes on body 4
2a. Stripes on belly, not on back . . . . Skipjack
2b. Stripes on back, not on belly 3
3a. Branched stripes on back . . . . Little Tunny
3b. Straight or wavy stripes on back . . . . Atlantic Bonito
4a. Finlets dark 5
4b. Finlets yellow 6
5a. Tail edged in white . . . . Albacore
5b. Tail not edged in white . . . . Blackfin
6a. Pectorals reaching second dorsal fin 7
6b. Pectorals not reaching second dorsal fin . . . . Bluefin
7a. Second dorsal and anal fins yellow . . . . Yellowfin
7b. Second dorsal and anal fins dark . . . . Bigeye

To confirm the identity of a bluefin, count the number of gill rakers on the first gill arch. Simply lift up the gill plate and look at the backward-pointing, V-shaped bone with soft red filaments on the outside and hard, bony bumps inside.

The bumps are the gill rakers. There are more than thirty in the bluefin tuna, and less than thirty in all similar tuna. Other characteristics are less reliable. Rows of white dots on the belly also occur in yellowfin, and corduroy-like striations on the lower side of the liver also occur in albacore and bigeye.

Bluefin tuna don't breed until they are 6 years old, and aren't important breeders until 15 or 16 years old. Virtually all bluefin tuna on this side of the Atlantic spawn from April through June in the Straits of Florida, off northwest Cuba, and on the east side of the Florida Current near Bimini. Bluefin tuna spawn in deep water about 30 feet below the surface.

For a successful year class of bluefin tuna, there must be plenty of food in the water at the right time. What do tiny tunas eat? Japanese workers looked inside the stomachs of 535 larval Southern bluefin tuna, a related species. One-quarter- to three-eighths-inch tuna are loaded with little shrimplike crustaceans, but rarely eat fish, either their own or any other kind.

Bluefin tuna grow rapidly in length up to about age 15, live to at least 32 years, and get fatter rather than longer with increasing age. Top size is about 1,500 pounds.

How tuna are able to migrate has been a mystery. A clue recently appeared when, in 1984, magnetite crystals in association with nerve endings were discovered inside a pocket of the skull of yellowfin tuna. There seems no doubt that this nerve-magnetite complex is the heart of a biological compass.

Not all bluefin tuna migrate the same distance or direction. Giants and smaller fish differ in where they make landfall and their northward extent into cold water. In April, giant tuna occur off the coast of Yucatan and Grand Cayman Island, probably heading for the Gulf of Mexico. They spawn in May. Late in the month, they begin their northern migration. They appear to remain in cold, deep water,

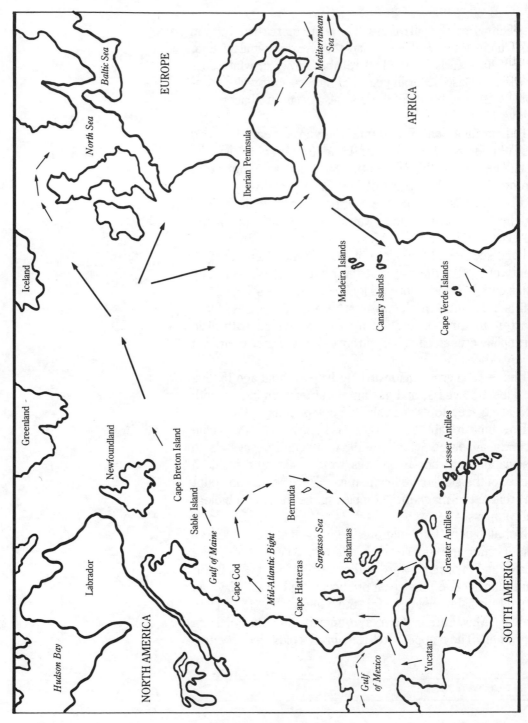

Migratory Paths of the Bluefin Tuna

avoiding the Gulf Stream. They reappear about a month later from Block Island to the Gulf of Maine. Their most northerly migratory point appears to be Hamilton Inlet, Labrador. By November and December, they begin migrating to the Caribbean, presumably along the continental shelf. They have never been located during this southern trek. In January and February, they arrive off Central and South America and begin moving toward the Lesser Antilles. By March and April, they have moved into the Gulf of Mexico for spawning, to complete the annual cycle.

A lot of the next generation of giants (fish in the 700- to 800-pound range) will be taken off Montauk, New York, in Cape Cod Bay and offshore, and off Rhode Island. The largest and oldest of the giants are usually found in the far north, from Maine to Prince Edward Island. It all has a lot to do with different migration patterns for fishes of different sizes.

Small and medium fish arrive off the middle Atlantic coast in May and June from the Sargasso Sea. They are occasionally seen on the surface in the cold, near shore green water off northern North Carolina, and in 1987 a huge number of 40-pound-class fish were landed at Oregon Inlet, not far from the Virginia line. Skippers in the area believe these fish come from far offshore, crossing the shelf above Cape Hatteras and reaching the Virginia line before migrating northward along the coast.

From July through October, medium fish are scattered throughout the upper two-thirds of the Mid-Atlantic Bight and into the Gulf of Maine as far as Newfoundland. They stay close to the 68-degree isotherm, feeding on herring, menhaden, mackerel, silver hake, and squid. With winter temperatures plummeting toward 55 degrees, the fish head for deep offshore water and begin migrating to the Sargasso Sea, where they remain until spring.

Small fish migrate north and south even less than medium fish. They spend the winter in the Sargasso Sea and the summer in the Mid-Atlantic Bight, not passing north of Cape Cod.

Until fifteen years ago, we were certain that bluefin tuna were on the verge of disappearance. That changed with an excellent 1973 year class that has grown into 300- and 400-pounders. Virginia fishermen now enjoy an excellent inshore fishery for these medium bluefins.

In 1835, a British physician in the Mediterranean noted that freshly butchered tunas were as much as 19 degrees warmer than the surrounding sea. In 1923, a Japanese worker investigating strange mounds of capillaries in tunas recognized their similarity to mechanical heat exchangers. (Look at the tightly compressed coils on your air conditioner, and you'll see a typical mechanical heat exchanger.)

In all higher animals (including fishes), arterial blood, enriched with oxygen, goes to the muscles and other organs. These organs do their work, in the process eliminating carbon dioxide and other waste products. Since work generates heat, heat is one of the waste products carried away by the venous blood to be eliminated from the body. In fishes, oxygen-rich blood leaving the gills travels along the arterial system to the muscles and organs. The arteries break up into smaller blood vessels, finally becoming capillaries, through which the blood and organs exchange their loads. Leaving these organs through the far ends of the same capillaries, the blood, now carrying waste heat and carbon dioxide, travels up through the venous system and back to the heart; from the heart the blood is pumped to the gills. At the capillary-enriched gill surface, the wastes are carbon dioxide and heat, dissipated to the outside world, and oxygen is taken up from the cool water.

In the larger tunas, capillaries connecting the venous and arterial systems are stacked into a mound (rete) of parallel tubules which transfer, and thereby conserve, heat while allowing other waste products to go on their way. With retes, tunas accumulate heat rather than dissipate it. At 44 degrees Fahrenheit, large tuna (with lots of red muscle mass for generating energy and heat) can have bodies as hot as 79 degrees Fahrenheit.

Tunas have their enemies. In Goode & Bean's *American Fishes* (1888), a Captain Atwood of Cape Cod Bay is quoted as stating, "There is nothing to trouble the horse mackerel until the killer (whale) comes, and then they know it, I tell you. Then the horse mackerel will run! Some fishermen will say that they have seen a killer poke his head out of the water with a horse mackerel in his mouth."

Bluefin tuna also fall victim to big, fast sharks like whites. Several pelagic sharks have also evolved heat-conserving systems and are able to run down a tuna.

By far, the bluefin tuna's most important enemy is man. The 1973 year class has given us a second chance to show what we've learned and manage bluefin stocks with sensitivity to their conservation, taking the excess rather than the essence of the species. Check current regulations for bluefin tuna fishing. You might need a permit to take a giant.

Tuna can be caught while anchored using cut bait or live bait in a chum slick, or by trolling artificial or natural baits. The size of the tuna determines the size of the tackle, which may range from 50-pound-class for 100-pound fish, to 80-pound-class for 400-pounders. Although the 1,000-pound giants are rare today, there are more 700- and 800-pounders caught than equal-sized blue marlin, and 130-pound-class tackle is the appropriate gear. Smaller tuna may occur well inshore in 30 to 50 feet of water, but the 800-pound-and-up giants prefer deep water, over 100 feet, especially around drop-offs or structures. It's more difficult to anchor there, but it pays.

Cut bait fishing with menhaden chum is the most popular method. For fish in the 50- to 100-pound range, the line is tied directly to 10 feet of 50- to 100-pound-test monofilament leader, and the leader snelled to a 5/0 to 9/0 short-shanked tuna hook. For larger fish, use 20 feet of 300-

pound-test leader on a 9/0 to 12/0 hook. The standard baits are menhaden, butterfish, chub mackerel, or other soft-meat, shiny fish. The head and tail of the bait fish is removed. Then the hook is inserted into the body from the rear, pushed all the way through and out the front, and then pulled back again to the bend, so that the point is buried in the meat. The boat is firmly anchored, a menhaden chum slick is established that is clear of the other boats, and the baits are free-lined into the slick about 50 to 100 feet off. If you need additional weight to push the baits down, add rubber-cored sinkers to the line just above the leader.

Live baits are more effective than cut baits. Smaller and lighter hooks are necessary or the menhaden (or bluefish or seatrout) will be dragged to the bottom. Hook the fish through the back just in front of the dorsal fin and let it drift out into the chum slick.

Trolling is best when you don't know where the fish are. The simplest trolling rig is a red-and-white cedar plug with a single 9/0 or 12/0 hook on 20 feet of wire. You can also troll Japanese feathers or hard-headed jigs, with or without a strip of meat as a sweetener. Skippers weaned on billfishing often rig a big, fresh, deboned mackerel with wire and a barrel sinker to get it down. Rich skippers may use a straight-lined daisy chain of expensive plastic squid, and still others use a spreader to lay out a horizontal array; in both cases, only the rear squid is armed with a 12/0 hook.

While bluefin tuna are good eating, most fishermen wouldn't pass up an offer of $10 a pound in the round from a buyer at the dock. One average tuna will buy you a lot of lobsters. The fishery is strictly regulated, and the fines substantial. Check with local officials before you go.

Your chances of catching a small or medium bluefin are pretty good in Virginia waters, but giants are rare. Your best shot at a giant is Prince Edward Island, Canada, in September and October. Charters during 1987 cost about $250 split six ways, but only one person can fish at a time and the fish belongs to the captain. Call Captain Clarence Guathier (902-963-2360), Captain Thomas Gallant (902-886-2491), Captain Hartley Jardine (902-357-2785), Captain Merrill MacDonald (902-357-2599), North Lake Tuna Charters (902-357-2055), Captain Parker MacDonald (902-583-2332), Captain Robert McFadden (902-961-2971), Captain Douglas Coffin (902-676-2991), or Captain Henry Coffin (902-676-2326).

Wahoo

The Blue Water Zone

In northern seas, marine life depends on drifting phytoplankton, which in turn supports zooplankton. The zooplankton consists of tiny drifting and swimming shrimp, crabs and other crustaceans, worms, jellyfish, fish eggs, and baby fish. The zooplankton is food for roving herrings, anchovies, jellyfish, and giant, filter-feeding sharks and whales.

In our temperate zone, coastal marine life depends mostly on detritus, fragments of grasses and algae that are broken down further by microbes. Detritus is eaten by barnacles, clams, mussels, worms, shrimp, crabs, and mullet, and the microbes on the detritus are digested. Those animals are then eaten by larger animals. In the tropics, both coastal grasses and mangrove trees provide the detritus.

In shallow, tropical waters with hard bottoms, coral reefs develop and provide important foods for higher animals. Corals only live in shallow waters because they require symbiotic algae in their tissues, and the algae need light. In deeper tropical seas, the corals are deprived of their algae and cannot survive. In these depths, sponges cover the rocks, and the reefs continue to provide food for higher animals.

What of our central Gulf of Mexico and the Gulf Stream? In this ocean environment the water is clear, there are no mangrove trees or grasses, no vast schools of krill or coral reefs. How does life survive in this oceanic, tropical desert?

Life survives and prospers in three ways. At the very surface, we have the sargassum forest that will eventually degrade to detritus. Through much of the water column, we have a plankton system. And on the very bottom, we have sponge-encrusted, deepwater tropical reefs. It all works on the energy of sun and wind. The sun provides the engine for photosynthesis, and the wind drives the currents that stir nutrients up into the water column. In short, the Gulf currents have many food chains.

In the central Gulf of Mexico, the wind-driven currents are not strong, and surface vegetation is sparse. As the water spews out between the Florida and Yucatan peninsulas, it turns northward along the continental shelf, joined by tropical ocean water moved inexorably eastward by the trade winds and by nearby hot, circulating water and vegetation from the Sargasso Sea.

Now the Gulf Stream becomes a distinctive water mass, its origins in the Gulf of Mexico, Atlantic Ocean, and Sargasso Sea waters lost in a new identity—hot, saline, and as clean and deep as blue-black glass.

And it's fast, tumbling forward in some places at five knots. Where the edges of the Gulf Stream brush colder water moving southward, violent eddies spin out, producing great undersea cyclones that stir up the bottom, sweeping nutrients into the turbulence. As the Gulf Stream rides over undersea mountains and against the steep continental slope, friction makes the bottom water swirl in frustration, and the water above caroms over and off the obstructions, further stirring the waters and nutrients upward toward the surface.

The upwelled nutrients are rapidly absorbed by phytoplankton so sparse that it fails to tint the water, then mixed by turbulence and tumbled down to feed zooplankton at all depths. The zooplankton feeds tiny jellyfish, swimming shrimp, and small ocean fishes that filter or pick tiny food out of the water—fishes like herrings, frigate mackerel, and argentines. You'll see some of them spat out on deck by a tuna or billfish brought on board, and sometimes see large schools 10 to 20 feet below the surface.

Other fish like sauries, ballyhoos, and flying fish remain at the top, where there's no abundance of zooplankton or vast schools of forage fish. They await the small creatures foolish enough to leave the shelter of the sargassum weed forest.

Unimaginable tons of sargassum may drift in a few square miles of ocean, making sargassum weed as important in the Gulf Stream as grass beds are in estuaries. Living attached to the sargassum weed are other algae, hydroids, barnacles, tubeworms, and bryozoans. Miniature predators seeking miniature prey roam the dense sargassum forest, including crabs, shrimp, filefish, triggerfish, sea horses, and pipefish. Some, like the sargassum anglerfish, have evolved here and are so perfectly camouflaged that they look like the weed itself. All of them are important forage in the Gulf Stream in the same way that anchovies and silversides are important in coastal waters.

Just as the wastes of living animals, the carcasses of dead animals, and the cracked and broken leaves of dying coastal grasses and mangrove trees add to the detritus, so dying sargassum weed provides detritus to the deep ocean. The sargassum weed forest and all its creatures will eventually join the sediments, and someday again provide nutrients for plankton, perhaps next year, and perhaps a million years from now.

What of the big predators in the Gulf Stream? Dolphin, wahoo, and billfish feed extensively on the creatures of the sargassum forest. Tunas feed mostly on the cruising squid and herrings below. But food is too precious and scattered in the Gulf Stream for any predator to specialize. All Gulf Stream game fish are opportunists, feeding anywhere their sharp eyes locate prey, at the surface or at a hundred fathoms. It's their only world, and they have to survive in it.

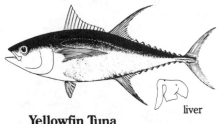

Yellowfin Tuna
Thunnus albacares

liver

Yellowfin Tuna

While northern sportfishermen are enjoying a resurgence of bluefin tuna stocks, southeastern fishermen have been enjoying a brand new fishery for yellowfin tuna. Well known to California fishermen, yellowfins are the mainstay of the Pacific tuna fleet, taken on short poles baited with live anchovies or feathered jigs, or snared in enormous nets (along with porpoises). They're the target of week-long sportfishing cruises on giant headboats out of San Diego.

Yellowfins are new to many Atlantic and Gulf coast fishermen, in part because they used to remain far offshore, and perhaps in part because the Japanese have eased up on longlining them. But that's history. The fish are here now in abundance, and any boat that can make the run to blue water will find them in spring, fall, and even mid-winter.

Although not highly migratory, they're worldwide in deep, warm seas. The various stocks in the North and South Atlantic, off Mexico, around Hawaii, and elsewhere may be separate populations. It is possible that the giants in the 250- to 350-pound class may school separately.

Yellowfins prefer a temperature of right at 70 degrees Fahrenheit. That's why they're abundant in spring and fall, move north of our area for the summer, and retreat into the Gulf Stream for the winter. Where the water is not moving, they remain within 300 feet of the surface. In the Gulf Stream, of course, they go to all depths.

They breed year-round in the center of their distribution, and seasonally at their northern and southern limits. In the

Atlantic, they breed in late winter and early spring off Central and South America. There doesn't seem to be any spawning off the Atlantic coast of the United States.

The larvae grow fast. By eight days of age they're a third of an inch long. By the end of the first year, they're one or two feet long, and a foot longer after the third year. At this time, they're old enough to breed, but don't. They'll spawn when they're three or four years old and three to five feet long. They vary a great deal in growth rates, and one particular 140-pound, six-foot-long fish was found to be only four years old.

Yellowfin tuna average 20 to 70 pounds, but 100-pounders are common. The largest on record, all Pacific fish, were close to 400 pounds. (Large yellowfins were called Allison's tuna years ago when they were thought to be a separate species.) The large, 300-pound-class Pacific yellowfins are off Clarion and San Benedicto islands off Mexico, and at Kona, Hawaii. In the Gulf of Mexico, 200-pounders are taken in June off South Pass, Louisiana. On the Atlantic seaboard, there's no clear pattern.

Unlike billfish and bluefin, there's no problem in having four or more fish on at a time. While it looks like a Chinese fire drill, yellowfins don't crisscross the whole ocean with blistering runs, reverse fields, and charges at the boat. They run away, and then down. The pandemonium is not crossed lines, but people trying to hold bucking rods and getting in each other's way on a tossing boat. After the fish sound, it's a simple matter of pumping them to the surface—simple if you're Arnold Schwarzenegger. Once on top, they're a long way from burned out, and continue to take line down and away several more times, not giving up. Some fish are lost immediately after hookup, in which case they were probably very thinly hooked, and others are lost close to the boat when worn-out fishermen give them two seconds of slack.

Yellowfins take anything at all. Because the baits are cheap, most charter skippers opt for 5- to 6-knot trolling with a skirted ballyhoo on a wire leader. Others troll at 8 to 10 knots with 300-pound-test, limp monofilament leaders on blunt plastic squids like the flat-headed Yap, Boone Striker, Flat-nose Clone, Sundance Flathead, or the Psychobead "green machine." Silver glitter, red beads, big eyes, and all kinds of other gimmicks do more to jack up the lure's price than its effectiveness, so go for the least gold. Everything works because yellowfins aren't the least bit picky.

Six to eight baits are run right at the surface, none off downriggers, and all at different distances from the boat, from right at the prop wash to way out. Four flatlines and two outrigger lines leave little room for teasers, which are unnecessary for yellowfins and just another item to get out of the way when a fish is on. While you'd run curves and turns for billfish to get the lures arcing to different depths, you can run straight for yellowfin. If they're around, they'll probably hit all the baits at once.

Six or Eight Line Trolling

Rods 1 and 2 are set far forward and lead to outriggers.

Rods 3 and 4 remain in the transom, fishing directly back.

Rods 5 and 6 may be fished off clips attached to the stern transom, or straight back, or off downriggers at the stern corners.

Rods 7 and 8 are optional. They may be fished directly off the bridge and straight back, or halfway out as a second outrigger line on each side. These positions may also be used for teasers.

All lines are out different distances, those on the rearmost rods closest to the boat and those off the outriggers farthest from the boat.

All lines should hold different baits.

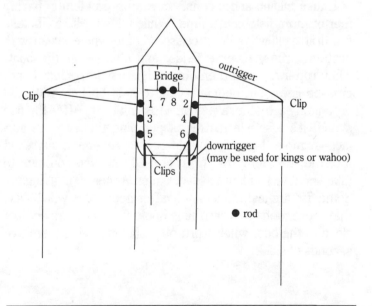

Sometimes you'll see birds and turbulence on the surface. As often as not, those are skipjack, blackfin, or other small tuna. But they could be yellowfin, so don't pass it up. The hot spots for yellowfin on the Atlantic coast are the tips and edges of Washington and Norfolk canyons off Virginia; the Point east of Oregon Inlet; Big Rock off Morehead City and Hatteras, North Carolina; and the Charleston Bump off South Carolina. Yellowfins are harder to find off Georgia and Florida, but appear again in the Gulf of Mexico, with the largest fish taken in June off South Pass, Louisiana.

BiGEYE TUNA

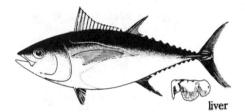

Bigeye Tuna
Thunnus obesus

liver

Far more abundant than reported landings would suggest, bigeye tuna rank right up there with mid-sized bluefin as top-notch targets of Atlantic coast tuna anglers. As improved techniques are picked up by more fishermen, expect more reports of bigeyes on the dock and new records established. The fish are there, just waiting for fishermen to smarten up and take their share.

Bigeyes are often regarded as intermediate in size between bluefins and yellowfins. In fact, bigeyes get hardly any bigger than yellowfins. The largest bigeyes known are a 375-pounder from the Atlantic and a 434-pounder from the Pacific. The largest yellowfin known is a Pacific 388-pounder, in the same ball park. The key difference between the two species is in their average size, and that's where bigeyes shine. Fishermen frequently take bigeyes in the 200- to 275-pound range, whereas a 150-pound yellowfin is a rare catch.

Bigeyes grow more slowly than yellowfins, but live a long time. It's been estimated that bigeyes, on the average, are 6 pounds and 18 inches long at the end of the first year; 16.5 pounds and 2.3 feet long at age two; 40 pounds and 3 feet long at age three; 70 pounds and 3.8 feet long at age four; 120 pounds and 4.5 feet long at age five; and 170 pounds and 5 feet long at age six. The average weight increase per year, after the third year, can vary from 15 to as much as 50 pounds.

Bigeyes mature when about three years old and 3 feet long, but we don't know how long they live. Since virtually all of the recreational catch, and much of the commercial catch, consists of fish much larger than 40 pounds (the average weight of a three-year-old), bigeyes get to spawn at least once before harvest, and therefore are in no immediate danger of being overfished.

They school by size, often mixing with other kinds of tuna. The larger ones seem to aggregate after dark, but this may reflect their continued feeding when other tunas have stopped for the night and only the bigeyes are still active. The really big fish tend to be loners.

We may already be landing more bigeyes than we think, but not recognizing them. Below Virginia, where the fish is not as well known, some fish being touted as big yellowfins may, in fact, be bigeyes.

Telling them apart is not easy. First, forget all about the size of the eye, the colors of the finlets, and the length of the pectoral fins. Forget about any blue band along the flank or rows of white spots. Several tuna can, under various conditions, overlap in all these characteristics. Those methods of identification are not reliable for bigeye. The surest way to separate a bigeye from a yellowfin is to look at its liver. The livers of tuna are divided into three lobes. In the bigeye, the blood vessels come very close to the skin of the liver on the underside, push against the liver skin, and appear as fine lines or striations. When you gut the fish, lift the liver and look for multiple, parallel, fine, elevated ridges on the liver skin. If these "streaks" occur, you've either got a bigeye or an albacore.

Albacores, in case you've never seen one, have a white-edged tail fin in addition to striations on the liver. Because the largest albacore known is only 88 pounds, pay close attention to the color of the tail on any large tuna. I suspect some larger albacores have been landed and thought to be bigeyes or yellowfins.

Well, suppose you're still at sea, you've got this great big fish without a white-edged tail fin, and the skipper doesn't want you to cut into its belly because the blood will mess up his boat. He suggests that the length of the pectoral fin is all you need to see. That's not reliable, but there is another way.

All tuna have distinctive scale patterns. The scales up front are bigger and thicker than the scales behind. These bigger scales encircle the fish and make up what is called the corselet. You have probably cut fillets following this pattern, since it generally follows the border of thick and hard skin up front.

The corselet is different in bigeyes and yellowfins. In yellowfins, it extends barely to the second dorsal fin, and the pectoral fin, when laid flat against the side, completely covers it. In bigeyes, the corselet extends back to the end of the second dorsal fin. When you lay a bigeye's pectoral fin flat, it doesn't nearly cover the corselet.

This outside, whole-fish method will only distinguish between bigeyes and large yellowfins. Because a bluefin has a corselet similar to a bigeye, and could be the same size (in the 150- to 400-pound range), you need to open the fish and check the underside of the liver back at the dock. Again, if there are striations on the liver, you've got a bigeye.

Bigeyes occur in the Pacific, Indian, and Atlantic oceans (but not the Mediterranean Sea), from roughly 42 degrees north to 42 degrees south latitude. Strictly oceanic, they range from the surface down to 125 fathoms. They won't come into coastal waters the way bluefin will, remaining well offshore in waters of 100 fathoms or more. You don't find that kind of water until you're 50 to 70 miles offshore at the outer shelf-break zone or over canyons along much of the East Coast.

That's one reason more bigeyes are not caught. Many boats troll offshore at the near edge of the shelf-break zone for dolphin, wahoo, blackfin tuna, white marlin, sailfish, and yellowfins. But bigeyes prefer deeper water. Of course, there's a big difference between 50 miles and 65 miles. The 30-mile, round-trip gas supply usually limits the average guy with a 24-foot boat to shallower water on the inside of the shelf break.

In June, however, larger boats head farther offshore to the 100-fathom curve, as that's the best place to search for migrating blue marlin. On these trips, bigeyes are much more likely to be encountered.

The optimal temperature range for bigeye tuna is 63 to 72 degrees Fahrenheit. Remember the old joke about the hen-chasing rooster who stopped to eat when the farmer threw him some grain? The farmer remarked that he hoped he never got that hungry. Bigeyes never get that hungry. Don't look for them at tide lines or weed lines, or migrating up and down with concentrations of plankton that in turn attract concentrations of baitfish. Read your thermometer. Bigeyes stay within their preferred 63 to 72 degree temperature range, and feed if the food comes there, not vice-versa.

Bigeyes are opportunists, feeding on whatever comes across their noses from the surface to at least 425 feet (71 fathoms) down. Nearer the surface, they tend to feed in schools, sometimes mixed with yellowfins or bluefins, while the deepest-caught fish are often loners.

Most tuna are daylight and surface or mid-depth feeders. Bigeyes feed day and night and at all depths. Their slightly larger eyes provide them with enhanced vision that enables pursuit in near-darkness. People long-lining at night for swordfish often take bigeyes, but not other tuna.

Four Pacific studies are of interest. The first study of 147 western Pacific bigeyes revealed that the most frequent and abundant food items were squid, followed by various ocean fishes. They also ate sea squirts, crabs, and other top-water and deepwater foods, representing a total of seven orders of invertebrates and lower chordates and twenty-one families of fishes. A second study of 40 bigeyes from the eastern Pacific indicated once again that squid dominated the diet, making up 63 percent of food volume compared with 22 percent fish and 15 percent crustaceans. A third study of 166 bigeyes from the central Pacific indicated that fish made up 62 percent of stomach volume, squid and other molluscs made up 35 percent, and crustaceans only 2 percent. All three studies were of fish taken by long-lining. In a fourth study of 52 eastern Pacific fish taken on live bait, half the fish had empty stomachs, and of the rest, 85 percent of the stomach volumes were fish, 9 percent were crusta-ceans, and only 5 percent were squid. The only conclusion is that bigeyes are opportunists. Squid may be high on their list of preferred food items at times, but they're not at all fussy about what they eat.

As big as they are, they're not completely safe in the open ocean. The main predators on bigeyes are toothed whales (not all whales eat plankton), billfish, and man. Commercial fishermen representing seventeen countries take about 170,000 to 200,000 metric tons a year. (Not all countries report landings.) Variations in annual landings indicate that only a portion of the stocks are being fished. Previously harvested mainly by the Japanese, 60 percent of the world catch is now taken by the Koreans.

Bigeyes have a lot more mercury in their meat than yellowfins, and that may indicate a difference in diet, growth rate, metabolic rate, or even metabolic pathways. The concentrations, however, should not be of concern to Americans, who do not consume vast amounts of fish.

In the Indian and Pacific oceans, bigeye spawn year-round. We haven't found any Atlantic spawning grounds yet. They breed twice a year. The egg is just over a millimeter in diameter, floats, and develops rapidly, with the embryo wriggling inside the shell at 19 hours. The egg starts hatching at 21 hours, and the 1.5-millimeter-long larva takes about 30 minutes to escape the shell. In a few days it is a quarter inch long and has the teeth of a predator.

In our area, bigeyes are taken at the canyons and over the outer shelf-break zone, usually in 100 or more fathoms of water. Surface temperatures are important, and should be in the high 60s. Because water quality, depth, and temperature are all important, look for bigeyes well offshore near the top in the early spring, but deeper as summer heats up the surface layers.

Favored methods are trolling during the day and live-baiting or drift-fishing with chum at night. Bigeyes won't cut your line and can be caught on monofilament straight to the hook (no leader) on medium tackle, or using 80-pound-test monofilament leaders on light tackle. Heavier or stiff leaders should be avoided. Trolling depth should be as low as possible, using weighted lures (large egg sinkers work well) to get the bait down. Even one foot can make a difference. Head shape, bubbles, beads, and all that other baloney don't make a bit of difference. How you work the lure is what counts. For the average guy, the best lure is one that costs the least. Lure size is not important, but the hook shouldn't be larger than the thickness of the lure or extend past the skirt. Tuna are color-blind, so color is irrelevant.

Best times are first and last light. Go slow, and don't skip the baits, as bigeyes are turned off by that. Putting the baits back away from the boat seems to help some guys, but makes little difference to others. Depth is more important.

Night-chumming for bigeyes is popular north of Virginia, where fishermen go out over the canyons to the 100-fathom line or deeper, and set out a steady, unbroken chum slick. Butterfish and alewives are preferred for chum, and squid for bait, with live squid best of all, but bluefish, jacks, or anything else is better than any dead bait. The fish might be at any depth at night, so the lines should be weighted and set at various levels, from 50 feet down.

Don't overlook daytime live-bait fishing, drifting in a chum slick, or slow-trolling with downriggers. The idea that bigeyes are too deep or not actively feeding during the day is all wrong. If you haven't caught them before, you're fishing in shallow water, too fast, too close to the top, or the yellowfins are charging in ahead of the bigeyes. Your 200-pound bigeye is out there. Go for it.

Blackfin TUNA

Blackfin are small tropical tuna with a top size of less than three and a half feet and 50 pounds. The average fish is 5 pounds and, like all Gulf Stream fish, the smaller the fish, the larger the bait it destroys. Common but not popular in the northern part of our range (where the top-drawer fish are bluefin, bigeye, and yellowfin), it is an important tuna off south Florida, and its action and numbers have mitigated many an otherwise quiet offshore sailfishing trip.

Blackfins are exclusively Atlantic in distribution, ranging from Cape Cod to Brazil, and always remain offshore. They eat fish, crabs, and planktonic animals from the surface to great depths, usually in mixed schools with skipjack tuna. They are eaten by larger tuna, blue marlin, and even dolphin.

liver

Blackfin Tuna
Thunnus atlanticus

Spawning occurs off Florida and in the Gulf of Mexico all summer long, and they live at least five years. Little else is known about them.

Blackfins have excellent white meat, although there isn't much of it on a five-pounder. Some skippers save any small, live blackfin, rig a wire loop through its nose, dangle a hook from the loop (rather than sticking it into the fish), and troll the live blackfin for a big, hungry blue marlin. Big blackfins go into the icebox.

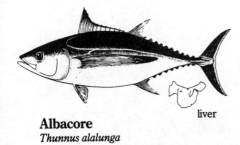

Albacore
Thunnus alalunga

liver

Albacore

Albacore are worldwide in distribution, but curiously absent from the Gulf of Mexico and the Caribbean. They may mix with bluefin, yellowfin, or other kinds of tuna, and can be quickly recognized by the white-edged tail fin.

Top size reported in the Atlantic is just over three feet, and the largest Pacific fish was just over four. The largest on record was well under a hundred pounds, so check any big tuna's tail; you might be a winner.

Although they might occur offshore anywhere from Cape Cod to Cape Canaveral, the largest fish tend to enter colder water, and they're not unusual where bluefin tuna and big bluefish are working in a chum slick. The best fish are taken from the northern part of our area.

Dolphin

Dolphin are the most abundant sport fish in the Gulf Stream, and frequently come inshore during the summer where the water is clean and warm. They've been taken from the surf at Cape Hatteras

Bull Dolphin

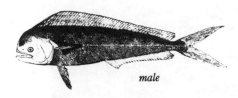

male

Dolphin
Coryphaena hippurus

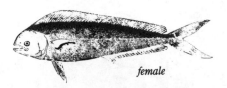

female

juvenile

and from fishing piers everywhere in our area. Errant strays occur in estuaries and harbors, indicating a tolerance of temperatures and salinities remarkable for a Gulf Stream fish. They've been held in cages at temperatures and salinities of 59 to 86 degrees Fahrenheit and 16 to 26 parts per thousand (normal seawater is 36 ppt) without ill effect.

The dolphin, in this book, is a fish. The mammal frequently called by that name is a porpoise or small whale. Restaurants, aware of the confusion in the public's mind and its aversion to cannibalizing Flipper, sell dolphin meat as mahi-mahi, the Hawaiian name. By any name, the meat is excellent.

Occurring in all the tropical seas of the world, dolphin are generally offshore fish that prefer oceanic warm-water currents like the Gulf Stream. Abundant in the Gulf of Mexico, off the coast of Florida, and off the Atlantic coast as far north as Virginia, they occur regularly off Montauk, New York, and have been taken off George's Bank, Nova Scotia. On the other side of the Atlantic, they range normally from the Iberian Peninsula and the Mediterranean Sea south to the mouth of the Congo River, and rarely to South Africa. They normally don't range into offshore water colder than 68 degrees Fahrenheit.

Dolphin are strictly surface fish; they don't even dive when hooked. Smaller dolphin associate with floating sargassum weed and aggregate around any floating object, including shipping pallets, boards, dead trees, sheets of newspaper, and rafts. They'll follow sailboats for days over great distances. Why they behave this way has been attributed to food on the object, shade, or even social attraction to inanimate objects. Nobody knows why they do it, but they're the only Gulf Stream fish that behave this way. Smart skippers never go by any floating object without making at least one pass, for they know that the size of the object has no relation to the number of small dolphin associated with it, and even a single two-by-four might yield dozens of fish. Very large dolphin seldom are found in these aggregations, tending to be open-water loners that appear out of nowhere, just like billfish.

The most commonly occurring foods of dolphin around the world, by frequency of occurrence and bulk, are flying fishes and ballyhoos. But dolphin are opportunists that eat anything they see, and gorge on whatever happens to be available at the time. Most of their foods are residents or associates of the sargassum weed forest, including small shrimp and crabs, filefishes and triggerfishes, small jacks and scads, herrings, sargassum frogfishes, pipefishes and sea horses, puffers, and other, smaller dolphin. Their stomachs sometimes contain coastal grasses, indicating feeding in near shore tide lines. Frequently they contain a great deal of sargassum weed. I recall one trip when the sargassum weed was loaded with matchhead-sized, bright red sargassum crab larvae. Going through large volumes of weed, I found a single red sea horse (they're normally brown) which apparently had fed on those crabs and picked up the pigment. When we dressed out the catch of dolphin, their stomachs were crammed with red sea horses and weed.

In a study of 2,632 dolphin stomachs from the Atlantic and Gulf coasts, several strange items appeared once or twice, including rocks, white paper, a green ribbon, a cigarette filter, a lid to a cooler jug, several colors of plastic, tar balls, corn kernels, bird feathers and bones, and a light bulb.

Another study of captive dolphin showed that they stop feeding entirely when the temperature drops to 66 degrees Fahrenheit, and feed and grow best between 74 and 85 degrees Fahrenheit. Captive fish were weaned from cut fish onto animal feed pellets soaked in fish oil, and finally just dry pellets.

Dolphin breed year-round, and have even spawned in public aquariums. Eggs collected at sea have been hatched and reared in captivity. The young fish, frequently associated with the sargassum weed, develop a barred pattern early in life, and eat anything, including each other. They grow rapidly. One aquarium-held fish grew from 1 pound to 37 pounds in eight months.

Most of those caught by hook and line are one-year-old fish. The very largest dolphin caught are four-year-olds, which seems to be the maximum age.

After the first year or so, males grow much heavier than females of the same length. By the time the fish are four feet long (age three or older), males might be twice as heavy as females. All the largest ones caught have been male "bull" dolphin, characterized by a vertical head profile. The top size appears to be about five feet and just over 100 pounds, but a fish half this weight is exceptional.

Fishing for small dolphin is simplicity itself. If there's no sargassum weed out there, don't expect to find many fish. Troll alongside weed lines or around floating debris. When dolphin are located, stop trolling and switch to light tackle. Use a cube of skinless cut bait free-lined out from the boat, but don't let it sink more than 20 feet down. If nothing happens right away, reeling it in fast will often provoke a strike. Chum with bits of meat to hold the fish close. You can also throw artificials, if that's your bag. Everything works.

Most charter skippers avoid fishing out the entire school, taking some and leaving the rest for another day. It's good conservation practice in general, but perhaps not necessary with dolphin, which have a very high natural mortality. Their populations seem more dependent on the current abundance of sargassum weed than on fishing pressure.

Pompano Dolphin

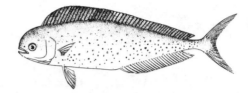

Pompano Dolphin
Coryphaena equiselis

here is a second species of dolphin that is not as well known in our waters. It also occurs around the world, but tends to be more of an offshore fish. The pompano dolphin is deeper-bodied than the common dolphin, and has a convex rather than concave anal fin. If you're still not sure, there's a patch of teeth on the tongue that is small and oval in the common dolphin, while larger and square in the pompano dolphin. Since you're likely to have commons in the boat before you get what may be a pompano dolphin, you'll have something with which to compare that oddly different fish.

juvenile

Pompano dolphin don't get very big, reaching a top size of perhaps 30 inches, but very few adults have been caught. They probably live no longer (if that) than common dolphin, and appear to prefer slightly warmer and more saline waters. They sometimes mix with common dolphin, and other times avoid them altogether. They don't eat flying fish to any great extent, and probably differ in feeding habits, since adults are so seldom caught.

The two species of dolphin have been hybridized under laboratory conditions, and produced viable fry which grew faster than normal. They don't seem to hybridize in nature.

Juveniles, at very small sizes, are uniformly black without any bars on the side; as they get older, they lose pigment all along the fork of the tail fin, producing a clear edge. Older juveniles of common dolphin lack pigment only at the tips of the tail.

Wahoo

Wahoo
Acanthocybium solandri

ahoo are the biggest, fastest, and meanest mackerel in American waters. Usually a by-catch of billfishing, they're most often taken while trolling offshore for marlin and tuna.

Offshore is the operative word. You'll hear about wahoo occasionally caught by hand in Florida bays, with accompanying speculation about their "normal" habitats and where to fish for them. Any wahoo caught that way was a fish that made the mistake of charging over the wrong reef, a reef with oceanic, deep water on the seaward side and an estuarine trap on the landward side. Trapped in shallow inshore waters, it's as good as dead.

The National Marine Fisheries Service did a survey of one northern Gulf Coast boat's fishing success over a 10-year period. Of 22,350 fish taken during the decade, 61 percent were king mackerel, 10 percent were bluefish and little tunny, 4 percent were Spanish mackerel, and 4 percent were dolphin. Only six wahoo were taken in all that time. From this list, it's clear that the boat rarely caught blue water fish (only dolphin and wahoo fit that category). And even then, they caught more than 100 dolphin for every wahoo. So, either they caught blue water fish that wandered inshore, or they occasionally made an offshore run. The bottom line, however, is that wahoo are strictly offshore fish.

In 1970, some 8,000 mid-Atlantic fishermen took over 170,000 wahoo weighing 4 million pounds. If you figure 6 fishermen to a charter, that averages to one 23-pound wahoo per 3.5 charters. In 1977-78, North Carolina fishermen alone took just under 3,000 fish each year, the average weighing 26 pounds.

But wahoo are not evenly distributed. Another National Marine Fisheries Service study of catches per hour of the top ten fish by offshore ocean trolling (excluding all near shore waters) showed that wahoo were not among the top five fish anywhere, and not among the top ten in either northwest Florida (the Panama City area of the Gulf Coast) or in south Texas. Does that mean that the Gulf of Mexico is not the best place to chase them? Not at all. The catch rate was the highest by far off Louisiana, with one wahoo caught for every five hours of offshore trolling. That's five times higher than off the North Carolina coast, and six times higher than off south Florida.

Although unevenly distributed, wahoo occur worldwide in warm seas. In our area, they might be taken anywhere that billfish and dolphin occur, but you can't count on them. If one comes along, it's a bonus.

Wahoo are not commercially fished anywhere, are not normally a by-catch of the worldwide Japanese longline fleet, are not vulnerable to traps, drift gill nets, or trawls, are difficult to hook on rod-and-reel, and are lost as often as landed. That means they're not under much pressure. The only place wahoo are recorded to be kept as a by-catch of commercial longlining is in Samoa, where the people only catch enough for local consumption (not by design, but because few of them are taken on longline baits).

Wahoo occur from Virginia to South America, erratically throughout the Gulf of Mexico, and into the Caribbean. They're uncommon off the Iberian Peninsula, but occur throughout the Mediterranean. According to published reports, they're supposed to be uncommon off the west coast of Africa. However, Mrs. Ailsa Schwartzkopf and her husband, who do a lot of billfishing off Nigeria, catch plenty of them. It's probable that few people billfish over there, so few wahoo landings are reported.

Wahoo have many names around the world, including queenfish (Caribbean), ono (Hawaii), peto (Bahamas), and springer (Brazil).

They are abundant from the east coast of Africa to the Arabian peninsula and Indian subcontinent, and in the Indo-Pacific region from Australia to southern Japan in the north and Hawaii in the east. On the American Pacific coast, they're abundant from Mexico to the Galapagos. In short, wahoo are sport fish around the world, and in no danger from any quarter. For that reason, they don't need management.

What exactly is a wahoo? In fact, it is a unique member of the mackerel family, the classification of which is based almost exclusively on their bones. A line of the tunas and mackerels leads to a group called the "Tribe" (smaller than a family) Scomberomorini (pronounced SCOMBER-OH-MORÉ-IN-EYE). That tribe contains the eighteen species of *Scomberomorus* (king and Spanish mackerels) around the world, the unique wahoo (*Acanthocybium solandri*), and the primitive genus *Grammatorcynus*, which doesn't occur in our waters. The wahoo has seventeen bone shape characteristics in common with all the king and Spanish mackerels, and the other genus (*Grammatorcynus*) has very few. Northern (Boston and chub) mackerel are not closely related to these others.

Despite all the knowledge of wahoo bones and distribution, surprisingly little is known of their biology. Wahoo larvae are very distinctive, and we know when and where they spawn. That will be covered below. But for many years, nobody studied their growth rates, top sizes, and other aspects of their feeding habits and biology. During the mid-1970s, however, Bill Hogarth earned his doctorate at North Carolina State University with a study of wahoo biology. Bill is now the Director of the North Carolina Division of Marine Fisheries, and was kind enough to let me have a copy of his unpublished doctoral dissertation.

Wahoo are distinctive. They're much bigger than king mackerel, sleeker, more powerful, with a long face, brilliant vertical banding on the sides, and big, close-set, razor-sharp teeth that can slice through 100-pound-test monofilament like butter. They have no gill rakers (and so don't strain small items from the water), and their gill membranes are remarkably similar to those of marlin and swordfish.

They're usually taken trolling with wired ballyhoos or feathers, but not plastic plugs. Out of San Diego, they're taken on live bait drifted deep down into a chum stream of anchovies.

Depth is the operable word. Wahoo feed deep. Running baits off drails, planers, or downriggers is more likely to bring a hit than running them on top, no matter how fast. Many skippers believe that wahoo prefer high-speed baits. If that were true, then people pulling plastic at eight knots should get more than those running rigged ballyhoo at three knots. But they don't. Meat baits catch more wahoo.

Wahoo don't school, but they will aggregate to a feeding area, and catching two to five fish in one place isn't rare. What's important is the place.

Search for wahoo in blue water between 30 and 100 fathoms (180 to 600 feet), below large masses of drifting sargassum weed, over undersea reefs, bumps, ledges, drop-offs, or other large features. Work in close to weed lines, and circle slowly or slow down to a crawl, letting the trolling baits sink deeply. Wahoo prefer to stay down, so meet them halfway. Surprisingly, the Schwartzkopfs catch lots of them off west Africa where there is no sargassum weed or any kind of drifting vegetation.

In our waters, live bait, free-lined while drifting near sargassum weed or over a major structure, is more likely to bring a wahoo hit than trolling. (Of course, you also risk hooking a big amberjack; it can be broken off by locking down on the drag and spool).

What's the best bait? Wahoo don't eat the small items that abound in drifting sargassum weed, nor do they eat deep-water ocean fishes. They feed in the upper layers of the deep ocean, but on larger fare. Their principal foods on the East Coast and in the Gulf of Mexico are small, forage species of mackerels, flying fish, butterfish, small herrings, spiny boxfish (burrfish), and squid. But they're likely to hit anything at all that's below the surface, six inches to two feet long, and far enough away from the sargassum weed to make an easy target. Big baits don't attract bigger wahoo; a wahoo of any size will attack (and slice apart) a bait of any size. Their diets seem to be virtually identical around the world.

Use a short-shanked, 5/0 to 9/0 hook (depending on the stiffness of your rod) with 10 feet of wire wrapped through the eye and around the shank, the wire leader tied through a small black swivel to a shocker of heavy monofilament if you're using 30-pound-class stand-up tackle, or through the swivel to your 50-pound-class sit-down trolling rig line.

Wahoo are line-burners, and are reputed to be the fastest fish in the ocean. They run fast, straight, and hard, but don't sound deeply, and fight a lot like a non-jumping billfish. Unlike king mackerel, they don't burn out; a fight with a big wahoo can last thirty minutes to an hour or more. I've known one skipper to radio the whole fleet that he was into a "blue marlin." A half hour later, the "marlin" was still on. After another half hour, the "marlin" was close to the boat, and was actually (he said sheepishly) a big wahoo of about 90 pounds. Well, I saw that wahoo at the dock and it was no more than 50 pounds. A good wahoo away from the boat can fool even an experienced skipper, and most skippers keep their mouths shut about the size of a fish until they see it close up.

The average size is 25 pounds, but 70- to 90-pounders are not uncommon. The IGFA world record is just under 150 pounds, and they get much larger, with a 183-pounder reported. Nobody knows how big a wahoo can get, because many ocean fish will continue to grow all their lives. Unlike tunas, sharks, and many other fishes (and people), wahoo don't get relatively stockier with age, but continue to be bigger and tougher, streamlined, athletic fish.

In our area, one-year-old wahoo start breeding in May, reach a peak in June, and keep at it until October. (Ah, to be young!) The major spawning area is between Cuba and Florida. Each female may carry a half-million to forty-five million eggs. Babies are two-thirds fish and one-third alligator. They grow fast, attaining a length of three-and-a-half feet the first year. Two- and three-year-olds are four to four-and-a-half feet long, and four-year-olds are five feet long.

They live at least five years, and probably more. That 183-pounder was almost seven feet long.

Natural mortality is about 35 to 38 percent per year, and additional mortality from fishing pressure is negligible. So long as wahoo remain recreational fish, the fishery won't need to be regulated.

Wahoo usually have two (sometimes more) huge, brownish black, parasitic worms in their stomachs, with leechlike suckers and ridges. They're not leeches at all, but digenetic trematodes, also known as internal flukes. How this worm, whose name is *Hirudinella ventricosa*, gets there is not known, but most digenetic trematodes have life cycles that work this way. The worms mate and lay eggs, which travel down the intestinal tract and are evacuated into the sea with the wahoo's wastes. It's likely that the eggs hatch in the water, and the ciliated larval worms (called miracidia) swim toward and infect a certain kind of snail that lives in sargassum weed. The worm multiplies and meta-morphoses inside the snail, and eventually becomes, at another stage of the cycle, hundreds or thousands of tailed, swimming larvae called cercariae. The cercariae leave the snail in huge bursts, probably around sunrise every day, and search for and penetrate a kind of fish or squid that wahoo normally eat. The cercaria sheds its tail and encysts on or in this intermediate host. Now it is called a metacercaria. When a wahoo attacks and eats this fish (or squid) host, the metacercaria is released, moves to the stomach of the wahoo, grows up, mates with another lucky worm that made the trip, and the life cycle is completed.

There could also be an abbreviated cycle, in which the snail (or reasonable facsimile) plays the role of both first and second intermediate host. Or, there could be one or more extra steps.

Since there isn't any sargassum weed off the west coast of Africa, and no obvious structures that might support a snail, another possibility is that the host is a sea hare, which

Probable Life Cycle of
the Wahoo Worm, Hirudinella ventricosa

Adult worms in the stomach of a wahoo mate and lay eggs (1), which are moved down the intestinal tract to the outside. In the sea, the eggs hatch (2) and the ciliated miracidium larvae swim toward the scent of a certain kind of snail that lives in sargassum weed (3). The larva penetrates the snail, shedding its cilia, and begins the process of growing and dividing into many individuals. Eventually, hundreds or thousands of daughter parasites, called cercariae, leave the snail (4), swimming by means of their whipping tails, seeking a certain kind of forage fish. They enter the forage fish (5), shedding their tails, and move to a particular organ or tissue where they encyst and become dormant. If the forage fish is eaten by a wahoo (6), the encysted, dormant parasites leave their cysts, attach to the wahoo's stomach, and grow up to complete the cycle, mating and laying eggs.

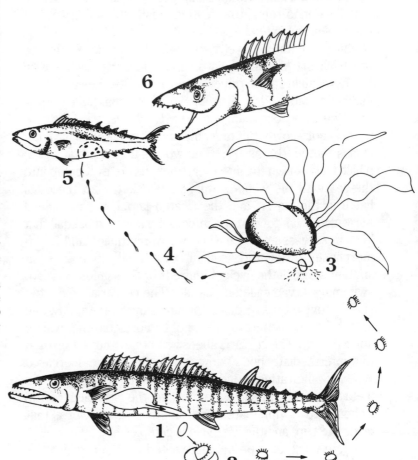

essentially is a swimming snail that has no shell. A sea hare would be ideal for an abbreviated cycle.

Recently, we've found the identical worm in the stomachs of sailfish and white, striped, blue, and black marlin. There are usually a lot of them in billfish, and they're smaller than the worms in wahoo (perhaps the numbers in a stomach affect the size of all individuals). Therefore, the intermediate fish or squid host is something that is eaten in common by wahoo and marlins all over the world. It should now be possible to solve the mystery of the life cycle of the "wahoo worm."

Wahoos have many other striking parasites, most notably a variety of bizarre crustaceans on their skin. And they're pretty common. Doctor Roger Cressey of the Smithsonian Institution, in a recent paper, listed the kinds of crustacean parasites he found on sixty-four specimens of wahoo. He found *Brachiella thynni* on thirty-nine fish, *Gloiopotes hygomianus* on twenty-seven, *Caligus productus* on eleven, *Shiinoa occlusa* on two, and *Caligus corphyaenae*, *Pennella* species, and *Tuxophorus cybii* on a single wahoo each.

Billfishing

There are two kinds of billfishing—day fishing for sailfish, white marlin, and blue marlin, and night fishing for swordfish. We'll talk about day fishing first, since that's what most people care about.

The ideal time and place for blue marlin is June and July off North Carolina. September is the best time for white marlin, and North Carolina and Virginia are the best places. Sailfish can be caught throughout our area at any time, but are most common from July through September along the mid-Atlantic coast, and in December or January in south Florida. All billfish can be caught virtually every month of the year in blue water, but their concentrations vary seasonally. Swordfish have declined in our area, but some Florida boats will take you for a night charter.

If you're not in great shape, don't worry about it. The way to beat a big marlin is to rely on your will when your wind gives out. Marlin fishing separates winners from quitters, and strength has little to do with it.

If you've never gone billfishing, I advise you to learn how from a professional captain. Charters are inexpensive when split six ways, and the education is priceless. If possible, visit the marina and ask to look over the book kept by the charter service (they usually record every boat's catch of billfish for every day of the season). Stay away from boats that come in empty-handed when everyone else has fish, and from dirty boats, which often indicate careless crews. Pick a boat and a fishing date, but plan on staying an extra day to search for another boat in case your date is blown out by the weather.

Many novices set themselves up for seasickness by staying up late and drinking excessively the night before, or eating a greasy breakfast (fried eggs, butter, home-fried potatoes) the morning of the trip. Eat a good dinner to help you sleep, and get to bed early. Get up in plenty of time, have a refreshing shave and a leisurely shower, and eat a light but substantial breakfast of dry cereal, perhaps some doughnuts, juice and milk or coffee, with no butter or margarine. Allow enough time for getting to the dock without rushing.

If you don't know whether you're prone to seasickness, take an over-the-counter motion sickness prevention pill or use a prescription scopalamine patch. The Office of Naval Research recommends two Sudafed (30 milligrams each) and one Dramamine, Bonine, or Marazine the night before

300-pound Blue Marlin

and again one hour before boarding. Wristlets, which press against acupuncture pressure points, are no gimmick; the British navy is currently testing them, following some impressive preliminary findings.

The run out may take up to three hours, depending on the distance to the right ledge, outcrop, contour, or other structure within the blue water zone. You'll recognize the glassy black Gulf Stream by its color and the sudden increase in drifting golden-yellow sargassum weed. When the boat slows and the mate begins putting out the rods and baits, get into a chair. Most outfits will be 50-pound-class gear, with one or two 80-pound rigs. Skirted ballyhoo are the principal bait; very few Atlantic and Gulf coast skippers run artificials. The baits are run submerged so the billfish can get them.

Sometimes the strike is sudden and unexpected. More often, it's not. Don't look for a bill behind the boat, flailing wildly at the baits. Marlin slither up like big black snakes, usually for a long inspection. You won't see much from deck level, but the captain will see it from topside and he'll shout instructions to the mate. The mate will pick up the rod with the bait nearest the fish, reel in, and drop back, trying to entice the fish into a strike. If the fish moves, the mate will put that rod down and pick up another. Most of the time, the fish loses interest and leaves. Perhaps one time in four the fish takes the bait and hooks itself.

If you're a beginner, get into a chair, let the mate work the slack out of the line, and then set the rod butt into the gimbal. Start cranking immediately, and do only what the mate tells you to do.

Don't jerk the rod! You'll only rip the hook out. When the mate jerked the rod earlier, he was only lifting the line out of the water to shorten the distance to the fish; he was not trying to imbed the hook deeper. In fact, billfish usually are lightly hooked in the bill, the fish held only by the hook point, not the barb. If the fish is on its first run, just hang on, rod held high as you can get it. The instant any slack appears imminent, reel for all you're worth. Pump and reel, and don't stop pumping for a second. All a billfish needs is an instant of slack line to shake that hook out. Don't fiddle with the drag; the mate will adjust it if needed.

Marlin are easy to lose. No game fish can run harder and faster simultaneously. You'll be hanging onto that bending rod while your line runs straight out under enormous pressure. Suddenly you'll see a marlin leaping off to the side and you'll think there are two of them out there. It's the same fish, going faster than the line can slide sideways and catch up.

When the fish comes close to the boat, you'll see its eyes turn toward you. If you can order that fish gaffed for a mount, you're harder than I am. I haven't killed one yet, and I don't buy that load of cow chips about the fish being used for food by the locals so it isn't wasted. People who say that just want an excuse to put a kill on the dock.

If you decide to have a billfish mounted, plan on spending $600 to $1500 for something that doesn't look like your fish at all. I've got a better idea. Tell the mate to turn the fish loose. When you get back to the dock, buy yourself a $7 pennant from the marina shop and hang it on your wall upside down, signifying a billfish release. That's something to be proud of. Killing a billfish isn't.

Sailfish

S ailfish are marlin that never grew up. They're among the smallest of billfish, about the same size as spearfish (which we'll cover later). They retain a post-larval character—the sail—which other marlins also have at an early age, but eventually lose. The sail

Atlantic Sailfish
Istiophorus albicans

may be a drifting aid to the larval fish, while in the adult it may be a temperature regulator, like an elephant's ear. Since sailfish occupy the shallowest and frequently hottest water of all billfish, temperature regulation seems a likely function.

The Atlantic sailfish is smaller than its Pacific cousin, and differs slightly in the length of the tail and pectoral fins. The average Atlantic sail is about 25 to 45 pounds. Top size is at least 175 pounds for a longlined fish (which may have been a Pacific sail that rounded the Cape of Good Hope), but the world angling record is much smaller.

Sailfish occur from France to South Africa and from North Carolina to Brazil. They like hot water, prefer the 82 degree Fahrenheit isotherm, and often venture practically onto the beaches; one Florida fishing pier accounts for about a dozen a year. Large concentrations occur off Yucatan and Central America from April through June and off Florida and Brazil in December. The largest Atlantic sails (those in the 100-pound class) come from Angola in west Africa and Cancun on the east coast of Yucatan.

Some tagged fish have traveled between Cape Hatteras and Venezuela, or across the Atlantic to the west coast of Africa. However, most of the tagging data indicate only short migrations, suggesting that few sailfish make major sojourns and that certain areas have local populations of big fish.

Temperature is important. Although sails occur in surface waters as cold as 70 degrees Fahrenheit, they follow the 82-degree Fahrenheit isotherm closely. Local movements are strongly influenced by weather, especially wind, which can alter surface temperatures quickly.

Sailfish may occur as single fish or in pairs, in small or in large groups. Double hookups are not unusual. They frequently aggregate for feeding, and will surround a school of bait fish on the surface just like amberjack or bluefish, balling the fish tightly before charging in to feed.

Most west Atlantic sailfish are thought to be 1- or 2-year-old fish, with the maximum age estimated to be 11 years. Males and females don't differ in size, and size may not be an accurate indicator of age. A female recaptured after 10 years and 10 months only weighed 54 pounds, just 10 pounds heavier than when she was tagged.

Breeding occurs in the second year, when the roes may grow to 10 percent of the fish's weight and hold up to 20 million eggs. They breed in May and June off Florida, in July and August off Georgia, and in September off the Carolinas. Several males may pursue a female, but spawning is by pairs. In the east Atlantic, they spawn year-round, with a peak in May.

Stomach analyses of 241 adult sailfish revealed little tunny (false albacore), halfbeaks like ballyhoo and balao, needlefish, cutlassfish, flying fish, small jacks like cigar minnows and blue runners, triggerfish, pinfish, herrings, anchovies, flying squid (a different kind than we buy for food or bait), swimming octopuses (nautiluses), and many other items associated with the surface, mid-depths, or the bottom. The same study came up with hardly any sargassum forest inhabitants, such as the specific shrimp, crabs, and fishes that live only here. That missing element suggests that sailfish are not dependent on Gulf Stream foods, but generally feed inshore in coastal waters, and from top to bottom.

You can take sailfish trolling rigged baits with 50-pound-class gear, but you can also fish for them with much lighter tackle. Anyone with a small boat in Florida, or a boat capable of making a blue water run elsewhere, can go after sails with 30-pound-class, stand-up gear. Sails are favorites with saltwater fly rodders and spinning tackle enthusiasts. Live-bait fishing by slow-trolling or with balloons or kites is ideally suited to sailfish. Fish caught on live baits may survive release better than those caught by other methods, but the data is not conclusive.

Sailfish are plentiful throughout our area, and in no danger of overharvesting. Recreational fishermen catch more sailfish than do longliners, and most of them are released alive. If you're going to kill any billfish for a mount, this one is sufficiently abundant to harvest, makes the prettiest trophy (if you think painted plaster-of-paris and plastic is pretty), and is the smallest and cheapest to do. Be aware, however, that actual skin mounts of billfish are rare; what you're likely to get is a model cast from a mold with the same dimensions as your fish, and then hand-painted and lacquered. The taxidermist most probably will never see your fish, but simply get its measurements over the telephone from the guy to whom you gave a deposit (that's his commission). Your fish will end up in the trash after you leave the dock.

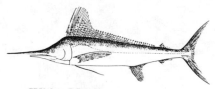

White Marlin
Tetrapterus albidus

White marlin

Two separate stocks of white marlin live in the North Atlantic and South Atlantic, and individuals from both stocks cross the ocean to Europe or Africa. They all overwinter together off the coast of Venezuela and Brazil. In late spring, the South Atlantic fish spawn off Venezuela, while the North Atlantic stock migrates to Cuba and the Greater Antilles for early summer spawning. After spawning, this stock divides into two groups; one group moves westward into the Gulf of Mexico, and the other races northward into the Mid-Atlantic Bight as far as Cape Cod. During this period, they're widely scattered, but groups of two and three are occasionally seen.

The Atlantic coast fish regroup in the fall, aggregating off Virginia and North Carolina for about a week in September and then rapidly moving southward, picking up the Gulf

Coast group before finally joining the South Atlantic stock off South America.

Like sailfish, white marlin have a preferred temperature isotherm (75 degrees Fahrenheit), which they follow very closely. They are relatively cool-water billfish, and have been taken as far north as Canada. They will enter water as shallow as 50 feet on occasion, but only become abundant beyond 40 fathoms (240 feet), and prefer 100-fathom (600-foot) water. Most charter skippers work the 60-fathom curve (if it drops steeply), the continental slope, or the canyons.

Ages and growth rates are not well understood. In common with other billfishes, post-larval white marlin have sails, which they eventually lose as they grow. During the 1950s, landing data indicated that the fish were increasing in size at about 10 pounds a year. Tag returns show that they can live at least 12 years.

The average white is about 60 pounds, but 100-pounders are not rare. Fish over 70 pounds are almost always females. The largest fish known were all between 171 and 182 pounds, all taken off the coast of Brazil between 1975 and 1979, and all probably from the same year class.

White marlin feed mostly on round herring, squid, small jacks like cigar minnows and blue runners, bait mackerel, dolphin, little tunny, flying fish, and sargassum-associated filefish and triggerfish. These items indicate that they feed mostly at mid-depth and at the surface, but not at all on the bottom. Other items found less frequently were cutlassfish, surgeonfish, puffers, small sharks, barracuda, remoras, and small crabs. A young swordfish was also found in a white marlin's stomach.

Most white marlin are taken trolling with skirted ballyhoo on 50-pound-class outfits. That's appropriate gear, although they can be taken on lighter, stand-up tackle by experts. Whites fight very hard and fast, and most (but not all) of them are jumpers that put on a spectacular display.

Longliners take many white marlin as a by-catch of tuna fishing, but cut them loose in United States waters, and many of these fish survive. Sportfishermen only fish the fringe of the populations, those fish within range of our boats. We catch a lot, but most sport-caught white marlin are released. On some September days, North Carolina and Virginia boats will come into port flying one or two dozen pennants upside down, signifying a phenomenal day, with all fish released.

Blue marlin

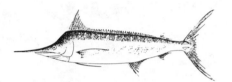

Atlantic Blue Marlin
Makaira nigricans

T he Atlantic blue marlin is a separate species from the Pacific form, and the queen of the billfishes in our waters. There are separate populations above and below the equator, our group concentrated at 25 to 45 degrees north and the southern group at 25 to 35 degrees south latitude. Both migrate to within 5 or 10 degrees of the equator, but don't aggregate there, preferring cooler climes. Both stocks also travel to the coast of west Africa, but are more common on this side of the Atlantic.

Our northern stock has a long breeding season, spawning from May to November near Cuba and the Greater Antilles. After spawning, they tend to migrate lazily northward with warm Gulf Stream water, not as a mass, but as singles or very small groups. Larval blue marlin have all been found right at about 83 degrees Fahrenheit, which points to that as the optimal, preferred temperature. Like other baby billfish, the post-larvae have sails, which are eventually lost.

Growth is very fast. Males mature at age 1, when they weigh 70 to 90 pounds. Adult males average 100 to 250 pounds, and the largest on record is 350 pounds. Females mature at age 1 or 2, when they weigh 100 to 135 pounds. All giants have been females. Based on both Atlantic and Pacific data, it appears that a 500-pound fish will be a 15-year-old female. A 1,376-pound world record Pacific fish was determined to be a 26-year-old female. In 1984, a 1,565-pound Pacific blue was taken off Hawaii on a big, white, skirted Kona-type plug. The largest Atlantic blue marlin on record are a 1,282-pounder and a 1,128-pounder; these two "granders" were taken off St. Thomas and North Carolina. A North Carolina monster estimated at 1,500 pounds was fought by several anglers for 30 hours in 1981 before breaking off. The largest Pacific fish on record was 1,805 pounds, but was disqualified from a record because it was fought by several anglers.

Many Atlantic blue marlin are taken from North Carolina to Montauk, New York. Skippers usually put out an 80-pound outfit (sometimes loaded with 100-pound-test line) rigged with a foot-long Spanish mackerel, deboned mullet, or big squid. They believe that bigger marlin go after bigger baits, which isn't exactly true.

Stomach analyses have shown that blue marlin eat fish almost exclusively (99 percent), with squid making up just 1 percent of the stomach volumes. In fact, blue marlin don't eat much and don't eat many large items. Of eighty-seven fish examined in one study, the average total food volume per stomach was under a pint, irrespective of what or how many of an item the marlin had eaten. In several studies in the Pacific and Atlantic, it was determined that blue marlin of all sizes ate food of all sizes, but primarily ate small items such as forage types of ocean fish about one to two inches long, a variety of small reef fishes, and the small filefishes and triggerfishes associated with sargassum weed. Their stomachs have contained dime-sized ocean sunfish, baby sailfish, baby swordfish, a rare spearfish on one occasion, half-inch-long tuna, and dolphin smaller than your little finger. But other, exceptional blue marlin had eaten a 60-

pound white marlin, a 63-pound bigeye tuna, and a 110-pound bigeye tuna! Because blue marlin sometimes eat big fish, many skippers like to rig a whole, small blackfin or skipjack tuna for them. But I haven't heard that this is particularly successful.

The two principal findings of the stomach analysis studies are that blue marlin don't normally eat squid at all, and usually don't eat big fish. You're more likely to get a hit on a small bait, and more likely to hook it.

Incidentally, they feed principally between 10:00 and 11:00 A.M. standard time in our waters, become inactive between noon and 1:00 P.M., have another binge between 2:00 and 4:00 P.M., and then taper off and don't feed at all after dark. Off the coast of west Africa, they appear to feed primarily between 11:00 A.M. and 2:00 P.M.. Blue marlin sometimes hunt in pairs or very small groups, but they don't school.

You probably think I'm now going to tell you what kind of tackle to use and how to fight a blue marlin. I'm not. They often defeat the heaviest tackle you can handle even with a top-notch boat and a well-equipped fighting chair. They're simultaneously so strong and fast that there's nothing with which they can be compared, and they're all different. Some are aerial acrobats, leaping into the sky first on one horizon and five seconds later on the other. Other blues never jump, but just run like wahoo from one end of the ocean to the other. Others sound like tuna, refusing to come up. When it comes to fighting a blue marlin, you can do everything right and still lose it. It's a magnificent, unpredictable, extraordinarily powerful animal in every way, and you'll doubt the possibility that it can be brought to the boat. If, after a half-hour or a few hours, you do manage to reach the leader, credit the captain and the mate as much as yourself. Then turn the fish loose.

Lonqbill Spearfish

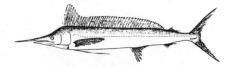

Longbill Spearfish
Tetrapterus pfluegeri

A spearfish looks like a sailfish run over by a steamroller and stretched out like a wahoo. It is very long and thin, doesn't have a sail, has pelvic fins (so you can tell it from a swordfish), has a straight profile (white marlin have a hump on the nape), and differs from all other marlins in having the vent located halfway back to the anal fin rather than right at the anal fin. If you catch a possible spearfish, boat it, ice it down, and radio the marina to have somebody from the National Marine Fisheries Service meet you at the dock. The stocks are in no danger whatever, and we need specimens for study.

Of the three or four kinds of spearfishes around the world, the only one in our area is the longbill. It has been reported once from Texas (Port Aransas) and many times from Florida. Its range extends from New Jersey and possibly New England in the north to Brazil and Argentina in the south. Perhaps the light tackle favored for billfishing in Florida is less likely to rip out of a spearfish than the tackle used to the north, and so more are landed, but not necessarily hooked, there.

Longbills are deepwater ocean fish which are an insignificant by-catch of the American and Japanese longline tuna fishery. Some 10.8 metric tons of spearfish were landed by tuna longliners in 1980, with Americans landing twice as many as the Japanese. (Surprised?) This is 1.5 percent of all marlins taken by longline, not counting swordfish. If we count swords, then spearfish make up 0.2 percent of the total billfish by-catch.

One-year-old fish are less than 3 feet long and weigh about 5 pounds. At this size, the dorsal fin is pretty high all along the length of the back, and the young spearfish might be confused with a baby sailfish. After two years, the fish are 5.3 to 5.6 feet long, weigh about 40 pounds, and are mature. Most fish caught by commercial longliners and by recreational anglers are two-year-olds. In the third year, the fish are still under 6 feet long, but weigh about 70 pounds. Few longbill spearfish live beyond three years, but those are the ones worth catching.

Longbills have a long spawning season with a peak in late winter. The principal spawning area is a narrow mid-ocean line from just northeast of French Guiana to the western tip of the bulge of Africa at about 17 degrees north latitude, across the entire North Atlantic Ocean. A second spawning area has been found in the middle of the South Atlantic, at about 10 degrees south and 15 degrees west.

The longbill spearfish feeds on squid and small fish associated with drifting surface materials like sargassum weed, and rarely contains anything from down below. However, we know little about its feeding habits and nothing about its parasites.

For most billfishermen, getting a spearfish is just plain lucky. All the spearfish caught by recreational anglers have been taken trolling, but that doesn't mean much. Longliners take them still-fishing with dead bait. The key to getting a spearfish anywhere is working well offshore with small baits and paying close attention before turning anything loose.

Swordfish
Xiphias gladius

Swordfish

The swordfish is the only billfish that's really in trouble, based on firm statistical data. That's because it's the only one being harvested for money by both commercial and recreational fishermen. Just like bluefin tuna, it's a rare swordfish that is released by any "sport" fisherman; the meat brings too good a price at the dock. Commercial fishermen take them by harpoon, longline, and drift gill net. Sportfishermen drift rigged squid and light sticks deep at night, a takeoff on a standard commercial longlining technique.

In the mid-1970s, a big swordfish population was discovered off south Florida. Night fishing for swordfish with Cyalume light sticks imbedded in or tied next to a rigged squid (as used by longliners) was adopted by recreational fishermen in small boats. The chances of getting a swordfish on any one night were better than 40 percent. Lots of people caught two or three in a night. Big fish were common, 400-pounders caught constantly, and 600-pounders not rare. You could catch a trophy fish (or more than one) and recover your costs, and then some, by selling it at the dock.

In response to the new, intense fishing pressure, the average size of swordfish dropped to under 100 pounds, and the local population was virtually wiped out. Today, a swordfish of any size off south Florida is as rare as a 1,000-pound bluefin tuna off Nova Scotia. Put simply, too many fishermen, both recreational and commercial, chased too few adult fish and began loading up on the babies.

In response to a rapid (less than 10-year) 25 to 40 percent or more worldwide reduction in swordfish stocks, and the shocking decline in average size to the point where virtually all landed fish were immature (never once getting the chance to breed and replenish the populations), the South Atlantic, Gulf of Mexico, Mid-Atlantic, Caribbean, and New England Fishery Management councils joined forces in an unprecedented cooperative agreement to stop the slaughter and give swordfish a chance to recover.

In 1986, the councils finalized a swordfish management plan, but it was never implemented. Believe it or not, the black hat in this disgraceful episode was an administrator of the National Oceanic and Atmospheric Administration (NOAA) who complained that the plan would hurt foreign and American tuna longliners. The councils will try again, as that incompetent administrator is now gone.

Swordfish don't move around much, and that makes local populations vulnerable to overfishing. They're still common where sportfishing pressure is minimal, but as soon as a population is discovered within range of small boats, its days are numbered. Swordfish cannot survive the combined pressure of commercial fishermen and sportfishermen in the absence of management.

There is only one species of swordfish worldwide, and it occurs in all the temperate, subtropical, and tropical seas, ranging some 50 degrees north and south of the equator. On our coasts, it ranges from Newfoundland to Argentina and from Oregon to Chile. Across the Atlantic, it occurs from Scandinavia to South Africa, and across the Pacific it ranges from north Japan to south Australia.

The heaviest aggregations are off the coasts of Saudi Arabia, south Japan, south California, east Australia, Argentina, and the Galapagos. There is also a very large area in the mid-Pacific at about 20 to 40 degrees north and 160 degrees east to 160 degrees west.

The swordfish is the only member of the fish family Xiphiidae, and has no close relatives. It is distantly related to the marlins (family Istiophoridae) and a strange, 250-pound ocean fish called the louvar, the only member of the fish family Luvaridae. The swordfish has lots of common names, including broadbill, pez espada, svaerdfisk, espadon, and mekajiki. The commonly written name "broadbill swordfish" is redundant.

Swordfish adults have a broad, flat bill rather than a rounded one; they have no scales and not even tiny teeth; they have one enormous keel on each side of the base of the tail rather than two; and (most obvious of all) they lack pelvic fins.

Swordfish occur all over the world's oceans because they have a temperature and depth range greater than any billfish. While their optimal temperature is 66 to 72 degrees Fahrenheit, they've been found in 53 degree Fahrenheit water. They frequently occur on the surface, but have been caught on deep-set lines in the canyons and on the high seas. Recently, a swordfish was seen outside the window of a deep-diving submersible at a depth of 2,060 feet. Based on what's been found in their stomachs, they are believed to go deeper and colder.

Breeding takes place year-round in 75 degree Fahrenheit waters. Swordfish move into shallower shelf waters or into the upper 250 feet of deep waters to spawn. Each female carries 2 to 5 million eggs. The eggs float and are less than two millimeters in diameter. In our area, larvae are abundant in the eastern Gulf of Mexico, along the south Atlantic coast northward to Cape Hatteras, in the Straits of Florida and Yucatan, and off the Leeward Islands and northern South America. Most larvae are found in surface waters where the depth is greater than 600 feet, and almost all of them at 75 degrees Fahrenheit and an ocean salinity of 36 parts per thousand (ppt).

Swordfish larvae are very different from the adults, and very different from other billfish larvae. They have two enormous, equal-sized jaws equipped with large teeth. The larvae also have scales and a long, low dorsal fin that extends all the way back to the tail, but they don't have a sail as do the marlins. Swordfish larvae feed on zooplankton until they're three-quarters of an inch long, and then eat fish.

They reach 16 inches their first year. Males mature at age three and females at age four. It is likely that swordfish must be age five or six before they are of any value to the breeding population. They live at least nine years, but the maximum life span is unknown.

The maximum size is probably about 1,200 pounds and 14 or 15 feet. The average offshore swordfish taken by the commercial fleet is 250 to 350 pounds, but inshore fish subjected to recreational fishing pressure average much less. Females get much larger than males, and any fish over 250 pounds is probably a female.

Swordfish eat anything, day or night, but prefer squid. A recent study of 168 swordfish confirmed that fish occurred in half the stomachs, while squid occurred in 82 percent. They're opportunists, taking pelagic fishes out at sea (mostly tuna, dolphin, snake mackerels, flying fish, and ocean squids) and mackerels, herrings, bluefish, needlefish, anchovies, and sardines inshore. They also feed on the very bottom in both shallow coastal and deep offshore waters.

Slashes found on cuttlefish and squid inside swordfish stomachs indicate that swordfish use their bills to club or slash their prey. There's an American report of a big swordfish in the stomach of a mako shark, and a Russian report of a 400-pound mako shark with a broken swordfish bill penetrating through the entire front half of the shark's body.

There is no significant long-range migration of swordfish. They may wander from top to bottom several times in a 24-hour period. It is only in northern climes that they bask at the surface.

In the early 1970s, the Food and Drug Administration prohibited the sale of swordfish with mercury levels greater than 0.5 parts per million (ppm) until the safe level was determined, and the industry collapsed. Later it was recognized that you would have to eat more than a pound of fish a day with mercury levels of 0.6 ppm to exceed the safe level. Today, the official FDA danger level is 1.0 ppm, and commerce in swordfish has resumed.

Swordfish are wonderful game fish, but they're in the precarious position of being vulnerable to sportfishermen and commercial fishermen before they're old enough to breed. There must be a minimum size on swordfish, with all shorts turned loose if alive and recorded (but not available for sale) if dead. There must be a rotating closure of the swordfish fishery everywhere to allow local recovery of stocks; this might be two consecutive years every decade in staggered portions of our coasts. And, because the swordfish alone among billfish is not strictly a game fish but also an important food fish, it must be managed as a food resource, with no harvest allocations made prior to assessments of what the stocks can stand.

Offshore Headboat Fishing

Headboats (party boats) may be modified, surplus naval PT boats or specifically designed fishing boats of the catamaran or single-hull type. Most of them sail daily and carry 35 to 100 passengers who pay individual fares. Headboats differ from charter boats, which contract with an individual to provide services for up to 6 people on a specific day for a specific fee, with certain conditions stipulated (who pays for the fuel, who keeps the catch, etc.).

There are too many people on a headboat to allow trolling, but headboats can anchor and fish the bottom, or they may drift over a productive bottom and fish unweighted baits at mid-depth. Along most of the United States coast, headboats typically fish rocky or grassy bottoms of shallow, near shore waters for black sea bass, scup (porgy), seatrout, flounder, red drum, bluefish, spot, and croaker. Many boats offer half-day trips which appeal to tourists, novices, and others unwilling or unable to devote a 6:00 A.M. to 6:00 P.M. day to fishing. Still others offer 24- and 48-hour trips to distant grounds where trout and redfish or other bottom fish are abundant.

Other headboats specialize in fishing coral reefs and rocky outcrops for red snappers and groupers. In south Florida, many of the best inshore grounds have been overfished, and half-day trips (which at one time were very productive) are not likely to yield memorable catches. Longer runs, particularly on the west side of the state, are now required to reach areas of good fishing. But fishing for red snappers and groupers is not confined to coral reefs off Florida. Texas and Louisiana have excellent snapper populations at oil and gas drilling platforms and at isolated reefs a long distance offshore. A similar snapper/grouper fishery extends northward as far as Virginia and North Carolina in deep Gulf Stream water at the edge of the continental shelf.

At near shore depths of 50 to 100 feet, the outcrops are occasionally washed in meanders of warm Gulf Stream water. In this warm environment where the light is too weak for photosynthesis, the rocks are covered with live sponges. Other invertebrates scurry and creep through the nooks and crannies of the sponge-encrusted rocks. This "live bottom" is home to very large black sea bass (two to five pounds) and equally large whitebone, longspine, and spottail porgies, pigfish, and white grunts, any one of which could make a meal for two people.

From 100 to 200 feet, all along the entire shelf, the live bottom is now constantly bathed in warm water, and the resident fishes change. Suddenly, red porgies ("silver snappers") appear in vast numbers, joined by white grunt, American red snappers, brilliantly colored vermilion snappers (beeliners), gray triggerfish, and hefty gag, red, and scamp groupers.

This is the inner edge of the continental shelf, and the region fished by headboats specializing in "red snapper" fishing.

Beyond 200 feet, the powerful currents demand two-pound weights, and sometimes electric reels. This is the shelf-break zone, where the bottom drops precipitously in the course of a couple of miles from 200 to 550 feet. Undersea cliffs, chasms, and deep ravines cut the steeply declining rocky bottom, dropping or rising in 20- to 30-foot increments into the blue-black Gulf Stream water above and the cold abyss beyond.

This is a different kind of habitat, and within this erratic shelf-break zone appear new and different fishes. Here, snowy and yellowedge groupers engulf anything smaller; an occasional lumbering Warsaw grouper yawns from its cave; and blueline tilefish rise out of submarine foxholes in the mucky slopes alongside the rocks, seeking red crabs and other deepwater delectables, then quickly rush back into their underground lairs.

Many of these offshore outcrops are very small and difficult to locate. For many years, this was a hit-or-miss fishery—a hit if you managed to locate a productive outcrop on a trip and a miss if you did not. The introduction of Loran changed all that. Small and secret locations could be precisely charted. For traditional netters, it was out of the question to work a trawl in these waters. But for hook-and-line fishermen with Loran to mark the hot spots, it was a bonanza.

A cold-water-induced mass mortality of red snapper occurred in 1981, and it wasn't in the Gulf of Mexico or off the Florida Keys, but off Morehead City, North Carolina. Such events underline the fragility of these habitats.

GROUPERS

The standard headboat tackle is an 80-pound-class rod and 4/0 to 6/0 reel with 80-pound-test monofilament line. The high-low, two-hook bottom rig is tied with 125-pound-test monofilament, one 8/0 hook on a two-foot leader tied two feet above the 16- to 20-ounce sinker and the other 8/0 hook on a two-foot leader tied one foot below the sinker. Headboat tackle is, in my view, too heavy. It often is in poor condition, with rickety reels half-filled with old, knotted, or brittle line, and every chromed

Grouper Rig

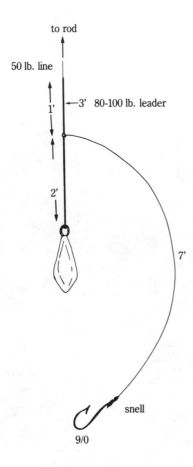

to rod

50 lb. line

1'

3' 80-100 lb. leader

2'

7'

snell

9/0

surface of the reel or rod covered in corrosion. I advise you to carry your own tackle. Use a 3/0 or 4/0 reel loaded with 50-pound-test monofilament line, and a short rod with a slightly flexible tip and plenty of spine. The terminal rig should consist of 80- to 100-pound-test monofilament leader, enough lead to get down (16 to 20 ounces on deep reefs), and 7/0 to 10/0 grouper hooks like the Mustad 95160 (Siwash) or 7731 (Big Game). Tie a single grouper hook above the sinker on a leader six to eight feet long. Add a smaller 5/0 hook on a short leader three feet above your grouper hook. It will catch snappers, grunts, and porgies (silver snappers), which you can eat or use for bait.

For normal snapper/grouper fishing, anglers are advised by headboat skippers (who supply the tackle and rigs) to lift the sinker about eight turns on the reel up from the bottom. That puts the top hook in the territory of vermilion snappers, which feed well above the bottom, and the bottom hook in range of everything else. It also enables the angler to feel a tug and react quickly, and it cuts down on rigs lost among the rocks.

Let's talk about bait. I have a stack of scientific papers on groupers that comes up to my knees. It includes, among other things, stomach content analyses. However, I've been a fisherman long enough to know that the best way to catch fish is to throw out the scientific studies and ask the local guys with overflowing coolers. Studies are great for when and where they were done. To catch fish here and now, you need to know what they're eating right here and right now. Different baits will produce fish on different days, even when you're fishing the same place.

To catch groupers in deep water, the best baits are iced (not frozen), soft-bodied, whole fish about eight inches long, such as scads (cigar minnows) or round herring. Hard, deep-bodied, whole fish like spots, pigfish, pinfish, and grunts aren't as good, perhaps because they're spiny. A lot of mates on headboats say that the best grouper bait is an

418-pound 2-ounce Warsaw Grouper
North Carolina state record—caught by
Paul Vissicchio aboard *Shadow* off Hatteras, North Carolina

Photo by C. R. Cannon, Dare County Tourist Bureau

eight-inch by three-inch rounded slab filleted from a grunt or porgy. Live baits have not been very productive for me.

Bury the hook point in the bait and drop your rig all the way to the bottom. Then slack off and forget it for a while. Periodically, take in slack and quickly raise your rig off the bottom. If you feel as though you're stuck in the rocks, the odds are a grouper has your rig.

Slack off again and wait a full two minutes. Then take in slack and raise up fast and hard. If you catch him outside the rocks, you'll know a grouper from anything else. A grouper is an extremely strong fish, smart enough to know that it's better off deep inside a rock cavern. When you've got him (as opposed to her) coming, you cannot afford a moment's respite. And remember, you haven't got him until he's in the box.

If you don't have a boat capable of making the run to the offshore wrecks, rocks, reefs, or platforms, you can take advantage of the offshore headboats that run out to Gulf Stream water. A full-day trip will cost $35 to $60, depending on the distance to the grounds. Some boats run deep-reef overnight trips, but I don't recommend them; even fishing buddies can get on your nerves after so long.

There are about 380 species of groupers in all the world's oceans, mostly in the tropics. Many of the larger groupers are important to both commercial and sport fisheries. They excel in just about every category from size to intelligence and from the quality of their meat to the quality of their powerful fight.

The average grouper begins life as a female, which will produce eggs from age 5 or 6 to about age 12. It then turns into a male and will live, on average, another 3 years, although 30-year-old fish are known.

Grouper larvae are thumbnail-sized monsters with spikes on their fins and gill covers. The functions of their huge spines may be to assist them in drifting, to protect them from predation, or to regulate temperature.

Groupers will gulp down crabs, shrimp, squid, octopus, and all kinds of small fishes. They're mostly sight feeders, but some of the very deepwater forms may also rely on other senses. Big groupers will suddenly open wide, as if in a yawn, drawing in water and prey at the same time. At one time it was believed that most groupers fed on small fare, their enormous open maws creating a suction that no tiny prey could resist. Today we know that groupers often use those big mouths to eat big prey animals.

Many groupers, like jewfish, are solitary fish. Except for some bellowing and snorting that goes with being a big male accustomed to living alone in a private territory, they're generally non-aggressive to their own kind, so long as their feeding stations remain private property. Some, however, like the deepwater gag (gray grouper), will aggregate in huge swarms, much like a pack of forage fish.

Groupers can be identified only with care, and you would be wise to pay little attention to the names applied by headboat mates; commercial fishermen have their local, traditional names for different species, but we'll use proper names in this book. You should be able to identify any common grouper from the following descriptions, irrespective of its local name.

The colors of groupers are variable, and you have to pay attention to specific markings rather than overall appearance; but markings are only partially useful. You may have to count the spines (stiff, single spikes) in the front part of the dorsal fin and the rays (soft, flexible, branched spikes) in the anal fin. We'll initially look at those groupers with nine dorsal fin spines.

The coney and graysby are small groupers, only about a foot long, which come in a myriad of colors. Both have nine hard spines in the dorsal fin. The graysby has a series of four black spots along its back just under the dorsal fin, and its body is densely covered with reddish brown spots. It has a rounded tail fin, unusual in small groupers. The spectacu-

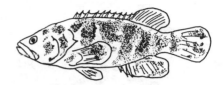

Jewfish
Epinephelus itajara

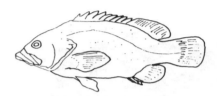

Coney
Epinephelus fulva

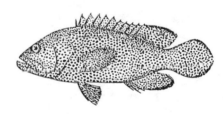

Graysby
Epinephelus cruentatus

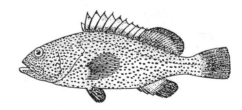

Red Hind
Epinephelus guttatus

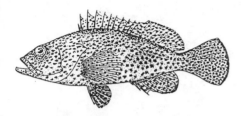

Rock Hind
Epinephelus adscensionis

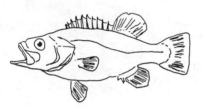

Speckled Hind
Epinephelus drummondhayi

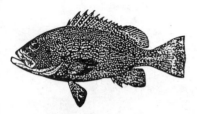

Wreckfish
Polyprion americanus

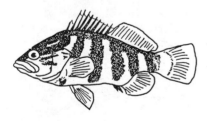

Nassau Grouper
Epinephelus striatus

lar coney has two black spots on the front and back of the top surface of the base of the tail (the peduncle), two side-by-side black spots on the lower lips, and oblique rows of tiny, dark-ringed, blue spots scattered over the upper two-thirds of the body.

Hinds are confusing, variable fish, but you can identify them with these guidelines. The rock hind, red hind, and speckled hind have eleven hard spines in the dorsal fin and eight or nine soft rays in the anal fin. Red and rock hinds have reddish brown spots all over the body. In the red hind, the spots are all the same size. In the rock hind, the spots are much larger toward the bottom of the fish; in addition, there are four saddlelike blotches on the back, three under the dorsal fin, and one on the root of the tail. The speckled hind has tiny white spots.

There are four giants: the deepwater wreckfish that occurs north of the Carolinas, the deepwater Nassau and Warsaw groupers which occur from the Carolinas southward, and the shallow-water jewfish, which is typically southern. Wreckfish get up to five feet long, but they're flattened from side to side, so they only attain about 100 pounds. They're distinguished by bumps and protuberances on the head and over the eyes and large fins which make them look like mutant tripletails. Jewfish get up to eight feet and 700 pounds, are mostly dark with marbling and speckles, have a very smooth, almost velvety appearance, and are the only large groupers with rounded tails. Jewfish have been dangerously overfished and are now protected by law in many federal management zones. The Warsaw grouper is dark, with virtually no markings. It can be recognized by the extremely long second spine in the dorsal fin. The Nassau grouper attains over 400 pounds. It has an oblique band through the eye, like an amberjack, and its second dorsal spine is about the same size as the third.

The red grouper is common everywhere. This reddish brown, marbled, velvet-bodied fish is the only grouper whose spiny dorsal fin has a smooth edge, the spines not protruding beyond the fin membrane.

Now we come to a group that all have ten to thirteen soft rays in the rear part of the anal (lower median) fin. The gag (gray grouper) is a common grouper throughout its range. Generally gray with darker squiggles on the face, it also has a sharp bone on the lower edge of the topmost gill plate. This is the only grouper in which the larvae drift inshore and settle down in dense vegetation on rocky bottoms and in estuaries, where they eventually metamorphose into small groupers. I dip-netted many of the spiny, clear orange larvae from a clump of sargassum weed attached to a rock in Beaufort, North Carolina, and I understand that they're abundant in the grassy zones of the estuaries. In an aquarium, they eat prodigious amounts of fish meat and gradually metamorphose into miniatures of the adults. Young gags remain in inshore waters until they reach almost a foot in length, and then gradually move offshore with increasing size. This is the common northern grouper of rocky shorelines and black-sea-bass banks.

The scamp is browner than the gag, and often occurs farther offshore. It has spots on the face, not lines, and its rear nostrils are larger than its front ones. Big scamps get extensions of the tail fin rays, making them broom-tailed. Certain Pacific groupers share this characteristic.

Some groupers only occur at the deepest part of the continental shelf. Among the offshore types is the snowy grouper, a dark fish with small, snowflake-like white blotches on the body. Young fish have a dark blotch on the base of the tail and more prominent snowflakes than older fish.

Black and yellowfin groupers have about three to five rows of very large, ovoid blotches, while yellowmouth groupers have—you guessed it—yellow pigment inside the mouth. Black groupers are almost always gray or black, and have several rows of horizontal, ovoid blotches on the sides.

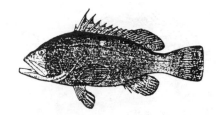

Warsaw Grouper
Epinephelus nigritus

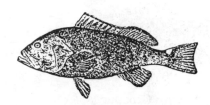

Red Grouper
Epinephelus morio

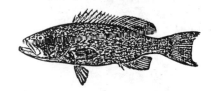

Gag
Mycteroperca microlepis

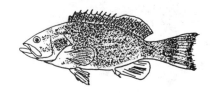

Scamp
Mycteroperca phenax

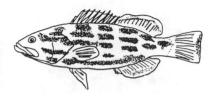

Black Grouper
Mycteroperca bonaci

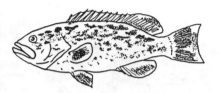

Yellowfin Grouper
Mycteroperca venenosa

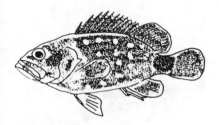

Snowy Grouper
Epinephelus niveatus

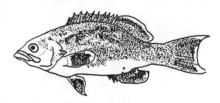

Yellowmouth Grouper
Mycteroperca interstitialis

Yellowfins have similar but smaller ovoid blotches on their sides, and they have yellow edges on their pectoral fins. The real yellowedge grouper has similarly colored fins but an unmarked body.

There are several more groupers in our area, but they're less common than these. Certain tropical groupers also enter our waters, particularly on offshore reefs, so this list is not complete by any means. Furthermore, we have records of a partially albino red grouper and a solid yellow speckled hind. It's not enough that these fishes vary normally; we now know that they vary abnormally as well.

Armed with this scientific knowledge, you should now be able to identify any offshore grouper with a 25 percent probability of being right! If you still don't know what you've got, send me a photograph of the live fish.

Some of our Atlantic groupers occur on the European side and in the Mediterranean Sea. The wreckfish, for example, is more common there than here. There are other groupers found only on that side of the Atlantic, like the dusky perch, which looks like a muscle-bound tautog.

The National Marine Fisheries Service (NMFS), in cooperation with the South Atlantic and Gulf of Mexico Fishery Management councils, has studied the effects of fishing pressure on the stocks of snappers and groupers. They've documented imminent growth overfishing, which, in plain English, means that the fish are getting smaller because of heavy pressure, and the populations could suddenly collapse if that pressure continues. They've recommended a minimum size of 12 inches on Nassau and red grouper, and prohibitions on the taking of jewfish. Additional groupers will probably need some kind of protection as the commercial fishery continues to decimate stocks on isolated outcrops.

There are all kinds of protection. You'll discover that headboat skippers often leave a good spot before the action lets up. It's because groupers (and snappers) are very slow-growing fish and don't migrate, so reefs are not repopulated by incoming fish. One boat can fish out all the groupers on a small reef in a matter of hours and make that reef barren for the next three years. However, if only a few of the big fish are taken and the boat moves on, smaller fish will grow more quickly and the reef will be productive again in a shorter time.

If you're a sportfisherman with your own boat, try not to fish an outcrop or a particular Loran station more than a couple of hours once a month. It's an effective way to manage the resource for maximum productivity.

Other Reef Fishes

C oral reefs and sponge-encrusted rocky out-crops are home to many kinds of fishes. Some are specialists and others generalized feeders. Feeding habits can sometimes be ascertained by looking at teeth.

Snappers, grunts, and porgies are easily distinguished from one another, yet have few technical differences. In general, snappers are colorful and not very deep-bodied, and they have long, sloping faces, very large mouths, and prominent canine teeth. Porgies are deep-bodied, flat-tened, and silvery, with convex faces, small mouths, conical or incisor teeth (sometimes blunt, funny-looking canines) up front, and big, flat molars on the sides of the jaws. Grunts have rather straight faces, are usually colorful, often have red or orange mouths that open downward, and have simple teeth throughout.

Ciguatoxin

B ecause snappers eat a broad range of foods, they sometimes carry CTX, the ciguatera toxin produced by the planktonic microscopic alga, *Gam-*

bierdiscus toxicus, and concentrated up the food chain. CTX is the fifth most powerful toxin known, the lethal dose only 0.00000045 gram per kilogram of body weight in mice. Dog snappers from the east Virgin Islands are frequent carriers of the toxin, but snappers of any kind (including cubera and red snappers) and in any area might be toxic. Generally, the carriers of CTX are fish-eaters of inshore bottoms, rather than pelagic fish or those that eat coral, plankton, or vegetation. But don't count on it. Among the most frequently implicated species other than the cubera and dog snapper are barracuda and several kinds of jacks. A 1987 episode involved a barracuda caught offshore from North Carolina.

The symptoms may appear as late as 30 hours after eating, and include tingling of the lips, tongue, and throat, followed by numbness, then nausea, vomiting, stomach cramps, diarrhea, severe headache, sore teeth, and convulsions. About 7 percent of these cases are fatal due to respiratory collapse, but the other 93 percent of the victims are sure they will be among the 7 percent who don't survive. There is no specific treatment, but injections of steroids, antihistamines, non-respiratory depressants, antidiuretics, and vitamins all alleviate symptoms somewhat. Anything that induces vomiting may help. Even after recovery, symptoms may persist for months or years.

Red Snapper

Now that you're properly warned, let's ignore the risk and go snapper fishing. There are about 250 kinds of snappers around the world, including 15 in our area. Young of the gray (mangrove), schoolmaster, dog, lane, and mahogany snappers are common at shallow-water Florida reefs and rocky areas, and even run up into estuaries, but only the gray snapper stays in brackish water as an adult. The most important in the offshore fisheries are the red, vermilion, silk, and blackfin snappers.

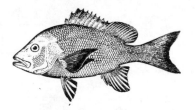

Red Snapper
Lutjanus campechanus

Red snappers (American reds, chicken snappers) occur along the continental shelf from Cape Hatteras to Yucatan. You can identify them by their red irises and lack of black armpits. Adults typically occur at depths of 60 to 300 feet, have been caught at over 1,300 feet, and are suspected to range down to 8,000 feet. In the Gulf of Mexico, juveniles are common at inshore jetties and oil platforms. Attaining more than 35 pounds and averaging 15 or 20, red snappers are prime target fishes of offshore headboats. Small fish eat sea squirts, jellyfish, crabs, shrimp, and other fish, and big ones are almost wholly fish-eaters.

Red snappers breed in the warm months, the adults spiralling up into the water column during spawning. The eggs are 0.8 millimeter in diameter and float, hatching just over 25 hours later. The larvae are rare in the plankton, where they spend a long time before settling down on a hard inshore bottom. After transformation into the adult form, they gradually move offshore into deeper waters and attain sexual maturity when they're 12 to 15 inches in length and 2 years old. At 7 years of age, red snappers weigh almost 10 pounds; they reach almost 17 pounds at age 11 and almost 30 pounds at age 15. Red snapper landings have declined with increased pressure from commercial fishermen and sport fishermen. The stock is suffering from growth overfishing, a condition in which fishing mortality is higher than natural mortality, and total landings by weight would increase if the smaller ones were released or not caught at all. We already know that many deepwater fishes, even those with protruding swim bladders, can be released and will survive. Recent studies have demonstrated that protruding bladders can be punctured to allow the fish to get back to the bottom, and there will be no long-term ill effects.

Silk Snapper

The silk snapper (yellow-eye, yellow snapper, day snapper, longfin snapper) is similar to the red snapper but has a yellow iris. Ranging from the Carolinas to northern South America, it is common between 250 and 350 feet on the edge of the continental shelf and abundant between 500 and 800 feet in the Bahamas. Silk snappers prefer low-profile hard bottoms, and are the only snappers on deep, muddy bottoms in the Gulf of Mexico. Most fish are 10 to 25 pounds in weight, but they get up to about 40 pounds. Silk snappers are opportunists that eat fish, shrimp, crabs, and molluscs. They mature at 20 to 24 inches in length (and of unknown age) and breed in the warm months. Larvae are rare in plankton, and juveniles have been found in water as shallow as 100 feet.

Blackfin Snapper

The blackfin snapper is a red snapper that is distinguished by its black armpit, red iris, and orange-yellow upper base of the tail. Ranging from the Carolinas to northern South America, it is most abundant from 250 to 450 feet, ranges down to at least 650 feet, yet also enters shallow water (30 feet) on occasion. In our area, the average fish is 2 feet long and about 9 pounds, but blackfins get up to 30 pounds. Caribbean fish are smaller, perhaps due to overfishing. Blackfin snappers eat shrimp, crabs, spiny lobsters, isopods, octopus, squid, and fish. They mature at 12 to 16 inches in length, but the ages of these fish haven't been determined. Spawning occurs year-round, with a peak in April. One juvenile under 3 inches was collected in 140 feet of water.

Mutton, Mahogany, and Lane Snappers

Mutton Snapper
Lutjanus analis

The mutton snapper is common from Cape Canaveral southward, and into the Gulf of Mexico. A typical member of the snapper fishery in this area, it is greenish above and reddish below, with red fins and a large black blotch and tiny blue dots on the side. The mutton snapper frequents shallower waters than the red, silk, and blackfin, and often roves over open, sandy bottoms at depths of 65 to 200 feet. The young enter grassy bays and mangrove flats in the Bahamas. Attaining a weight of 25 pounds, it is an important sport fish. It feeds largely on fishes, especially small grunts, and all kinds of invertebrates. Maturity is attained at 16 inches and at unknown age.

In the lower Florida Keys, the similar but smaller mahogany snapper is also important to the headboat fishery. Mahogany snappers get up to about 15 pounds and lack the tiny blue dots on the side.

Lane snappers range throughout our area, from shore to 1,300 feet and from both hard bottoms and muddy bottoms. A brown fish, it has characteristically thin yellow lines and a large, dark smudge on each side. The top size is about 16 inches at 10 years of age, but a foot-long fish is big; they're usually too small to be hooked before 4 years of age. Lane snappers are most abundant in Florida waters, where they're commonly taken from private boats and headboats using two-hook bottom rigs baited with cut fish or squid.

Vermilion Snapper

Vermilion Snapper
Rhomboplites aurorubens

Vermilion snappers (beeliner, night snapper, mingo) are the most common of the deep-water "red" snappers of the Atlantic coast shelf-break zone, and the least snapperlike in shape. Vermilions are characterized by their deep red color, thin yellow streaks, and sharply forked tail. More common in large areas of broken bottom than on isolated outcrops, vermilions become abundant beyond 200 feet over most of their range, and as little as 100 feet off the Carolinas. Schools of vermilion snappers cruise 6 to 25 feet above the outcrops, feeding day and night on amphipods, euphausiid shrimp (krill), planktonic lobsters, larval crabs, minute planktonic shrimp, small fishes, squid, worms, and other swimming invertebrates. Squid make up over a third of the stomach volumes of the largest vermilions. The average fish is just over a foot long and weighs between two and three pounds, but they get up to 26 inches in length and just over six pounds in weight. Vermilions first breed at age 4, when they're 14 to 16 inches long. They spawn from spring to fall, releasing 150,000 to ten times that many floating eggs per female. Maximum age is 8 years for males and 10 years for females.

Yellowtail Snapper

Similar in size and shape to the vermilion snapper is the yellowtail snapper, a shallow-water, Florida fish that feeds in the water column above inshore hard bottoms, especially isolated patch reefs. Light colored, with a broad, bright yellow streak along the side, most individuals are less than a foot long, but they are known to get up to 30 inches and five pounds. Don't confuse the yellowtail snapper with the west coast fish called yellowtail, which is a species of amberjack.

Cubera Snapper

The cubera snapper is our rarest, largest, and strangest snapper. Known from the Chesapeake Bay to Brazil, it prefers ledges, patch reefs, deep cuts, and channels not far from shore, enters mangrove swamps, grass flats, and tidal creeks, and is not known to occur deeper than about 165 feet. Maximum size is almost 5 feet in length and 121.5 pounds in weight for a fish from Cameron, Louisiana. An earlier (smaller) world record was a fish caught on a pier in North Carolina. Cubera snappers have caused ciguatera poisoning.

Red Porgy

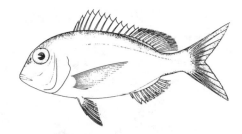

Red Porgy
Pagrus pagrus

Even fishermen who have never been out to the Gulf Stream are familiar with porgies. We've all caught some types, whether scup off New Jersey, sheepshead in southern waters, or pinfish from a dock anywhere. In most of our area, porgies can make up a third to a half of the total headboat landings. A few porgies that are uncommon inshore may be abundant in deep water far offshore. We'll look at those that associate with snappers and groupers on the rocky reefs at the edge of the continental shelf under the Gulf Stream.

The red porgy (pink porgy, silver snapper) is the most abundant species in the shelf-edge headboat fishery, making up almost half the catch. Occurring at depths of 50 to 550 feet with the larger fish progressively farther offshore, it concentrates at the shelf-break zone from the Carolinas to Texas, and never occurs inshore. It is absent from the south Gulf of Mexico to French Guiana, but is abundant off South America. Another stock occurs in the east Atlantic from the Iberian Peninsula south to Angola.

The red porgy is a metallic lavender fish covered with rows of tiny, dark blue dots and a bold blue streak over the eye. When brought up from the bottom, it may have shadowy bands on the sides that quickly disappear. Many have a blush of blue or yellow across the snout. The average red porgy caught at the shelf-break zone is 18 inches long and

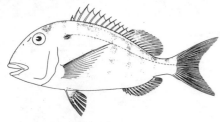

Grass Porgy
Calamus arctifrons

Saucereye Porgy
Calamus calamus

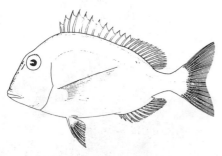

Knobbed Porgy
Calamus nodosus

Jolthead Porgy
Calamus bajonado

weighs almost 3 pounds. A two-foot-long fish would weigh over 6 pounds. The largest one known was 29 inches long and weighed over 11 pounds.

Like all groupers, a few kinds of porgies are hermaphroditic, developing first as one sex and much later changing to the other. Red porgies become sexually mature females at about age 3, and become males about 3 years later. They spawn mostly during the spring. The tiny, floating eggs hatch in about a day and a half, and growth is slow. Most of those taken by hook and line are 4 to 8 years old, and few live more than 11 or 12 years. The oldest fish found was 17 years of age. Because porgies mature and spawn before they're big enough to be taken by hook and line, they are in no danger of being overfished.

Red porgies are non-discriminating feeders that eat anything on or near the bottom. Crabs, sea urchins, brittle stars, snails, and clams make up much of the diet, but many kinds of small, slow-swimming bottom fish are also eaten. On headboats, red porgies are caught on cut fish or squid baits, and will probably take anything. Statistically, the average offshore headboat angler catches 26 pounds of fish, including five red porgies weighing 14 pounds.

Saucereye Porgy

A bundant at the shelf-break zone, the spectacular saucereye porgy is distinguished by a profusion of yellow or brassy spots overlaying a blue face. The top size is probably 16 inches. Saucereyes are second in abundance to red porgies.

Knobbed and Jolthead Porgies

T he knobbed and jolthead porgies are large, silvery fish that prefer deep water. The jolthead is shaped like the red porgy and has been reported from New England to Belize in water as deep as 150 feet. It attains 22 inches and 8 pounds. The knobbed porgy has a very steep head profile. It occurs only from the Carolinas to the Yucatan, attains 24 inches in length and probably 10 pounds in weight, and extends into at least 260 feet of water.

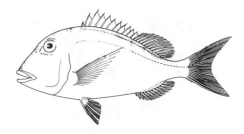

Whitebone Porgy
Calamus leucosteus

Whitebone and Longspine Porgies

The whitebone is a small porgy that occurs at depths of 30 to 300 feet on both sponge/coral rocky outcrops and sandy bottoms near patch reefs from the Carolinas to the Gulf of Mexico. The fish matures at just a year old, when it is 7 to 10 inches long, and spawns in the spring. Most fish caught are 4 to 6 years old, but may live 12 years. The maximum size is about 14 inches. Just over half of all whitebone porgies change from female to male, usually at age 2 or 4. The great age spread of the population, early spawning, and the ability of part of the population to change sex at different ages protect this porgy from the effects of overfishing.

Longspine porgies are also small, seldom attaining 8 inches in length, and are common inshore, but range into deep water. Longspines occur over both hard and grassy bottoms throughout our area, but are only abundant in the Gulf of Mexico. They breed their first year, and live only 2 or 3 years.

Longspine Porgy
Stenotomus caprinus

Grunts

The grunts are abundant, small fishes that range from Virginia to the tropics. Similar to both snappers and porgies, they differ in having sharp, tiny teeth throughout the jaws. The floor and roof of the mouth also have modified teeth, and the fish rub them together to

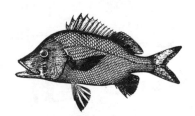

White Grunt
Haemulon plumieri

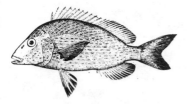

Pigfish
Orthopristis chrysopterus

create the grunting sound typical of all members of the group. Grunts are common both inshore and far offshore on deep reefs. Most are small species, almost all of them have red mouths (inside), and several are large and abundant, making them important sport fishes.

Perhaps the most abundant of the edible species is the white grunt. Ranging from Chesapeake Bay southward, the white grunt is common from inshore rocky bottoms all the way to the shelf-break zone, where it is taken along with vermilion snapper and red porgy. The top size is about three pounds and 16 inches; inshore fish average half this length; and one foot in length and one pound in weight is about the average size offshore. White grunts aren't white but dusky, with blue and copper spots on the sides and prominent blue lines on the face. The inside of the mouth is bright red-orange. Fresh fillets of white grunt are excellent grouper bait.

Other grunts occur on the deep offshore reefs throughout our area, but seldom get large enough or sufficiently abundant to be important. Most large grunts are important only on Florida reefs. The hogfish (pigfish) is a good-sized (one foot) grunt that is common as far north as Chesapeake Bay, but is typically an inshore, bay fish, which will not be covered here.

Gray Triggerfish
Balistes capriscus

Triggerfish

The triggerfishes are flat-sided fishes with stout, powerful teeth that can tear apart any shellfish. They have two prominent spines on the back, but the large one can only be unlocked and depressed if the small one (the trigger) is pressed down first. The skin is leathery and rough, and the entire fish looks decidedly inedible. But that's a big mistake.

The most common triggerfish in our area is the dull-colored gray triggerfish, ranging from Virginia (and occasionally Canada) southward, and across the Atlantic to the coasts of Europe and Africa. Abundant over the offshore rocky reefs out to the shelf-break zone, gray triggerfish get up to 22 inches in length and about 10 pounds in weight, and live up to 13 years. Gray triggerfish feed on shellfish of all types on the bottom, also eat fish, and will chase a bait far up above the reef, so that they are frequently hooked when an angler is retrieving his rig. Very hard fighters, gray triggerfish are, pound for pound, tougher than amberjacks. Be careful of their powerful teeth when unhooking them. Triggerfish should be skinned first and then filleted. The meat is comparable to that of groupers.

Queen triggerfish are less common throughout most of our range but abundant in the Florida Keys, where they feed largely on sea urchins. They range to the Carolinas on offshore reefs, and have been reported as far north as Canada. Queen triggerfish are spectacular blue, green, and yellow fish, the small ones popular in the marine aquarium trade. Normally edible, they are occasionally implicated in ciguatera poisoning. They attain about the same length as gray triggerfish, but are not quite as heavy.

Tilefish

T he tilefish (golden tilefish, rainbow tilefish) was first discovered in May of 1879 by a Captain Kirby, who was fishing in 150 fathoms (900 feet) of water off the southern coast of Nantucket. Just 3 years later, in March and April of 1882, boats entering New York harbor reported dead tilefish spread out over an area 170 miles long and 25 miles wide at the northern edge of the Gulf Stream. The mortality was later estimated at 1.4 billion

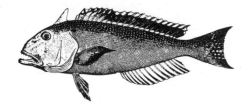

Tilefish
Lopholatilus chamaeleonticeps

tilefish with an average weight of 10 pounds, equivalent to 288 pounds of fish for every person living in the United States at the time. Subsequent searches indicated that the species might have become extinct. However, a few tilefish were captured 10 years later. By 1897, 15 years after the massive kill, the fishery had recovered.

Tilefish occur in deep, soft-bottomed submarine canyons from Nova Scotia through the Gulf of Mexico and northern South America. Most of the 2.5 million-pound commercial catch is made between Hudson Canyon off New York and Lydonia Canyon east of Cape Cod, and from Cape Canaveral to Key West, in 300 to 1,400 feet of water.

Recreational fishing only dates back to 1963, and occurs from Maryland to Long Island, New York, and off Georgia and South Carolina. Sportfishermen now account for a half-million pounds. The typical tackle is a standard boat rod with 4/0 to 6/0 reel; electric reels get lots of use. Off the north-eastern states, the round trip is about 200 miles to the canyons. Off the Carolinas, as elsewhere in the South, the distance to deep water is much less, but no fishery has yet developed. That's sure to change, and the first guys out there should have the best fishing.

Tilefish excavate holes in clay bottoms or in steep walls in canyons. Their burrows are often occupied by crabs and other species taking advantage of this deepwater "prairie-dog town." The key conditions are depth, a soft sub-stratum, and stable water temperatures between 49 and 58 degrees Fahrenheit.

Male tilefish attain 3.5 feet in length and a weight of almost 60 pounds, while females are much smaller (40 inches and 35 pounds). The average fish is 5 to 20 pounds, but 40-pounders are not unusual. They appear to live more than 20 years. Breeding occurs during the warmer half of the year, and it's possible, based on the sex ratios of fish of different size classes, that they change sex. Tilefish feed mostly between 10:00 A.M. and 3:00 P.M. within 10 feet of the bottom, consuming mostly squat lobster and spider crabs. They eat a great variety of invertebrates and fish, including other tilefish, and refuse baits that aren't absolutely fresh. Tilefish meat has been compared with lobster, but that's just hyperbole. It's a dense, off-white meat with an unusual texture, less tasty than pollock. Although the flavor is unusual, I'd rank it only about as good as gray seatrout.

Blueline Tilefish

The blueline (gray) tilefish is a small, subtropical species of tilefish that ranges from Virginia to Key West and throughout the Gulf of Mexico. The largest and oldest ones known are 2.5 feet long, just over 12 pounds, and about 15 years of age. Males get larger than females, and sex reversal is suspected in this species as well. The blueline tilefish prefers depths of 200 to 700 feet and is common in soft sediments and on sandy and shell hash bottoms between rocky outcrops of the shelf-break zone. It is frequently caught by headboats working outcrops for snappers and groupers, but there is no directed recreational fishery. That may develop as the snapper/grouper outcrops become overfished. The blueline tilefish's principal foods are crabs, shrimp, fish (flounders, cusk eels, morays, lizardfish), clams, sea squirts, starfish, and worms, but it eats just about anything.

The Missing Fishes and Other Thoughts

You've probably noticed that I have not covered several important fishes, such as striped bass, gray snapper, and snook. That's because they are usually caught from shore by foot-based fishermen, and not from boats. Other fishes have been excluded because, although they're common offshore and important in some places, they're not target fish of sportfishermen; Bermuda chub are a good example of this kind of fish. Still other fish like rays, skates, and lizardfish have been excluded because, although they may fight hard and are good to eat, American fishermen disdain them.

This is a book about fishing from boats for fishes that Americans like to catch and sometimes eat. It is not about fishes that biologists or Sea Grant extension agents or seafood industry specialists insist that we ought to pursue and eat, or about what we should eat. Right or wrong, informed or ignorant, what we do these days reflect American cultural characteristics, and my culture isn't any better than yours. So I won't tell you to eat raw fish (although I love it) or to steam your fish rather than fry it. I won't tell you that olive and peanut oils are the healthiest of all fats, if you insist on frying fish. I won't tell you that fish must be quickly dressed and placed in plastic bags and the bags (not the fish) covered with ice to maintain the best flavor. I won't tell you that the fresh, cucumbery smell of newly caught fish is due to t2,c6-nonadienal, and that this compound breaks down to awful-tasting c4-heptenol when the fish is frozen without lemon juice. Hell, you don't want to know any of that.

As the old refrain goes:

> *I'm an old hippie, and I don't know what to do. I ain't tryin' to change nobody. I'm just tryin' real hard to adjust.*

WHERE TO GO

The following pages contain a state-by-state list of Loran C coordinates for offshore hard bottom areas, a list of charter boats with their ports and telephone numbers, a list of the appropriate charts for that area, and sources of additional information.

The NOAA charts listed all include Loran C overlays, cost $7.50 each, and can be ordered from the Distribution Branch, N/CG33, National Ocean Service, NOAA, Riverdale, Maryland 20737-1199.

The NOAA bathymetric maps, available with or without Loran C overlays, are all different prices. For information on availability and cost, contact the National Ocean Service, NOAA, 6001 Executive Boulevard, Rockville, Maryland 20852, or phone them at 301-443-8361.

Boats change ports, phone numbers change, new clubs form, and old ones disappear. New hot spots are found and new artificial reefs built. I hope you'll write me, c/o John F. Blair, Publisher, 1406 Plaza Drive SW, Winston-Salem, North Carolina 27103, with updated information that can be incorporated into future editions.

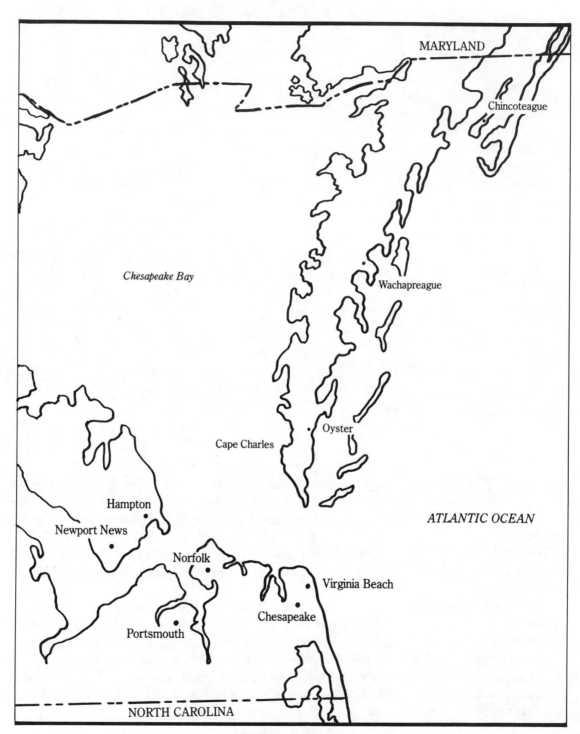

Virginia Coastline

Virginia

T he northernmost state of the Old South is the best in our area for bluefin tuna, tautog, and big black drum. It's the only state in range of codfish and Boston mackerel. The vast fishing grounds vary from massive Chesapeake Bay with its beaucoup bluefish, persistent striped bass, large weakfish (gray trout), and huge flounder, to the deep, distant offshore canyons where fast charter boats pursue white marlin, yellowfin tuna, and swordfish. Near shore headboats fish the wrecks and outcrops for tautog, sea bass, and amberjack, and pursue schools of Boston mackerel in early spring. Virginia has the pending world record for tautog (24 pounds) and the record for black sea bass.

The inshore waters are dominated by Chesapeake Bay. The upper Bay, including Smith Island and Tangier Island, yields spot, croaker, flounder, weakfish, and bluefish. Buoy 48 and the cut channel on the western side of Delaware Bay are hot spots for small boats, as is the series of rocks (actually holes) on the eastern side on the edge of the channel, particularly Stone Rock, Bird Rock, Crammyhack, Ditch Bank, and Hack's Rock. In the vicinity of the middle Bay, hot areas are the Cell, the Cape Charles artificial reef, Gwyan's Island and the artificial reef located there, and the area near the York and Rappahannock rivers. The Cabbage Patch and the C-10 buoy on the eastern side are premier locations for big black drum. The lower Bay hot spots include Bluefish Rock off Hampton (for cobia and blues) and Thimble Shoals in the Ocean View area. The Chesapeake Bay Bridge-Tunnel is terrific for all bay species, including tautog. Best bets are the hard bottoms at Islands 1, 2, 3, and 4 of the Bay Bridge, the North Channel Bridge, and the tunnel between Islands 3 and 4; tautog are most common in the outer Bay.

Wachapreague and Chincoteague inlets on the eastern shore are excellent locations for flounder, gray trout, bluefish, and black drum. The barrier islands are also great for red drum, but that's another story (and another book).

The principal offshore grounds off Chincoteague in north Virginia are the Lump, Winter Quarter Shoal, Monroe Slough, and the Jack Spot. South of this area, off Accomac, are the near shore Blackfish Bank and offshore Submarine Slough. East of Little Machipongo Inlet, you can head far offshore to 3-Mile Hill, the Monroe Wreck, 21-Mile Hill, 20-Fathom Finger, and the Washington Canyon. Out of Virginia Beach, you can fish the Triangle Wrecks, the Fingers, Norfolk Canyon, the Hot Dog, the Lumps, the 100-Fathom Curve, the Fish Hawk, and the Cigar. All are outstanding white marlin and yellowfin tuna hot spots. Use the NOAA charts to locate fishing grounds.

Off Cape Henry, numerous artificial reefs have been developed by the Virginia Marine Resources Commission, and the Virginia Sea Grant Marine Advisory Service can provide you a chart with Loran and latitude/longitude coordinates to the sites.

NOAA Charts

12211	Fenwick Island, Chincoteague Inlet, Ocean City Inlet
12210	Chincoteague Inlet to Great Machipongo Inlet
12221	Chesapeake Bay Entrance
12207	Cape Henry to Currituck Beach Light
12225	Chesapeake Bay, Wolf Trap to Smith Point
12228	Chesapeake Bay, Pocomoke and Tangier Sounds
12230	Chesapeake Bay, Smith Point to Cove Point
12231	Chesapeake Bay, Tangier Sound, Northern Part
12263	Chesapeake Bay, Cove Point to Sandy Point
12271	Chesapeake Bay, Eastern Bay and South River
12273	Chesapeake Bay, Sandy Point to Head of Bay
12222	Norfolk Harbor and Approaches
12223	Norfolk Harbor and Approaches
12253	Norfolk Harbor and Elizabeth River
12245	Hampton Roads
12248	James River, Newport News to Jamestown

NOAA Bathymetric Maps

NJ 18-8	Chincoteague. Inshore north.
NJ 18-9	Baltimore Rise. Offshore north.
NJ 19-7	Jones. Extreme offshore north.
NJ 18-11	Currituck Sound. Inshore south.
NJ 18-12	Hyman. Offshore south.
NJ 19-10	Wilmington Valley. Extreme offshore south.

Loran Coordinates of Wrecks and Reefs

Cape Henry area		
Cape Henry Wreck	41294.2	27180.3
Westmoreland	41288.9	27165.3
Santore	41277.7	27117.1
Tower Reef, Dry Dock	41286.2	27103.0
Owl & Kingston Celonite	41218.1	27121.5
Tiger	41188.0	27101.6
Salty Sea II	41241.7	27087.7
Walter Hines Page on Parramore Reef	41746.3	27095.5
Mona Island on Parramore Reef	41744.0	27096.0
John Morgan	41390.2	27032.9
John Morgan	41390.7	27033.3
John Morgan	41391.4	27033.7
Wreck south of John Morgan	41388.7	27032.9
Lillian Luckenback	41372.7	27032.0
Webster Liberty ship, Triangle Reef	41391.4	27020.2
Garrison Liberty ship, Triangle Reef	41390.2	27020.7
Garrison Liberty ship, Triangle Reef	41390.7	27020.5
Haviland Liberty ship, Triangle Reef	41389.6	27020.0
Edgar Clark Liberty ship, Triangle Reef	41386.2	27018.8
Clark	41387.4	27020.2
Gulf Hustler	41272.7	27069.7
Spring Chicken	41320.4	26958.5
Capt. Rick	41245.2	27035.7
Francis E. Powell	41270.4	27014.1
Francis E. Powell	41269.7	27013.5
Margaret P. Hanks	41188.9	27048.3
Concrete pipes, ODU Test Reef	41784.1	27125.4
Concrete igloos, ODU Test Reef	41741.0	27126.0
Concrete igloos, Cape Charles Reef	41541.2	27231.0
Concrete pipes, Cape Charles Reef	41539.4	27230.8
High surface tire units, Cape Charles	41539.0	27231.2
Gwynn Island Reef, composite	41637.2	27299.4
Concrete igloos, Little Creek	41259.8	27225.3

Offshore Charter Boats

Area Code (804)

Lower Peninsula

Al Hartz Marina	Poquoson	868-6821
Sandra	Poquoson	868-6821
Chesapeake Bay Charters	Hampton	723-9818
Jones Marina	Hampton	723-9818
Dandy Haven Marina	Hampton	877-2721
After Five	Hampton	851-0511
Skipjack	Hampton	851-7622
Reel Time Charter Service	Hampton	877-2721
Miss Charlie	Hampton	723-0998
Third Lady	Hampton	851-6836
Gray Cat	Newport News	595-8177

Middle Peninsula

Susan Carole	Deltaville	776-6283
Dawn II	Deltaville	776-9885
Patty Lee II	Deltaville	776-9394
Pretty Lady	Deltaville	358-8691
Buddy Lee	Deltaville	776-6694
Sweet Pea	Deltaville	758-4036
Bay Bear	Deltaville	776-6694
Snafu	Deltaville	776-9841
Miss Ruth	Deltaville	776-9661
Captina Q	Deltaville	776-9684

Myrtle M	Deltaville	776-9786		High Hopes	Rudee Inlet	425-9253
Cindy H	Deltaville	776-9394		Mar-Kim	Rudee Inlet	425-9253
Miss Nan	Deltaville	776-9656		Miss Va. Beach	Rudee Inlet	425-9253
Florence Marie	Gloucester Point	642-2786		Bros. Pride	Rudee Inlet	425-9253
Locklies Marina	Greys Point	758-2871		Fisherman's Wharf Marina	Rudee Inlet	480-3113
Wild Bill	Greys Point	758-2871		Smith Limited	Rudee Inlet	428-2111
Modema	Greys Point	758-2871		Cherokee	Rudee Inlet	473-1633
Tamara	Greys Point	758-2871		Teaser	Rudee Inlet	428-2111
Bonita	Greys Point	758-2871		Ocean Atlantic	Rudee Inlet	428-2111
Locklie's Lady	Greys Point	758-2871		Ocean Master	Rudee Inlet	425-9253
Frances G	Greys Point	758-2871		44 Magnum	Rudee Inlet	425-9253
John Boy	Greys Point	758-2871		O-Four	Rudee Inlet	425-9253
Sherwood	Greys Point	758-2871		Our Dream	Rudee Inlet	425-9253
Miss Florence	Greys Point	758-2871		Pinafore	Rudee Inlet	425-9253
Davea	Greys Point	758-2871		Poor Girl	Rudee Inlet	425-9253
Pat	Greys Point	758-2666		Top Hook	Rudee Inlet	425-9253
Kathy	Greys Point	758-2871		Anxious	Rudee Inlet	425-9253
Lee	Greys Point	758-2871		Wilkat	Rudee Inlet	425-9253
Ginger II	Greys Point	758-2871		Virginian	Rudee Inlet	425-9253
Miss Ruth	Greys Point	758-2871		Virginia Darling	Rudee Inlet	425-9253
Muriel Eileen	Cobbs Creek	776-6790		Follow the Sun	Rudee Inlet	425-9253
Miss Ellie	Cobbs Creek	776-6790		Chelsea	Rudee Inlet	425-9253
				Iemanja	Rudee Inlet	460-3711
				Great Expectations	Rudee Inlet	460-9443

Norfolk - Virginia Beach

Harrison Boat House	Norfolk	587-9630				
Little Creek Marina	Little Creek	583-3600				
Fish Virginia, Inc.	Little Creek	587-8835				
Sean	Little Creek	583-4130				
Elmon	Little Creek	588-5401				
Grand Slam	Little Creek	588-3042				
Screaming Eagle	Little Creek	588-5401				
Gusto	Little Creek	588-5401				
Hustler Jr.	Little Creek	588-5401				
Cobb's Marina	Little Creek	588-5401				

Eastern Shore

Bubba's Marina	Lynnhaven Inlet	481-9867		Cape Charles Harbor	Cape Charles	331-2121
D & M Marina	Lynnhaven Inlet	481-7211		Safari I	Cape Charles	331-3235
Four Winds	Lynnhaven Inlet	481-7211		SST	Cape Charles	331-1612
Big D	Lynnhaven Inlet	481-7211		Mako II	Cape Charles	331-1013
Nancy Ann	Lynnhaven Inlet	481-7211		Buccaneer	Cape Charles	331-2722
Kristen B	Lynnhaven Inlet	481-7211		Safari	Cape Charles	331-3235
Cap'n Mad	Lynnhaven Inlet	481-7211		Elizabeth	Cape Charles	336-5433
Faircee III	Rudee Inlet	484-3728		Kings Creek Marina	Cape Charles	331-2058
Kingfisher	Rudee Inlet	482-2939		Nancy May	Cape Charles	331-2369
Alibi	Rudee Inlet	490-3581		Miss Jennifer	Cape Charles	331-3063
Virginia Beach Fishing Center	Rudee Inlet	422-5700		El Pescadore	Cape Charles	331-2058
Relentless	Rudee Inlet	497-6377		Aralee	Cape Charles	331-2058
Sea Sport	Rudee Inlet	497-6394		Regina S	Chincoteague	336-6490
Four T's	Rudee Inlet	425-6088		Roie Lee	Chincoteague	336-6265
Hustler	Rudee Inlet	425-9253		Osprey	Chincoteague	336-6374
Rainbow	Rudee Inlet	425-9253		Canyon Connection	Chincoteague	336-5456
				Raider	Chincoteague	336-5722
				Pinecove	Chincoteague	336-6669
				Eva K	Chincoteague	336-3809
				The Virginian	Chincoteague	336-5430
				Anjina	Chincoteague	336-5433
				Betty J	Chincoteague	336-6865
				EC II	Sanford	824-5068
				Wanda Fay	Oyster	331-2044

Little Bit	Oyster	331-2111
Mary Page	Oyster	678-5498
Helen J	Oyster	331-3295
Kelley Marie	Quinby	665-5011
Fish 'N Fin	Quinby	787-3399
J-Mar	Quinby	442-6285
Ron-Jo	Quinby	442-9324
Timmy Kay	Quinby	442-7214
Canyon Lady	Wachapreague	787-3272
Melissa D	Wachapreague	787-3272
Sea Fox	Wachapreague	787-4576
Capt. n' Bill	Wachapreague	787-4506
Wachapreague Marina	Wachapreague	787-2105
Scorpio	Wachapreague	787-3010
Rebel	Wachapreague	787-2781
Lulu	Wachapreague	787-2550
Margo A	Wachapreague	787-2105
Fern A	Wachapreague	787-2105
Nomad	Wachapreague	787-2105
Foxy Lady	Wachapreague	787-2105
Sea Bird	Wachapreague	787-1040
Janie-Mac	Wachapreague	787-2105
Scorpio	Wachapreague	787-2105
Lu-lu	Wachapreague	787-2105
Rebel	Wachapreague	787-2105
Bonnie Sue	Wachapreague	787-2467
Virnanjo	Wachapreague	787-3341
Aqua-Gem	Wachapreague	787-2334
Nellie L	Saxis	824-4642

Northern Neck

Pur Sang	Callao	529-6801
Betty B	Coles Point	472-2903
Titonka	Kinsale	472-3282
Gay Ruth	Harry Hogan Point	529-6566
Sweet Thing II	Harry Hogan Point	529-7370
Gracie D	Harry Hogan Point	529-6931
SuBek	Harry Hogan Point	472-2358
The Fishing Center	Harry Hogan Point	529-7370
Sweet Thing	Harry Hogan Point	529-7370
Fun	Harry Hogan Point	529-7370
Miss Pam II	Lewisetta	529-6773
Ken-Ma-Ray	Lewisetta	529-6725
Willie B	Lewisetta	529-7345
Playtime	Lewisetta	472-3717
Marnie	Lewisetta	472-2486
Kathy L	Lewisetta	529-6276
Meg C	Lottsburg	262-2857
Cin-Cat	Lottsburg	333-3891
Blurok	Lottsburg	529-6645

Sherry Jerry	Reedville	633-6045
Jett's Hardware	Reedville	453-5325
Virginia Breeze	Reedville	443-4612
Mar-chelle	Reedville	453-4554
Marchelle II	Reedville	453-4554
Big Dipper	Reedville	224-0896
Crying Shame IV	Reedville	443-2298
Challenger II	Reedville	493-8557
Wahoo	Reedville	453-3491
Misty	Reedville	453-4077
Betty Jane	Reedville	580-5904
The Dudley	Reedville	453-3568
Little Gull	Reedville	453-3413
Sunchaser	Reedville	222-8819
Ventura	Reedville	453-3658
Southern Belle	Reedville	462-7149
Fair Wind	Reedville	453-3509
Misty Blue	Reedville	453-3525
Hiawatha	Reedville	453-5852
Kit	Reedville	453-3251
Don El	Reedville	580-7452
Midnight Sun	Reedville	224-7082
New Life	Reedville	453-3521
Miss Cathy II	Reedville	453-3513
Corsair	Reedville	798-5183
Iona	Reedville	453-4474
Hobo II	Warsaw	333-4329

Headboats

Raider	Chincoteague	336-6498
Adventurer	Chincoteague	336-5126
Osprey	Chincoteague	336-6374
Miss Charlie	Hampton	723-0998
Harrison Boat House	Norfolk	587-9630
D & M Marina	Norfolk	481-7211
Patricia Lynn	Norfolk	587-1381
Virginia Beach Fishing Center	Virginia Beach	422-5700
Sea Sport	Virginia Beach	425-9253
Rainbow	Virginia Beach	425-9253
Miss Virginia Beach	Virginia Beach	425-9253

Sources of Information

Virginia Division of Parks and Recreation
(list of marinas)
1201 Washington Building
Capitol Square
Richmond, Va. 23219

Commonwealth of Virginia Marine Resources Commission
(artificial reef news)
P.O. Box 756
Newport News, Va. 23607-0756
804-247-2200

Virginia Peninsular Chamber of Commerce
(accommodations)
P.O. Box 7269
Hampton, Va. 23666

Virginia Saltwater Fishing Tournament
968 Oriole Drive South, Suite 102
Virginia Beach, Va. 23451

Virginia Sea Grant
(free publications)
203 Monroe Hill House
University of Virginia
Charlottesville, Va. 22903
804-924-5965

Virginia Sea Grant Marine Advisory Service
(chart of fish havens with Loran coordinates, $1.00,
Marine Resource Bulletin, free.)
Virginia Institute of Marine Science
Gloucester Point, Va. 23062
804-642-7164

Virginia State Travel Service
(map, accommodations)
202 North Ninth Street
Richmond, Va. 23219
804-876-4484

Virginia Beach Sharkers
P.O. Box 12025
Norfolk, Va. 23502

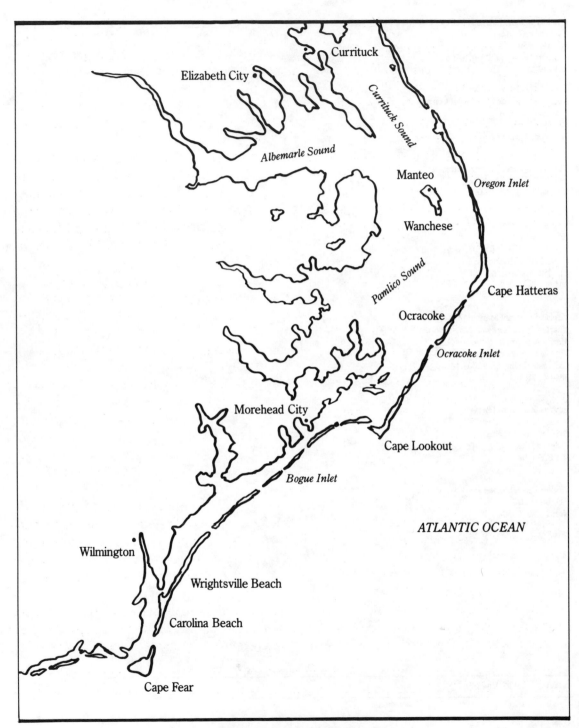

North Carolina Coastline

North Carolina

T he Tar Heel State takes top honors nationwide for giant red drum on the Outer
Banks and big blue marlin offshore. The charter boat fleet at Hatteras boasts
the shortest distance to the Gulf Stream north of Florida. The fleet at Morehead City has a good
record of blue marlin and sailfish catches, but the fleet at Oregon Inlet claims more blue and
white marlin than anywhere else. Best of all, the charter boat rates throughout the state are
about the lowest in the nation.

The principal offshore grounds out of Oregon Inlet are the 100-Fathom Curve and the area
south of the Cigar, both northeast of the inlet, and the Point, southeast of the inlet. Diamond
Shoals, east of Cape Hatteras, drops into Gulf water and is productive in late summer.
Morehead City boats converge on the undersea mountain called Big Rock, while boats out of
Hatteras fish the Rockpile. Fish abound in 60- to 100-fathom water beyond Cape Lookout
Shoals. Boats operating out of Wilmington work the drop-off beyond Frying Pan Shoals, but the
emphasis here is on king mackerel, not billfish.

Onslow Bay, between Cape Lookout and Cape Fear, offers excellent king mackerel fishing
for the guy with a 22-foot boat. These kings may be a native population that heads offshore in
the winter rather than south. The Wilmington group of king mackerel tournament fishermen
developed slow-trolling with live menhaden, and take top prizes wherever they compete. The
shoals off Cape Fear are a hot spot for big tarpon. Working from small boats and using live
pinfish as bait, the locals generally release all the tarpon they catch.

Less than an hour offshore, the rocky outcrops support black sea bass in the summer and
porgy (scup) and tautog in the winter. Two hours offshore, the sponge-encrusted rocky
outcrops at the edge of the Gulf Stream are rich in vermilion snapper and gag grouper. Two big
Gulf Stream headboats operate out of Morehead City, and others out of Manteo and Carolina
Beach. Most of the southern headboats offer half-day, short-distance trips for black sea bass.

The best inshore fishing is at the capes and inlets. Oregon Inlet is dangerous with shoals and
currents, but there are big red drum there.

Striped bass fishing on the Outer Banks is history. In the winter, the Chesapeake Bay
breeding stock was found a mile or more offshore south of Cape Hatteras, where commercial
fishermen sank gill nets to the bottom and devastated them. State stocking programs in the
rivers to Pamlico Sound continue, but don't work. Virtually every hatchery-reared fish stocked
in the sounds is taken by commercial netters within two years, and none of these fish enters the
coastal migratory group.

Pamlico and Albemarle sounds dominate the inland waters. Albemarle Sound is virtually
freshwater, tops for black bass fishing in its upper reaches, but heavily polluted in places from
agricultural runoff. Pamlico Sound is virtually the size of Chesapeake Bay, but shallower. Its

vast area and lack of structures make navigation by eye difficult; its thin waters (generally less than six feet deep) make groundings inevitable. Natives who ply the unmarked, shifting channels know where to find giant summer red drum and commercial supplies of seatrout. Non-natives are advised to stick to the ocean inlets, where depths, marked channels, and traffic make fishing safer than in the monotonous, empty interior.

The beach at Cape Hatteras is excellent for red drum, bluefish, and sharks. Hatteras and Ocracoke inlets are excellent for red drum, cobia, and grey seatrout. Drum Inlet is famous for flounder, but not for drum! The bight of Cape Lookout is protected, safe, deep, clean, and excellent for everything from Spanish and king mackerel to big sharks. Access is shortest from Harkers Island.

The shallow, inshore waters between the barrier islands from Cape Lookout to Cape Fear are good for flounder drift-fishing, but crabbing and night flounder gigging are the major activities.

NOAA Charts

12207	Cape Henry to Currituck Beach Light
12200	Cape May to Cape Hatteras Offshore
11520	Cape Hatteras to Charleston Offshore
12204	Currituck Beach Light to Wimble Shoals
11555	Cape Hatteras–Wimble Shoals to Ocracoke Inlet
11544	Portsmouth Island to Beaufort
11543	Cape Lookout to New River
11539	New River Inlet to Cape Fear
11536	Approaches to Cape Fear River

NOAA Bathymetric Maps

NJ 18-11	Currituck Sound. Inshore north.
NJ 18-12	Hyman. Offshore north.
NJ 19-10	Wilmington Valley. Extreme offshore north.
NI 18-2	Manteo. Inshore central.
NI 18-3	Wraight. Offshore central.
NI 19-1	Lippold. Extreme offshore central.
NI 18-4	Beaufort. Inshore south.
NI 18-5	Russell. Offshore south.
NI 18-6	Hatteras Ridge. Far offshore south.
NI 19-4	Evans. Extreme offshore south.
NI 18-7	Cape Fear. Inshore extreme south.
NI 18-8	Marmer. Offshore extreme south.
NI 18-9	Lanier. Extreme offshore, extreme south.

Artificial Reefs

AR 130	RR cars 12 mi from Oregon Inlet	26979.1	40726.0
AR 140	RR cars 9 mi from Oregon Inlet	26975.0	40690.0
AR 145	LCU 8 mi from Oregon Inlet	26941.4	40685.5
AR 220	RR cars 5 mi from Hatteras Inlet	26951.0	40182.0
AR 225	RR cars 6 mi from Hatteras Inlet	26945.0	40175.0
AR 250	RR cars 5 mi from Ocracoke Inlet	26987.0	40024.0
AR 255	RR cars 6 mi from Ocracoke Inlet	26995.9	39998.0
AR 298	BT 6400 Barge	27019.5	40132.7
AR 320	Clifton Moss near Beaufort Inlet	27138.5	39636.9
AR 330	Howard Chapin near Beaufort Inlet	27139.7	39569.5
AR 340	Paul Tyndall near Bogue Inlet	27162.4	39545.3
AR 342	Bogue Inlet 4-mi Reef	27177.0	39549.8
AR 345	RR cars 8.4 mi from Bogue Inlet	27160.2	39524.8
AR 355	New River Inlet RR cars	27210.0	39324.4
AR 362	New Topsail Inlet 9-mi Reef	27233.1	39224.5
AR 364	Billy Murrell near Masonboro Inlet	27267.4	39161.0
AR 366	New Topsail Inlet 14-mi Reef	27214.7	39226.0
AR 368	New Topsail Inlet 15.5-mi Reef	27211.7	39195.0
AR 372	Masonboro Inlet 5-mi Reef	27261.0	39068.7
AR 376	Masonboro Inlet 10-mi Reef	27243.1	39077.2
AR 386	Masonboro Inlet 18-mi Reef	27217.7	39082.9
AR 420	Tom McGlammery Cape Fear Reef	27300.7	57421.7
AR 425	Yaupon Beach Reef	27303.0	57426.8
AR 440	Brunswick County Fishing Club	27316.4	57390.2
AR 445	Lockwood Folly 9-mi Reef	27312.6	57375.5
AR 455	Shallotte Inlet 7-mi Reef	27325.9	57362.0
AR 460	Shallotte Inlet 3-mi Reef	27340.7	57350.1

Oregon Inlet Area Wrecks and Rocks

Liberty ship Zane Grey	26940.6	40575.2
Liberty ship Dionysus	26940.8	40573.5
Submarine	26917.0	40713.6
Nancy F.	26946.7	40816.6
Russian trawler	26844.7	40885.1
Ship	26882.5	40505.8
Wreck	26868.9	40931.9
Wreck	26893.5	40393.8
Wreck	26887.0	40278.0
Wreck	26919.0	40331.0
Asphalt barge	26868.4	40458.8
Ol' Ugly	26901.6	40503.0
Joe Doughty party	26877.4	40479.4
Alpha tower	26934.0	40910.0
Bravo tower	26855.0	40856.0
Charley tower	26915.0	40737.0
Gulf tower	26865.0	40660.0
The Point, dropoff	26785.0	40575.0
100-fathom slab rock	26810.0	40975.0
1140-1170 slab rock	26917.0	40392.0
Old green line 1250 rocks	26810.0	40400.0
Old green line 1250 rocks	26811.0	40415.0
530 hole at canyon	26797.0	40530.0
630 line	26803.0	40630.0
Green buoy	26847.5	40450.9
Platt Shoals	26925.1	40631.5
Large object	26816.9	40678.3
Bad rock	26891.7	40408.2

Cape Lookout Area Wrecks and Rocks

Morehead City Sea Buoy	27113.2	39668.7
Sea Buoy R2131	27113.5	39661.0
Swansboro Sea Buoy BW B1	27189.7	39546.1
Beaufort Sea Buoy	27113.2	39688.7
Beaufort Inlet	27114.4	39690.0
R2 Barden Inlet	27090.5	39680.0
R8	27092.0	38577.6
R6	27078.8	39595.8
1st NW Place	27090.4	39577.6
2nd NW Place	27069.1	39574.8
3rd NW Place	27089.1	39570.0
Little 10	27077.4	39553.6
Little 10	27081.1	39560.6
Big 10	27079.6	39555.2
Corner	27075.7	39518.8

West Rock	27072.1	39515.7
West Rock	27070.0	39520.0
South West Rock	27066.7	39594.8
South West Rock	27070.4	39507.5
100 Rock	27064.2	39601.2
120 Rock	27055.4	39621.8
210 Rock	27069.3	39488.0
210 Rock	27069.3	39493.1
210 Rock	27069.7	39493.1
210 Rock	27070.1	39491.4
240 Rock	27079.0	39495.3
240 Rock	27080.0	39494.6
Submarine	27063.5	39491.5
WW1 Wreck	27067.8	39463.3
Papoose	27074.0	39431.1
Papoose	27073.4	39431.2
Naeko	27065.6	39387.5
Naeko	27065.6	39386.8
SE Naeko	27035.0	39391.0
R14 Buoy	27040.5	39572.4
NW R14 Buoy	27046.1	39573.1
SE R14 Buoy	27032.8	39577.1
SE R14 Buoy	27032.9	39577.3
SE R14 Buoy	27023.2	39570.3
SE R14 Buoy	27024.4	39572.9
NE R14 Buoy	27034.4	39598.8
NE R14 Buoy	27037.3	39593.0
NE R14 Buoy	27037.7	39601.1
NE R14 Buoy	27037.9	39599.1
SW R14 Buoy	27046.6	39523.5
S R14 Buoy	27033.8	39542.6
S R14 Buoy	27027.4	39533.0
W R14 Buoy	27033.5	39543.9
W R14 Buoy	27033.2	39544.5
W R14 Buoy	27048.8	39562.3
190 from R14 Buoy	27031.5	39543.1
Corner	27031.5	39551.8
Corner	27031.5	39538.8
Corner	27043.6	39700.6
NW West Rock	27077.4	39521.5
Corner	27075.7	39518.8
Corner	27075.5	39518.5
Corner	27075.7	39517.9
90-foot Drop	27006.0	39576.0
Big Rock	26982.7	39595.5
W Big Rock	26987.2	39577.6
NE Big Rock	26984.2	39593.5
Southwest Rock	27066.7	39594.8
East Rock	27043.9	39681.5
East Rock	27048.5	39642.5
East Rock	27159.0	39561.4
Drop	27058.2	39634.7
R 2 P Buoy	27056.5	39652.0

1700 Rock	27043.4	39705.8
1700 Rock	27043.4	39709.8
Rock	27057.0	39700.0
Ario	27045.0	39747.5
"D" Wreck	27042.5	39740.8
Atlas Tanker	27023.6	39721.5-9
Shad Wreck	27025.3	39724.2
Shad Boat	27066.3	39610.3
Shad Boat Buoy R6	27078.4	39595.0
South Wreck	27143.2-6	39524.3
Amagansant Wreck	27026.9	39724.3
30-minute Rock	27054.6	39686.0
45-minute Rock	27176.0	39511.2
NNE of 1700 Rock	27052.4	39711.4
NE of 1700 Rock	27043.2	39710.9
Rock	26953.5	39775.0
Keypost Rock	27178.4	39567.4
Keypost Rock	27177.4	39563.7
Christmas Rock	27182.3	39393.8
Far East Tanker	26981.3	39788.9
John D. Gill (bow)	27198.5	39085.3
John D. Gill	27199.5	39085.3
WR 2	27129.0	39250.0
WR 2	27128.5	39249.5
WR 13 Buoy	27146.6	39551.6
S WR13 Buoy	27134.3	39470.0
SE WR13 Buoy	27128.4	39556.2
NW Rock	27159.2	39557.5
NE Rock	27037.2	39595.4
Hutton	27143.4	39524.3
Fewnwick Isle	27064.0	39607.9
195 Rock	27105.4	39553.2
Rock	27134.4	39470.0
Rock	27135.6	39466.9
Rock	27140.2	39518.1
Rocks SE of Sea Buoy	27161.7	39451.4
Rocks SE of Sea Buoy	27158.8	39451.6
Jerry's Reef	27140.2	39518.1
Knuckle, R4 Buoy	27061.2	39618.7
Russian Wreck	27037.1	39617.6
Russian Wreck	27047.2	39708.1
1400 Line	27936.0	39890.5
E Slough Buoy	27075.0	39670.4
W Slough Buoy	27083.3	39654.9
Trawler, R8 Buoy	27092.3	39633.3
Rock South 13	27134.3	39470.0
Ledge South of 13	27139.2	39487.0
Ledge SE of inlet	27112.6	39410.6
Ledge SE of inlet (another)	27111.2	39391.6
Artificial Reef	27127.9	39661.2

Bogue Inlet Area Wrecks and Rocks

Offshore Keypost	27175.9	39553.2
East Rock	27160.2	39560.1
Hutton Wreck	27143.2	39524.3
85-degree Ledge	27146.0	39415.4
Ledge	27151.8	39444.5
Contl Rock	27163.4	39458.7
Rough bottom	27162.0	39496.6
45-minute Rock	27175.5	39572.5
NW 45-minute Rock	27178.1	39512.2
Lost Rock	27183.0	39489.4
Bear Inlet Rock	27194.7	39497.8
Offshore Bear Inlet Rock	27193.0	39485.2
57-foot Rough bottom	27194.2	39445.9
Honeymoon Rock	27185.3	39434.3

Cape Fear Area Wrecks and Rocks

Sea Bouy, Masonboro Inet	27275.5	39097.2
Masonboro Inlet WR-4	27199.5	39091.0
Inshore WR-4	27214.7	39076.5
Offshore WR	27192.8	39069.2
Offshore WR-4	27170.3	39098.7
Offshore WR-4	27180.5	39100.0
Ledge south of WR-4	27208.2	39047.2
Ledge	27188.2	39068.9
Liberty ship	27268.0	39106.5
Pocahontas tug	27240.6	39048.3
SS Stone tug	27241.6	39046.0
Old dredge wreck	27241.2	39046.7
Peteroff wreck	59076.0	45322.9
Wreck	27263.4	39057.8
Wreck	27224.6	39068.1
Wreck	27179.2	39052.7
Fish Haven	27266.2	39164.8
Frying Pan Tower	27190.0	39025.0
Dallas rock	27252.5	39173.8
10-mile rock	27242.0	39097.0
10-mile rock	27241.0	39044.0
18-mile rock	27217.0	39136.0
23-mile rock	27190.9	39153.7
Rock	27177.0	39166.0
Rock	27202.5	39055.3
Rock	27240.0	39076.0
Rock	27195.0	39145.1
Rock	27177.0	39198.1
Rock	27230.3	39054.5
Rock	27255.8	39056.5
Rock	27227.4	39027.8
Rock	27213.2	39055.6

Offshore Charter Boats

(Area Code 919)

Grand Slam	Manteo	473-2280
Limited Edition	Manteo	473-5577
Salty Dawg Marina	Manteo	473-3405
Oregon Inlet Fishing Center	Oregon Inlet	441-6301
Capt. B.C.	Oregon Inlet	473-2348
Carolinian	Oregon Inlet	473-5224
Deepwater	Oregon Inlet	261-2063
Dream Girl	Oregon Inlet	473-5157
Fight-N-Lady	Oregon Inlet	441-4016
Fish-N-Fool	Oregon Inlet	473-2572
Gal-O-Mine	Oregon Inlet	473-3614
Gulf Stream	Oregon Inlet	473-3012
Honey	Oregon Inlet	473-2942
Hooker	Oregon Inlet	473-5965
Jo-Boy II	Oregon Inlet	473-2427
Marlin Fever	Oregon Inlet	491-8233
Mighty Wind	Oregon Inlet	473-2583
Miss Boo II	Oregon Inlet	473-2774
Outlaw	Oregon Inlet	473-5657
Sea Jay IV	Oregon Inlet	473-2675
Sinbad	Oregon Inlet	441-6301
Sportsman	Oregon Inlet	441-7295
Surfsider	Oregon Inlet	441-6301
Tarheel	Oregon Inlet	473-5791
Temptation	Oregon Inlet	473-5101
Temptress	Oregon Inlet	441-7705
Wildfire	Oregon Inlet	473-5961
Capt. Dean Johnson	Wanchese	473-2675
Pirates Cove Yacht Club	Nags Head	473-3906
Hatteras Fishing Center	Hatteras	986-2532
Hatteras Fever	Hatteras	995-4243
Hatteras Harbour Marina	Hatteras	986-2166
Anita Carol	Hatteras	995-5983
Sea Lady	Hatteras	986-2356
Eagle	Hatteras	986-2608
Tuna Dock	Hatteras	986-2467
Tiderunner	Hatteras	986-2395
Albatross Fleet	Hatteras	986-2515
Village Marina	Hatteras	986-2522
Willis Boat Landing	Hatteras	986-2208
Rascal	Ocracoke	928-5711
Sand Dollar	Ocracoke	928-5571
Harkers Island Fishing Center	Harkers Island	728-3907
Starflight	Harkers Island	728-6571
Second Glance	Harkers Island	728-2672
Ashley Renaie	Harkers Island	728-5780
Fisherman's Inn Marina	Harkers Island	728-5780
Fish Chaser	Harkers Island	728-5780
Morris Marina	Atlantic	225-4261
Anchorage Marina	Atlantic Beach	726-4423
Causeway Marina	Atlantic Beach	726-6977
Bill Collector	Atlantic Beach	726-7650
Charter Boat Booking Service	Atlantic Beach	726-2273
Fort Macon Marina	Atlantic Beach	726-2055
Eagle	Atlantic Beach	726-4989
Calcutta	Atlantic Beach	726-7878
Morehead City Yacht Basin	Morehead City	726-6862
Gould's Charter Boats	Morehead City	726-3821
Great Escape	Morehead City	726-7703
Mako	Morehead City	728-3520
Tom'N Jerry	Morehead City	726-6607
Offshore and Offshore III	Morehead City	729-3441
Sea Wife Charters	Morehead City	728-5670
Southwind	Morehead City	726-2476
Sharyn Da Nes	Morehead City	726-7756
Tropic Isle Yacht Services	Morehead City	726-9338
Wavedancer	Morehead City	800-682-3423
Ebb Tide	Morehead City	728-7327
Lion's Paw	Morehead City	728-7908
Dudley's Marina	Swansboro	393-2204
Billyanna II	Swansboro	326-5512
Capt. Don Huneycutt	Swansboro	393-8589
Swan Point Marina	Sneads Ferry	327-1081
Althea B	Wrightsville Beach	256-2353
Black Hawk	Wrightsville Beach	256-2408
Estelle B	Wrightsville Beach	799-0009
Forego	Wrightsville Beach	256-2341
Idle Hour	Wrightsville Beach	392-0725
Island Girl	Wrightsville Beach	256-2910
Minnie Ann	Wrightsville Beach	392-0725
Seapath Marina	Wrightsville Beach	256-3747
Strike Zone	Wrightsville Beach	256-2776
Fired Up	Wrightsville Beach	458-5172
Seapath Marina	Wrightsville Beach	256-3747
Wrightsville Marina	Wrightsville Beach	256-5770
Gulfstream Marina	Wrightsville Beach	256-4796
Carolina Inlet Marina	Carolina Beach	392-0582
Bird Dog Charter Service	Carolina Beach	458-9345
Capt. Doug	Carolina Beach	458-8671
Capt. Rick	Carolina Beach	458-9230
Fish Witch	Carolina Beach	458-8419
Flo Jo	Carolina Beach	458-5454
Fired Up	Carolina Beach	458-5172
Sinbad	Carolina Beach	458-5043
Holiday Lady	Carolina Beach	458-8671
Patsy	Carolina Beach	458-5101
Stew Bird	Carolina Beach	458-8471
Blue Water Charters	Southport	278-6382
Watts Charter Boats	Southport	457-5441
Kingfisher	Southport	278-6382

Salty Dog V	Southport	278-9834
Idle-On	Southport	457-5441
Southport Marina	Southport	457-5261
Southport Marine Mart	Southport	457-6350
My Other Woman	Long Beach	278-5666
Drifter	Long Beach	278-6257
The Fugitive	Long Beach	278-3796
Navaho III	Long Beach	278-3294
Swag Charters	Holden Beach	842-2646
El Toro	Holden Beach	842-9299
Seahawk II	Shallotte	579-2702
Inlet View Marina	Shallotte	579-6440
Hughes Marina	Shallotte	754-8962
Mike's Marina	Shallotte	754-6080
Bald Head Island Limited	Bald Head	457-4758
Bald Head Island Marina	Bald Head	457-6763
Sportsman's Blue Water Point	Oak Island	278-5267
Ocean Isle Marina	Ocean Isle	579-2702
Scott's Hill Marina	Scott's Hill	686-0896
Carolina Beach State Park	Scott's Hill	458-8207
Sea Cruiz	Calabash	579-3660

Headboats

Country Girl	Manteo	473-5577
Miss Hatteras	Hatteras	986-2166
Capt. Stacy IV	Morehead City	726-4675
Lady Faye	Morehead City	726-3060
Carolina Princess	Morehead City	726-5479
Blue Heron II	Snead's Ferry	327-1081
SS Winner Queen	Carolina Beach	458-5356
Winner Speed Queen	Carolina Beach	458-5356
Stew Bird II	Carolina Beach	458-8471
Pirate III	Carolina Beach	458-5626
Skipper	Southport	457-6204

Sources of Information

Carteret County Chamber of Commerce
P.O. Box 1198
Morehead City, N.C. 28557
919-726-6831

Greater Jacksonville Chamber of Commerce
P.O. Box 765
Jacksonville, N.C. 28540
919-347-3141

National Marine Fisheries Service
(technical publications)
Southeast Fisheries Center
Beaufort Laboratory
Beaufort, N.C. 28516-9722

North Carolina Division of Marine Fisheries
(*Tar Heel Coast* and other publications)
P.O. Box 769
Morehead City, N.C. 28557
1-800-682-2632

North Carolina Sea Grant
(various publications)
North Carolina State University
Box 8605
Raleigh, N.C. 27695
919-737-2454

Outer Banks Chamber of Commerce
P.O. Box 1757
Kitty Hawk, N.C. 27948
919-441-8144

South Brunswick Islands Chamber of Commerce
P.O. Box 1380
Shallotte, N.C. 28459
919-754-6644

Southport-Oak Island Chamber of Commerce
Route 5, Box 52
Southport, N.C. 28461
919-457-6964

Wilmington Chamber of Commerce
P.O. Box 330
Wilmington, N.C. 28402
919-762-2611

Fishing Clubs

Raleigh Salt Water Sportfishing Club
4818 North Hills Drive
Raleigh, N.C. 27612

Brunswick County Fishing Club
Rt. 2, Box 85
Supply, N.C. 28462

Cape Hatteras Anglers Club
P.O. Box. 145
Buxton, N.C. 27920

N.C. Beach Buggy Association
P.O. Box 969
Nags Head, N.C. 27959

Cape Lookout Mobile Fishermen
Katie Morris
Star Route
Atlantic, N.C. 28511

Piedmont Offshore Club
P.O. Box 7044
High Point, N.C. 27264

Carolina Croaker & Marlin Club
P.O. Box 1172
Greenville, NC 27835

Winston-Salem Sportfishing Club
P.O. Box 4212
Winston-Salem, N.C. 27115

Got-em-on Live Bait Club
David Franklin
217 Peninsula Drive
Carolina Beach, N.C. 28428

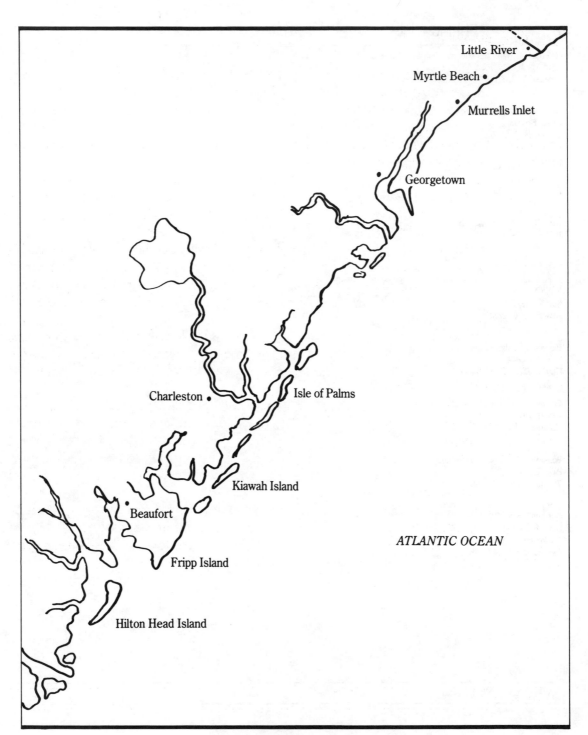

Little River

Myrtle Beach

Murrells Inlet

Georgetown

Charleston

Isle of Palms

Kiawah Island

Beaufort

Fripp Island

ATLANTIC OCEAN

Hilton Head Island

South Carolina Coastline

South Carolina

I f South Carolina is terrific for any kind of fishing, it is sharking. The world record tiger shark was taken from a pier at Cherry Grove, after the same fisherman had lost a bigger one the day before. Big sharks abound in the murky inshore waters near inlets and, because they are underfished to this day, remain abundant. Charleston has a shark club. The state has published *An Angler's Guide to South Carolina Sharks* (S.C. Wildlife and Marine Resources Dept., $3.50).

The principal fishing areas from north to south are Little River, Myrtle Beach, Murrells Inlet, Georgetown (including Pawley's Island), Charleston (including Isle of Palms, Folly Beach, Kiawah, Johns Island, and James Island), Edisto Beach, Beaufort (including Fripp Island), and Hilton Head Island (including Daufuskie Island).

The inshore waters have the same fishes that occur in North Carolina, but with noticeable differences. Giant red drum are less common at the inlets and along the beaches, but the small ones are abundant at cuts and structures. The bottom varies from grassy flats to rocky outcrops extending all the way to the beach. On the rocks, black drum, black sea bass, and spadefish are abundant.

Offshore has two meanings in South Carolina. To skippers of boats in the 20- to 30-foot class, it means trolling for king and Spanish mackerel in green water an hour or two out of port. Larger boats make the three-hour-plus run to the blue-black waters of the Gulf Stream for white and blue marlin, wahoo, barracuda, and sailfish.

The headboats that fish the rocky outcrops also differ. All the half-day and some full-day boats work the shallow (40- to 60-foot), inshore "snapper banks" (actually sea bass banks) for black sea bass, with porgies and just a few gag grouper and red snapper livening up the trip. Many of the full-day boats fish the 100- to 180-foot deep reefs at the edge of the Gulf Stream for vermilion and red snapper, red porgy, and a variety of groupers, with amberjack, dolphin, and tilefish adding sparkle to every outing.

The principal offshore features are the Gulf Stream beyond Frying Pan Shoals in the north, the Charleston Bump (an undersea mountain similar to Big Rock in North Carolina), and the artificial reefs and trolling alleys everywhere along the coast. The state's artificial reef program is very active, with the reef areas constantly being enlarged.

NOAA Charts

11009	Cape Hatteras to Straits of Florida
11520	Cape Hatteras to Charleston Offshore
11480	Charleston Light to Cape Canaveral Offshore
11536	Approaches to Cape Fear River
11535	Little River to Winyah Bay Entrance
11531	Winyah Bay Entrance to Isle of Palms
11521	Charleston Harbor and Approaches
11513	St. Helena Sound to Savannah River

NOAA Bathymetric Maps

NI 17-9	Georgetown. Coastal north.
NI 18-7	Cape Fear. Inshore north.
NI 18-8	Marmer. Offshore north.
NI 18-9	Lanier. Extreme offshore north.
NI 17-12	James Island. Coastal south.
NI 18-10	Richardson Hills. Inshore south.
NI 18-11	Wittman. Offshore south.
NI 18-12	Tibbet. Extreme offshore south.

Reefs, Wrecks and Rocks

BP-25 Reef 160-foot Tanker	45306.0	59551.4
Cape Romain Reef 100-foot Barge	45363.2	59996.2
Cape Romain Reef (nun)	45363.3	59996.4
Little River Reef Landing Craft (nun)*	45386.5	59418.5
Little River Reef Trolling Alley	45385.3	59419.0
Little River Reef Trolling Alley	45387.8	59419.0
Paradise Reef (nun)*	45465.0	59761.9
Paradise Reef Landing Craft (nun)	45464.0	59763.3
Paradise Reef Barge (can)	45463.7	59761.1
Paradise Reef Barge (can)	45463.0	59763.0
Paradise Reef Barge	45464.8	59762.1
10-mile Reef Trolling Alley (nun)	45418.1	59737.1
10-mile Reef Trolling Alley (nun)	45426.8	59741.0
10-mile Reef (can)*	45426.5	59742.2
10-mile Reef Ship	45427.1	59741.3
10-mile Reef Landing Craft	45426.4	59742.3
10-mile Reef Camel	45426.8	59741.3
Pawley's Reef, 2 Landing Craft (nun)*	45456.9	59814.9
Pawley's Reef, 2 Landing Craft (can)	45457.0	59814.0
Georgetown Reef (nun)*	45411.2	59882.7
Georgetown Reef (can)	45410.7	59882.3
Georgetown Reef Structure	45410.4	59882.3
Georgetown Reef Structure	45411.1	59882.7
Georgetown Reef Structure	45410.5	59882.0
Georgetown Reef Structure	45411.4	59882.9
Georgetown Reef Barge	45411.4	59881.5
Georgetown Reef Barge	45411.8	59881.1
Georgetown Reef Torungen	45410.3	59882.1
Georgetown Reef Trolling Alley	45411.7	59882.9
Georgetown Reef Trolling Alley	45410.1	59882.2
Capers Reef (R-8) State Buoy*	45438.2	60370.4
Capers Reef CG Buoy	45440.9	60367.5
Capers Reef M/V Pathfinder	45437.4	60368.4
Capers Reef Caisson	45437.6	60371.0
Capers Reef Landing Craft	45438.3	60370.5
Capers Reef Landing Craft	45438.1	60369.7
Capers Reef Landing Craft	45438.2	60370.0
Capers Reef Landing Craft	45438.2	60369.9
Capers Reef concrete pipes (88)	45438.5	60369.0
Kiawah Reef (4KI) State Buoy*	45493.1	60693.6
Kiawah Reef Dry Dock	45493.2	60693.4
Kiawah Reef LCU	45493.6	60693.9
Kiawah Reef Pontoons	45493.4	60693.5
Kiawah Reef Lifeboats	45491.1	60693.8
Kiawah Reef Tug	45492.7	60692.5
Kiawah Reef Tug	45494.4	60694.5
Kiawah Reef 200-foot Barge	45491.2	60691.4
Kiawah Reef Trolling Alley	45495.0	60690.4
Kiawah Reef Trolling Alley	45493.1	60693.6
Kiawah Reef 260-foot Barge	45494.9	60688.2
Kiawah Reef Tug	45492.6	60693.7
Kiawah Reef Barge	45492.7	60693.1
Kiawah Reef Barge	45495.4	60688.1
Edisto Reef Trolling Alley (nun)	45381.9	60689.6
Edisto Reef Trolling Alley (nun)	45380.5	60700.1
Edisto Reef Ship*	45382.7	60692.2
Edisto Reef Ship	45380.3	60699.2
Edisto Reef wreckage	45380.3	60699.2
Hunting Island Reef (nun)*	45525.1	60964.6
Hunting Island Reef (nun)	45523.2	60964.5
Hunting Island Reef Structure	45525.4	60964.8
Hunting Island Reef Structure	45525.0	60964.7
Hunting Island Reef Structure	45525.7	60964.9
Hunting Island Reef Structure	45522.9	60964.0
Hunting Island Reef Structure	45525.5	60965.1
Fripp Island Reef (nun)*	45546.0	60969.0
Fripp Island Reef (can)	45547.3	60970.1
Fripp Island Reef Structure	45546.8	60969.8
Fripp Island Reef Structure	45546.8	60969.3
Fripp Island Reef Structure	45546.7	60970.2
Fripp Dry Dock (can)	45566.6	60981.3
Outer Bar	45632.3	61263.2
Betsy Ross Reef (nun)*	45504.3	61062.8
Betsy Ross Reef (nun)	45504.0	61061.2
Hilton Head Reef (nun)*	45548.0	61178.5
Hilton Head Reef Trolling Alley (nun)	45549.6	61175.7

Hilton Head Reef Trolling Alley (nun)	45544.4	61176.0
Hilton Head Reef Barge	45547.5	61178.1
Hilton Head Reef Barge	45545.6	61176.5
Hilton Head Reef Boat	45549.6	61177.8
Hilton Head Reef tires	45549.4	61175.7
Gaskin Banks Reef	45615.0	61180.0
FishAmerica Reef NW (can)	45617.9	61180.1
FishAmerica Reef SW (can)	45616.7	61186.2
FishAmerica Reef NE (can)	45612.4	61176.1
FishAmerica Reef SE (can)	45612.4	61182.3
Gray Bay Reef	45521.3	28374.5
South Edisto Inshore Reef	45633.3	28772.7
General Sherman Wreck (nun)	45413.3	59455.6
City of Richmond Wreck	45343.7	59925.7
Hector Wreck wreckage	45379.6	60026.8
Hector Wreck	45379.6	60027.2
Hector Wreck BK Barges (4)	45379.8	60027.3
Savannah Tybee Tower	45562.7	61240.1
2 PR	45567.3	61140.2
General Gordon (nun)	45580.7	61096.9
General Gordon Wreck	45580.6	61097.2
Boiler Wreck	45609.8	61200.9
St. Cathan Wreck	45237.8	59616.3
Hebe Wreck	45237.1	59612.7
New Wreck	45306.0	59551.4
L Buoy	45480.0	61264.6

Reefs marked with an asterisk are federal Special Management Zones (SMZs). The use of traps or nets is prohibited.

Offshore Charter Boats

Area Code (803)

Split Decision	Edisto Beach	549-7503
Virginia	Little River	249-3970
Johnny Junior	Little River	249-3970
Carol Annes Bounty	Little River	249-5294
Dolphin	Little River	249-5294
The Other Woman	Little River	249-5294
Bon Jon	Little River	249-2226
Cyclone	Little River	249-3571
Shannon Marina	Little River	249-1222
Plantation Marina	Little River	249-5294
North Side Marina	Little River	249-1222
Vereen's Marina	Little River	249-4333
Hurricane Fleet	Little River	249-3571
Cyclone	North Myrtle Beach	249-3571

Tom Cat	Myrtle Beach	249-1409
Captain Monroe	Myrtle Beach	249-4333
Sharon K	Murrells Inlet	651-3900
Marilyn J	Murrells Inlet	651-3900
Mariner	Murrells Inlet	651-3900
Catch 22	Murrells Inlet	651-3900
Connie D	Murrells Inlet	651-3900
Silver Lining	Murrells Inlet	651-3900
Cousins II	Murrells Inlet	651-3900
Mermaid II	Murrells Inlet	651-3900
Inlet Port Marina	Murrells Inlet	651-3900
Marlin Quay Marina	Murrells Inlet	651-4444
Capt. Dick's Marina	Murrells Inlet	651-2125
Nomad	Murrells Inlet	651-2125
Sweet Moma	Murrells Inlet	651-2125
Lit' Birdie	Murrells Inlet	651-2125
Gulf Auto Marina	Georgetown	546-4250
Hustler	Georgetown	546-4250
Palmetto Lady	Georgetown	546-1776
Waterproof	Georgetown	546-1776
Bullship III	Georgetown	546-1776
Mar Har VI	Georgetown	546-1776
Jackpot	Georgetown	546-1776
Georgetown Landing Marina	Georgetown	546-1776
Barrier Island Charter	Isle of Palms	886-4396
Isle of Palms Marina	Isle of Palms	886-5100
Henry's Honey II	Isle of Palms	886-5100
23 Formula	Isle of Palms	886-5100
244 Formula	Isle of Palms	886-5100
Toler's Cove Marina	Mt. Pleasant	881-1888
Sea Spirit	Mt. Pleasant	884-3225
Crowdpleaser	Mt. Pleasant	884-2133
Highlander	Mt. Pleasant	871-2015
Dragon Lady	Mt. Pleasant	884-6680
Amie C	Goose Creek	747-9064
Charleston City Marina	Goose Creek	724-7356
Thunderstar	Goose Creek	747-9064
Ashley River Marina	Charleston	722-1996
Sea Spirit	Charleston	884-3225
Island Charters	Charleston	795-9192
Justavacation	Charleston	577-6515
Mariners Cay I	James Island	588-2487
Bohicket Marina	Johns Island	768-1280
Blue Water	Johns Island	768-1280
Bumpsie II	Johns Island	768-1280
Sandy Kay	Johns Island	768-1280
Sea Datsun	Johns Island	768-1280
Second Love	Johns Island	768-1280
Hot Pursuit	Johns Island	768-1280
Lickety Split	Johns Island	768-1280
Last Nickel	Johns Island	768-1280
Osprey	Johns Island	768-1280
Winjoy	Johns Island	768-1280

Rookie IV	Johns Island	768-1280
Rappid Dan II	Johns Island	747-8367
Stono Marina	Johns Island	747-8367
Holiday Inn	Beaufort	524-9703
Fripp Island Marina	Fripp Island	838-2832
Sea Hawk	Fripp Island	838-3124
High Seas	Fripp Island	524-5498
Warrior	Fripp Island	846-4820
Sea Wolf	Fripp Island	524-1174
Hilton Head Marina	Hilton Head	842-5253
Outdoor Resorts Yacht Club	Hilton Head	681-3241
Palmetto Bay Marina	Hilton Head	785-3910
Harbor I	Hilton Head	681-3241
Broad Creek Marina	Hilton Head	681-7335
Lucky Lady	Hilton Head	681-7335
Shelter Cove Marina	Hilton Head	842-7001
Gullah Gal	Hilton Head	842-7001
Miss Chief	Hilton Head	842-7001
Waterway	Hilton Head	842-7001
She Worthy	Hilton Head	842-7001
Kahlua	Hilton Head	842-7001
Echo	Hilton Head	842-7001
Micabe	Hilton Head	842-7001
Ric-A-Rue	Hilton Head	842-7001
Harbortown Yacht Basin	Hilton Head	671-4534
Manatee	Hilton Head	671-4534
Manatee Two	Hilton Head	671-4534
Point Comfort	Hilton Head	671-4534
Porbeagle	Hilton Head	671-3060
Fiesta	Hilton Head	671-4534
Hero	Hilton Head	671-4534
Dorado	Hilton Head	671-3060
South Beach Marina	Hilton Head	671-3060
Rebel	Hilton Head	671-3060
Strip	Hilton Head	671-3060

HeadboaTs

Helen Jean	Little River	249-2845
Hurricane	Little River	249-3571
Swift Ship	Little River	249-1222
Carolina Princess	Little River	249-5294
Hurricane	North Myrtle Beach	249-3571
Flying Fisher	Murrells Inlet	651-5700
New Inlet Princess	Murrells Inlet	651-2125
New Capt. Bill	Murrells Inlet	651-2125
Capt. Bill	Murrells Inlet	651-2125
Summer Sun	Murrells Inlet	651-3900
Gulf Stream II	Mt. Pleasant	884-7586
Carolina Clipper	Isle of Palms	722-4240
J-J	Charleston	766-9816
Drifter	Hilton Head	842-4155

Sources of Information

Beaufort County Chamber of Commerce
P.O. Box 910
Beaufort, S.C. 29901
803-524-3163

Charleston Chamber of Commerce
P.O. Box 975
Charleston, S.C. 29402

Hilton Head Island Chamber of Commerce
P.O. Box 5647
Hilton Head Island, S.C. 29938
803-785-3673

Myrtle Beach Chamber of Commerce
1301 North Kings Highway
Myrtle Beach, S.C. 29577

South Carolina Sea Grant
(Coastal Heritage)
287 Meeting Street
Charleston, S.C. 29401
803-727-2078

South Carolina Wildlife and Marine Resources Department
(Saltwater Conversation)
P.O. Box 12559
Charleston, S.C. 29412
803-795-6350

Fishing Clubs

Greater Charleston Shark Club
Joyce Schultz
P.O. Box 32171
Charleston, S.C. 29407

Columbia Offshore Fishing Association
Phil Wilson
1331 Wellington Drive
Columbia, S.C. 29204

Florence Blue Water Fishing Club
Larry Heiden
P.O. Box 3653
Florence, S.C. 29502

Sea Island Sportfishing Society
P.O. Box 324
Isle of Palms, S.C. 29451

Atlantic Billfish Club
Ross Swygert
P.O. Box 308
Johns Island, S.C. 29455

Saltwater Sports Club
P.O. Box 12852
Charleston, S.C. 29412

Edisto Beach Sportfishing Club
Bill Hackett
P.O. Box 197A
Edisto Beach, S.C. 29438

South Carolina Saltwater Sportsfishing Association
P.O. Box 2086
Charleston, S.C. 29403

Sumter Saltwater Fishing Association
Clyde McManus
c/o Sumter Cut Rate Drugs
32 South Main Street
Sumter, S.C. 29150

Hilton Head Fishing Club
P.O. Box 2196
Hilton Head, S.C. 29925

Springmaid Kingfishing Club
Springmaid Pier
P.O. Box 423
Myrtle Beach, S.C. 29577

Georgetown Sportfishing Association
Bob Coggins
Belle Isle Villa No. 42
Georgetown, S.C. 29440

Grand Strand Saltwater Sportfishing Association
Donnie Griffin
P.O. Box 3327
Myrtle Beach, S.C. 29587

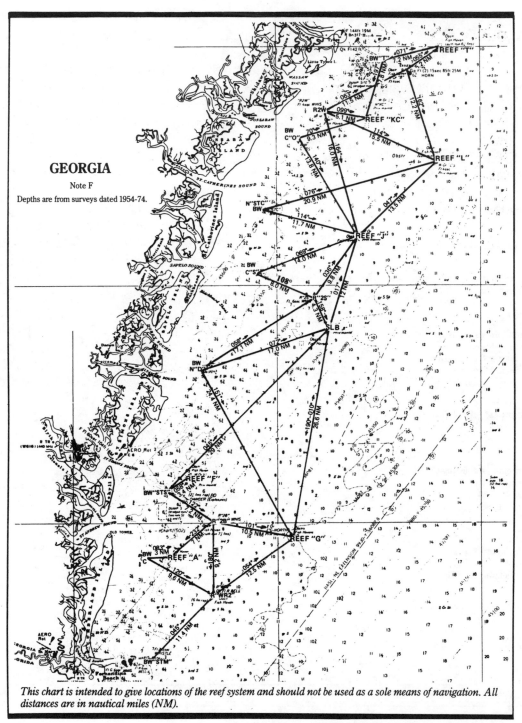

GEORGIA

Note F

Depths are from surveys dated 1954-74.

This chart is intended to give locations of the reef system and should not be used as a sole means of navigation. All distances are in nautical miles (NM).

GEORGIA

Georgia lies smack in the middle of the South Atlantic Bight, a flat, shallow plate that ranges from Cape Hatteras to Cape Canaveral. The Georgia portion of this sandy plate is very wide, extending 65 miles to sea before reaching the rocky edge of the continental shelf. This considerable distance has retarded development of big game fishing for deepwater blue and white marlin (but not shallow-water sailfish) and headboat fishing at the shelf edge. However, it also means excellent opportunities exist today to fish virtually untapped grounds, either in your own boat or on a charter. The new Savannah Bluewater Sportfishing Tournament has promoted billfishing by demonstrating that they're out there and can be caught. Several nice blue marlin and bull dolphin have taken honors in recent years.

The principal offshore features are the Savannah Snapper Banks 40 miles offshore, the Brunswick Snapper Banks, and the live bottom area some 18 miles east of Sapelo Island, recently designated Gray's Reef National Marine Sanctuary. The Savannah Snapper Banks have yielded the best catches of groupers.

The state has been actively developing an artificial reef program. Just recently, many of Georgia's artificial reefs were designated Special Management Zones (SMZs) by the National Marine Fisheries Service. This designation means that trapping and netting are prohibited in those zones, so that the reefs are preserved for hook-and-line fishing, scuba, and conservation purposes. These reefs offer excellent fishing for amberjack, cobia, gag grouper, and red snapper. They're also loaded with spadefish and black sea bass, so don't worry about a lack of action.

The near shore waters of Georgia have not received national attention, perhaps because it took so long to build an interstate from Atlanta to the coast. Nonetheless, the waters are rich in big flounder, croaker, spot, spotted seatrout, black drum and small red drum. Inshore fishing for tarpon with red-and-white plugs or live pinfish is excellent at the mouth of the Altamaha River and other major Georgia rivers, and a lot less crowded and expensive than it is farther south. Tarpon fishing will be the big draw to the Georgia coast when fishermen get the word.

NOAA Charts

11009	Cape Hatteras to Straits of Florida Offshore
11480	Charleston Light to Cape Canaveral
11513	St. Helena Sound to Savannah River
11509	Tybee Island to Doboy Sound
11502	Doboy Sound to Fernandina

NOAA Bathymetric Maps

NH 17-2	Brunswick.	Coastal north.
NH 17-3	Hoyt Hills.	Inshore north.
NH 18-1	Harrington Hill.	Offshore north.
NH 18-2	Taylor.	Extreme offshore north.
NH 17-5	Jacksonville.	Coastal south.
NH 17-6	Stetson Mesa.	Inshore south.
NH 18-4	Blake Spur.	Offshore south.

Reefs, Wrecks and Rocks

Reef T, Buoy	45548.0	61178.5
Reef T, tires and Wreck	45549.5	61177.7
Reef T, Barge	45545.5	61176.7
Reef T, 200-foot Barge	45547.9	61178.1
Reef KC, Buoy*	45564.3	61324.2
Reef KC, Motherlode Barge	45563.9	61324.6
Reef KC, tires	45566.0	61324.1
Reef L, Buoy*	45480.0	61263.6
Reef L, Dredge Bacon	45480.0	61264.5
Reef L, Tug Senasqua	45479.3	61268.3
Reef L, latex Barge	45480.9	61266.1
Reef L, Saylor Barge	45479.4	61266.1
Reef L, concrete culvert	45479.5	61262.2
Reef L, concrete culvert	45478.1	61263.0
Reef J, Buoy*	45495.5	61411.7
Reef J, Tug Elmira	45496.0	61413.0
Reef J, Liberty ship Daniels	45497.5	61412.8
Reef J, Liberty ship Daniels	45497.8	61413.8
Reef F, Buoy*	45485.4	61787.7
Reef F, tires	45486.0	61787.2
Reef F, 55-foot LCM	45483.0	61784.6
Reef G, Buoy*	45348.4	61700.1
Reef G, Tug Tampa	45348.1	61700.5
Reef G, Liberty ship Nettleton	45349.2	61695.7
Reef G, Tug Recife	45345.9	61691.7
Reef A, Buoy*	45447.2	61862.1
Reef A, tires	45447.0	61861.0
Reef C ("WR2"), Buoy*	45372.5	61829.7
Reef C ("WR2"), Wreck	45375.2	61832.1
Savannah Snapper Banks, 3-4-foot ledge	45345.1	61066.6
Savannah Snapper Banks, 3-4-foot ledge	45344.2	61066.7
Savannah Snapper Banks, rockpiles to 3 feet	45348.3	61074.2
Brunswick Snapper Banks, 2-3-foot ledge	45183.8	61516.5
Brunswick Snapper Banks, 6-10-foot ledge	45188.0	61541.3
Brunswick Snapper Banks, 3-4-foot ledge	45191.3	61525.4
Gray's Reef National Sanctuary, Buoy*	45460.3	61518.5
Gray's Reef, SW ledges to 5 feet	45462.9	61527.6
Gray's Reef, SW ledges to 5 feet	45465.4	61528.5
Gray's Reef, W ledges	45465.2	61528.9

Reefs marked with an asterisk are federally protected Special Management Zones (SMZs), at which the use of nets or traps is prohibited.

Offshore Charter Boats

Area Code (912)

Capt. Emmit Bridges	Savannah	897-2694
Helmey Charter Boat Co.	Savannah	897-2478
Coffee Bluff Fish Camp	Savannah	925-9030
Fishin Magician	Savannah	897-2609
Neva Miss Charter Boats	Savannah	897-2706
Miss Judy I and II	Savannah	897-4921
Miss Jerry	Savannah	897-4921
Smooth Operator	Savannah	897-2611
Lucky One Charters	Savannah	897-3474
Turner's Creek Marina	Savannah	897-5495
Adventurer	Savannah	354-9651
Adventurer III	Savannah	927-4516
The Lois Layne	Savannah	925-7988
Unreel	Richmond Hill	727-2470
Isle of Hope Marina	Isle of Hope	355-2310
Tuten's Fishing Camp & Marina	Isle of Hope	355-9182
Tybee Island Charters	Tybee Island	786-4801
Tybee Island Marina	Tybee Island	786-4996
Chimney Creek Fishing Camp	Tybee Island	786-9857
Skipjack	Brunswick	267-9498
Dolphin	Brunswick	267-7494
Wild Turkey	Brunswick	264-9723
Jet Lag	Brunswick	264-6834
Magic II	Brunswick	264-5461
Brunswick Marina	Brunswick	265-2290
Bell Bluff Island Marina	Townsend	832-5323
Fisherman's Lodge	Townsend	832-4671
Capts. L. & C. LaRoche	Townsend	832-4966
Capt. Walter Hewitt	Kingsland	729-5834
Capt. C.C. Higginbotham	Woodbine	576-5724
Inland Charter Boat Service	Sea Island	638-3611
Coastal Charter Services	St. Simons	638-3452
St. Simons Marina	St. Simons	638-9146
Cap Fendig Charter Boats	St. Simons	638-5678
Gone Fishin	St. Simons	638-7717
Sparrow II	St. Simons	638-8560
Capt. Maxwell Smith	St. Simons	265-8302
Tradewinds Fleet	Jekyll Island	635-2891

Headboats

Seecruise	Brunswick	265-1471

Sources of Information

Georgia Department of Natural Resources
Coastal Resources Division
(DNR Outdoor Report, Coastlines Georgia)
1200 Glynn Avenue
Brunswick, Ga. 31523-9990
912-264-7218

Georgia Sea Grant
Ecology Building
University of Georgia
Athens, Ga. 30602
404-542-7671

Golden Isles Sport Fishing Club
600 G Street
Brunswick, Ga. 31520

Savannah Area Convention and Visitors Bureau
301 W. Broad Street
Savannah, Ga. 31499
912-233-6651

Savannah Sport Fishing Club, Inc.
P.O. Box 1072
Savannah, Ga. 31402

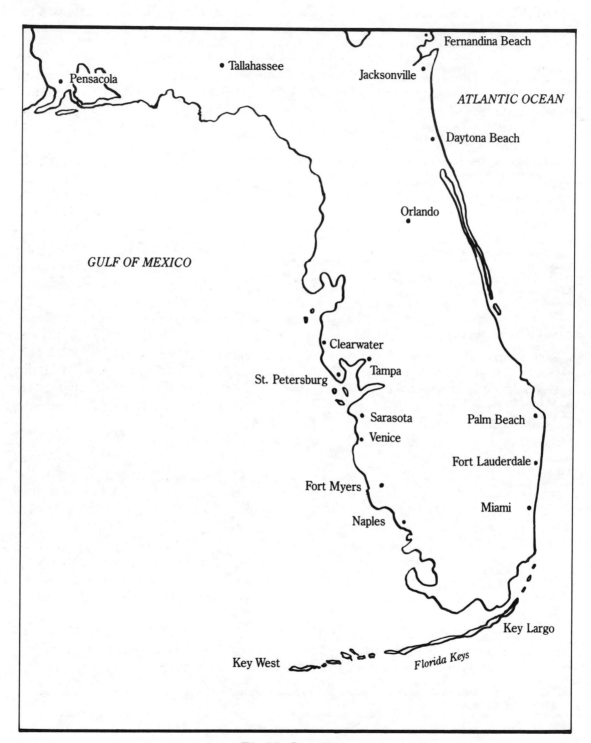

Florida Coastline

Florida

Florida is many places, many seas, many different fauna, and many different kinds of fishing. The northeastern corner, south to the mouth of the St. Johns River at Jacksonville, marks a southern distribution limit for fishes that range northward to Cape Lookout, Cape Fear, and Cape Hatteras. Below Jacksonville, the fauna of the Florida east coast changes suddenly and becomes subtropical like that of Bermuda and the Caribbean. This fauna is highly developed on the reefs off West Palm Beach, and continues seaward and southward offshore from the Keys.

The Florida Keys are unique. The Overseas Highway connecting the string of Keys all the way to Key West overlooks blue-green tropical Gulf of Mexico water to the west and subtropical blue-green Atlantic water to the east as it traverses the Straits of Florida. Rips under the bridges often provide good fishing. The crystalline (except after a storm) water is shallow around the myriad islands, but depths of 100 feet or more are not far away. Coral rubble and patch reefs dot the near shore flats, interspersed with vast sandy stretches rich with sea grass beds. As you move farther offshore, the drop-offs are marked with extensive reefs some 30 feet down on the landward side, dropping into blue-black depths seaward. The reefs are rich in snappers, grunts, porgies, and groupers, but the average size of the fish is much smaller than in years past due to overfishing. The grass beds and sand flats are seemingly barren, but smart anglers know they yield good catches of snappers, bonefish, and permit, which have not been overfished. The Florida Keys, with their vast expanses of shallow flats accessible by small boat, are the top location in the entire United States for light tackle, ultralight, and saltwater fly-fishing. The myriad islands and tiny islets, some of them not on the charts, are also confusing to non-natives, and I don't recommend that you head into the boonies without good electronics and compass or the company of an experienced guide.

Rounding the lower peninsula and heading northward along the Gulf Coast, the water changes dramatically. From Sarasota to Fort Myers, the Gulf now changes to a giant mud puddle, the distance to blue water even farther offshore the more northward you venture. The northeastern corner of the Gulf of Mexico is shark and mullet country. Heading westward along the Gulf Coast, blue shores appear once again at about Panama City and continue all the way to Destin, where they abruptly end.

The best offshore big game fishing is off the Atlantic coast. The Cape Canaveral area has big drum at the inlets and offshore. Tarpon are everywhere you find current and clean water. For snapper/grouper bottomfishing, the reefs off southeastern Florida have been severely over-fished, and your best bet is to fish out of west coast ports, where several headboats work the Dry Tortugas.

Shark fishing can be done everywhere, but the northern Gulf of Mexico probably has the largest inshore shark population in the United States. I used to set lines out from docks in three feet of water and get strikes (or destroyed docks) almost every night.

NOAA Charts

11009	Cape Hatteras to Straits of Florida Offshore
11013	Straits of Florida and Approaches Offshore
11006	Gulf Coast—Key West to Mississippi River Offshore
11480	Charleston Light to Cape Canaveral
11460	Cape Canaveral to Key West
11450	Fowey Rocks to American Shoal (Southern Tip)
11434	Florida Keys—Sombrero Key to Dry Tortugas
11420	Havana to Tampa Bay
11400	Tampa Bay to Cape San Blas
11360	Cape St. George to Mississippi Passes

NOAA Bathymetric Maps

NH 17-5	Jacksonville. East coastal extreme north.
NH 17-6	Stetston Mesa. East offshore extreme north.
NH 18-4	Blake Spur. East extreme offshore, extreme north.
NH 17-8	Daytona Beach. East coastal north.
NH 17-9	Adams. East offshore north.
NH 18-7	McAlinden Spur. East extreme offshore north.
NH 17-11	Orlando. East coastal north-central.
NH 17-12	Pillsbury. East offshore north-central.
NG 17-2	Fort Pierce. East coastal south-central.
NG 17-3	Walker Cay. East offshore south-central.
NG 17-6	Bahamas. East south-central.
NG 17-8	Miami. Far south coastal.
NG 17-9	Bimini. Far south offshore east.
NG 17-11	Key West. Extreme south-central offshore.
NG 17-12	Andros. Extreme south, east offshore.
NG 17-10	Dry Tortugas. Extreme south, west offshore.
NG 16-12	Rankin. West extreme south, extreme offshore.
NG 17-7	Pulley Ridge. Far south offshore west.
NG 16-9	Howell Hook. Far south extreme offshore west.
NG 17-4	Charlotte Harbor. West south coastal.
NG 16-6	Vernon Basis. West south offshore.
NG 16-5	Henderson. West south far offshore.
NG 16-4	Lund. West south extreme offshore (see Alabama).
NG 17-1	St. Petersburg. West coastal south-central.
NG 16-3	The Elbow. West offshore south-central.
NG 16-2	Lloyd. West far offshore south-central.
NH 17-10	Tarpon Springs. West coastal north-central.
NH 16-12	Florida Middle Grounds. West offshore north-central.
NH 16-11	DeSoto Canyon. West far offshore north-central.
NH 17-7	Gainesville. West coastal north.
NH 16-9	Apalachicola. West offshore north.
NH 16-8	Destin Dome. West extreme offshore north.
NH 16-6	Tallahassee. West extreme north coastal.
NH 16-5	Pensacola. Extreme west, north coastal.

Reefs, Wrecks, and Rocks*

Nassau, Duval, and St. Johns Counties

Sahlmans Gully	45308.1	61874.1
Whittakers Snapper Hole	45314.4	61907.1
Fernandina Snapper Banks	45292.6	61899.0
Amberjack Hole	45210.5	61849.0
Tanziers Waters	45151.8	61814.5
Montgomery Reef	45235.5	61958.0
Buseys Bonanza	45196.0	61918.5
Jacksonville 9-mile Reef	45192.2	61944.9
East 14 & 15	45156.2	61901.2
Harms Ledge	45077.0	61813.7
Pablo Grounds	45190.0	61976.0
Blackmars Reef	45182.4	61975.3
Paul Mains Reef	45181.3	61976.4
Claytons Holler	45117.0	61912.5
Middle Grounds	45141.7	61947.7
Casa Blanca	45012.7	61795.2
Jacksonville Beach Wreck	45166.0	62001.0
4-mile Reef	44998.0	62045.6
Dorothy Louise	44903.0	61938.0
9-mile North Reef	44953.5	62008.3
9-mile South Reef	44946.0	62022.7
Desco Boat	44903.3	61976.0
Inner Plane	44873.0	61964.9
Outer Plane	44858.0	61960.0
Shipwreck	44818.0	61962.5

Volusia, Brevard, and St. Lucie Counties

The Wreck	44461.7	61989.3
Liberty Reef	44457.8	61982.0
9-mile	44473.4	62035.3
Cracker Ridge	44410.9	61968.7
Concrete Rubble	14486.0	43940.0
Concrete Blocks	14460.9	43912.7
Autos and Rubble	14392.7	43344.9

Martin and Palm Beach Counties

Bill Donaldson Reef	43090.0	61990.1
Al Sirotkin Reef	43107.3	62013.8
Edgar Ernst Reef	43065.2	62002.0
Palm Beach Artificial Reef	14331.4	43012.6

Broward and Dade Counties

Barges, Tanks, and Fish Attractors	14268.8	62098.9
Dry Dock and Barges	14262.1	62107.5
Midwater Fish Attractors	14261.5	62109.7
Fireboat	14234.8	62128.5
Minesweeper	14233.7	62130.1
Lotus	14233.8	62129.2
Walka K	14233.1	62129.1
West End	14232.4	62130.3
LCI	14231.7	62130.9
Deep Freeze	14230.7	62133.0
Dry Dock	14231.5	62129.9
Hopper Barge	14229.5	62132.1
Bear Cut	14217.3	62156.2
Shrimp Drift Boats	14218.6	62144.4
Biscayne Wreck	14218.5	62145.0
Dade County Reef	14220.3	62142.8
Arida	14219.7	62143.7
Lakeland	14218.6	62143.7
Star Trek	14219.0	62142.2
Orion	14217.4	62145.0
Cement Mixers	14218.4	62144.6
Hopper Barge and Crane Boom	14210.3	62149.9
Railroad Barge	14206.9	62152.8
Santa Rita	14188.9	62170.7
Almirante	14187.5	62173.8
Belcher Barge	14187.0	62174.4

Monroe County

Alva Chapman Reef	14160.4	43185.8
Elbow Wreck	14149.4	43199.4
Crocodile Reef	14093.2	43292.6
Nimrod	14092.6	43292.0
Marathon Reef	14038.6	43397.4
Marathon Reef	14022.4	43432.8
VACA Cut Reef	14033.7	43404.8
7-mile Reef	14006.8	43460.6
American Reef	13984.7	43507.2
Big Pine Shoal Reef	13968.2	43548.6
American Shoal	13951.8	43570.2
Key West Tournament Reef	13923.5	43639.5

Collier County

5-mile Fish Haven	14075.8	43713.4
2-mile Fish Haven	14083.8	43708.3
Naples Reef	14100.1	43765.1

Lee County

Number 1 Sanibel	14100.0	43913.0
Unnamed	14116.0	43849.0
Marker 1 & 2	14123.8	43863.5
Marker 3 & 4	14124.3	43871.1
Marker 5 & 6	14125.0	43880.6
Point Ybel	14122.4	43897.4
Lighthouse Channel	14121.5	43896.5
TOR Point	14116.0	43898.7
Headboat area, General	14046.0	44022.0
Headboat area rock	14045.6	44022.3
Headboat area rock	14047.6	44020.4
Headboat area rock	14050.1	44016.2
Headboat area rock	14050.7	44015.5
Headboat area rock	14050.8	44015.3
Headboat area rock	14075.2	43971.6
Spanish Mackerel spot	14064.8	43989.6
Spanish Mackerel spot	14063.7	43991.1
Spanish Mackerel spot	14075.3	43970.9
Spanish Mackerel spot	14069.2	43981.0
Spanish Mackerel spot	14072.2	43976.1
Jewfish Mountain	14021.1	44073.0
Jewfish Mountain	14021.1	44072.9
Monster Hole	14044.9	43958.8
West Ledge	14067.0	44060.0
58-foot Headboat area	14045.0	44047.8
58-foot Headboat area	14065.5	43933.5
58-foot Headboat area	14068.6	43975.7
58-foot Headboat area	14069.7	44024.1
Pinnacle—Headboat area	14046.1	44027.5
Pinnacle—Headboat area	14046.6	44023.6
Pinnacle—Headboat area	14046.1	44024.6
Pinnacle—Headboat area	14046.2	44024.1
Marker 3-4 Estero Bay	14127.7	43879.1
SW of Big Carlos Pass	14123.0	43836.8
SW of Sanibel Light	14112.0	43902.2
West of Captiva	14072.9	44118.3
Marker 8 San Carlos Bay	14124.8	43892.1
Redfish Pass	14110.0	44022.5
Drawbridge A	14125.3	43903.9
Marker 5 San Carlos Bay	14119.7	43925.3
Bridge C	14119.6	43918.6
DA-2	13956.5	44110.0
DA-2	13957.6	44107.2
DA-2	13958.0	44108.1
DA-2	13958.4	44105.0
DA-1	13930.4	44164.2
DA-1	13929.9	44163.4
DA-3	13921.9	44153.0
Reef #7	13914.6	44148.8
Reef #7	13911.0	44151.5
Reef #7	13911.5	44151.1
Reef #7	13914.4	44148.8
Boiler	13899.1	44133.4

Baja	13920.6	43961.5
CR-2	13928.7	43981.3
CR-2	13926.6	43982.0
CR-1	13954.8	43966.9
CR-1	13954.6	43965.6
CR-1	13954.2	43969.5
40-mile Headboat area	14015.7	43994.6
25-mile Headboat areas	14075.2	43971.4
25-mile Headboat areas	14050.5	44016.4
25-mile Headboat areas	14050.2	44016.7
25-mile Headboat areas	14048.9	44013.8
25-mile Headboat areas	14047.2	44020.5
25-mile Headboat areas	14046.0	44020.8
25-mile Headboat areas	14045.7	44021.8
25-mile Headboat areas	14038.1	44043.3
25-mile Headboat areas	14038.0	44045.3
Far Headboat area	14035.2	44073.2
Far Headboat area	14035.5	44071.8
Far Headboat area	14035.3	44072.5
Far Headboat area	14035.3	44072.7
NW May Reef - San Carlos Pass	14122.4	43842.9
Center May Reef	14122.5	43839.6
SE May Reef	14122.6	43836.3

Charlotte County

Boca Grande Reef S Buoy	14114.2	44070.6
Boca Grande Reef N Buoy	14113.8	44077.1
Boca Grande Fishing Reef	14112.1	44089.2
#5 Reef G, NW	14115.1	43849.0
#5 Reef, Barge	14115.1	43847.7
#5 Reef H, SE	14115.0	43845.5
Sanibel Reef C, east	14111.8	43906.6
Sanibel Reef D, west	14110.4	43910.1
Fish Haven	14141.4	44183.2
Fish Haven	14169.4	44064.9

Sarasota County

Reef D (Venice)	14154.5	44302.1
Reef A (Lido Key)	14166.1	44422.9
Reef B (Lido Key)	14166.1	44438.1
Reef C (Lido Key)	14169.5	44426.2
Wreck off Gasparilla	14056.8	44376.0
Spring off Wiggins Pass	14096.9	43865.4
Spring off Wiggins Pass	14097.1	43865.0
Redfish Pass Barge	14085.2	44111.8
Stoney Point Wreck	13966.5	44252.4

Dry Tortugas Area

Grouper area N	13794.4	44013.2
Grouper area N	13800.3	44016.7
Grouper area NE	13812.1	43983.3
Grouper area NE	13813.9	43987.5
Grouper area SE	13795.3	44001.8
Grouper area SE	13795.5	44002.8
Grouper area SE	13795.9	44000.6
Grouper area SE	13795.1	44005.2
Grouper area SW	13773.8	44032.4
Grouper area SW	13781.4	44022.1
Grouper area SW	13773.4	44030.8
Pulaski Light area	13812.3	43990.6
Pulaski Light area	13812.4	43990.3
Grouper area NW	13780.9	44059.9
8-fathom rock	13781.0	44060.1
NE Ridge	13811.9	43996.2
NE Ridge	13811.8	44200.0

Manatee County

1-mile Reef	14180.0	44566.6
Reef B	14175.0	44593.3
Sarasota Bay Reef	14182.9	44462.6
Reef A	14168.5	44654.5
Metal junk	14141.4	44183.2
Tires	14169.4	44064.9
Cars, metal	14072.9	44118.3
Tires and concrete	14100.1	43765.1
Barge, crane, trucks, and tires	14075.8	43713.9
Tires	14083.8	43708.3
Tires and concrete	14111.9	43902.2
Tires and concrete	14109.0	44022.5
175-foot Patrol Boat and Ships	14122.6	43836.3
Weighted tires	14091.8	43920.8
Tires, rocks, and concrete	14153.3	43301.6
Shell and coral	13976.1	44783.4
Shell	14056.8	44376.0
Rocks	14045.1	44290.6
Shell and rocks	14132.1	44154.0
Rock	13957.6	44039.3
High ridges and rock	13812.2	44435.7
Rock and coral	14090.6	43725.3
Shell, sponge, and coral	14064.7	43934.9
Rock in depression	14079.2	44049.4
Steep rock sides	14086.9	43850.9
Sand and rock	14124.1	44077.2
Patch rock	14093.6	44079.9
Rock and gravel	14073.5	44001.2
Irregular rocky bottom	14126.1	44435.7
Rock	14098.4	44504.7

Rock and coral	14079.0	44514.1
Rocks	14138.5	44464.4
Rock and coral	14088.0	44429.1

Pinellas County

Sand, shell, rock, and sponge	14098.3	44844.0
Sand, shell, and rock	14126.4	44718.7
Sand, shell, some grass	14179.0	44644.1
Sand, shell, and grass	14184.4	44623.8
Rocks	14091.7	44856.1
Rock ledges	14254.2	45005.8
Limestone ridge	13997.9	45320.5
Sand and shell with rock	14171.2	45065.2
Scattered low rocks	14222.9	44853.8
Sand, shell, sponges	14140.9	44989.6
Artificial Reef on rock	14189.6	44821.5
St. Pete Beach Reef	14192.9	44694.1
St. Pete Reef	14242.6	44615.6
Treasure Island	14200.8	44738.7
Madeira Reef	14201.0	44768.0
Indian Shores Reef	14200.1	44859.6
Pinellas 2 Reef	14181.6	44943.3
Rube Allyn Reef	14212.3	44886.4
Clearwater Reef	14233.3	44851.1
Dunedin Reef	14247.9	44887.3
Tarpon Springs	14259.3	44935.3
Sand, shell, rock	14175.1	44757.0
Mud, sand, rock	14093.9	45128.7
Exposed rock in sand	14201.6	44948.7
Flat rock, barge, car, junk	14186.6	44731.7
Sand, mud, rocks	14171.1	44705.9
Sand, shell, rock	14179.4	45155.5
Sand, shell, rock	14221.7	45069.9
Rocky bottom	14227.4	44961.3
Sand, shell, rock	14246.3	44889.3
Sand, shell, rugged rock	14211.4	44809.7
Patches of flat rock	14124.2	44740.9
Rock ledges	14142.6	44540.7
Barge, junk, concrete pipe	14180.0	44566.6
Tires, concrete, tile	14182.9	44462.6
Tires, concrete pipe	14168.5	44654.5
Tires, concrete pipe	14175.0	44593.3
Tires, concrete pipe	14161.4	44589.4
Tires, concrete pipe	14170.9	44553.5
Cars	14180.2	44563.0
Junk, tires	14207.8	44652.2
Junk, tires	14210.4	44658.5
Junk, tires	14212.8	44665.6
Junk, tires	14211.2	44673.5
Concrete pilings, steel barges, tires	14243.3	44863.6

Tires, junk, and rubble	14213.5	44733.9
Tires, junk, and rubble	14215.1	44725.9
235-foot LSM, concrete pillbox	14199.8	44859.1
Tires, rubble	14240.4	44613.1
Tires, rubble	14221.7	44592.6
110-foot barge	14212.3	44886.2
Tires, concrete culverts	14258.5	44934.1
Concrete rubble	14247.7	44887.2
Tires	14201.0	44767.7
Concrete rubble	14192.6	44702.8
Tires, concrete culvert	14200.6	44738.5
Concrete rubble, 32-foot steel hull	14242.4	44616.2
Junk, rubble	14167.0	44434.0
Junk, rubble	14169.1	44425.7
Junk, rubble	14165.8	44423.0
Concrete pipe	14192.7	44624.9
Cars	14222.5	44560.3

Pasco, Hernando, Citrus, and Taylor Counties

Pasco Reef No. 1	14275.4	44997.5
Pasco Reef No. 2	14274.9	45048.6
Cars, rubble	14390.3	45232.4
Cars, drums	14428.3	45668.1
Cars, junk	14410.0	45498.5
Cars, junk	14405.9	45484.6
Cars, junk	14411.0	45464.0
Tires	14393.6	45496.4
A.H. Richardson	14325.3	45111.1
Liberty ship	14459.4	46014.4
Steinhatchee Reef	14459.9	46010.7
Keaton Schooner Reef	14474.8	46140.0
Taylor County Reef	14449.8	46152.0
Tires, rubble	14463.1	46490.7
Tires, rubble	14454.0	46422.5
Tires	14477.7	46430.3

Wakulla, Franklin, and Gulf Counties

Cars, tires, rubble	14487.9	46383.0
Cars, rubble	14152.1	46537.8
Tires	14351.0	46518.9
Car, junk	14426.8	45653.1
Rock ledges	14345.4	45523.5
Rock ledges	14360.9	45404.8
Exposed rocks	15280.4	45130.7
Broken rock on sand	14373.3	46075.3

Limestone ridges	14174.9	46288.5
Limestone ridges	14349.1	46402.8
Grass flats	14425.2	46393.9
Sink holes, rock	14322.2	45258.4
Ledges and rock	14245.8	45255.8
Broken rock	14122.0	45663.4
St. Marks Town Reef	14478.2	46426.6
V Tower	14306.6	46210.8
K Tower	14330.2	46262.5
S Tower	14223.7	46238.5
O Tower	14287.3	46375.7
C Tower	14195.0	46392.8
Rubble	14151.6	46537.7
Rubble	14111.6	46802.0
Cluster of 10 Reefs	14105.3	46819.9
Cluster of 10 Reefs	14088.0	46818.1

Bay County

Mexico Beach Site	14111.6	46845.5
Liberty ship	14056.4	46948.9
Liberty ship	14065.1	46918.6
Midway Site	14072.6	46949.6
Grey Ghost	13891.1	46991.7
Warsaw Site	14036.8	46977.2
Loss Pontoon	14078.5	46873.8
Stage 1 Site	14011.3	46925.5
PCMI Site	14043.8	47000.0
Fountainbleau Site	14019.8	47028.2
Junk, tires	14065.0	46974.3
Three barges, concrete rubble	13300.5	47105.4
Liberty ship	13302.6	47098.2
Concrete rubble	13332.8	47115.3
Plastic	13199.8	47113.8
Plastic	13263.3	47073.7
P5M aircraft tires	13331.5	47106.6

Walton, Okaloosa, and Santa Rosa Counties

Unnamed	13933.2	47151.7
Unnamed	13883.2	47160.9
Unnamed	13885.9	47173.8
Rubble, tires, tile	13668.8	47138.9
Rubble, tires, tile	13717.9	47136.7
Rubble, tires, tile	13767.5	47136.6
Unnamed	13786.4	47055.1
Christmas Tree Reef	13768.0	47136.5
Pole spot	13720.4	47131.0
Elgin barge	13720.4	47132.8

Pier rubble	13664.9	47138.0
Brown barge	13660.7	47134.1
Thomas Hayward Liberty ship	13648.2	47115.8
Diamond barge	13544.2	47062.7
Joseph E. Brown Reef	13515.2	47083.9
Metal junk, concrete	13906.8	47157.5
Tires, junk, cars	14008.9	47146.1
Liberty ship	13987.5	47091.4
Liberty ship	13511.4	47101.7
Tires, rubble	13933.2	47151.7
Tires, rubble	13883.2	47160.9
Tires, rubble	13885.9	47173.8
Tires, rubble	13847.3	47152.6

Escambia County

Tenneco Reef	13323.0	47013.0
P5M Reef	13326.3	47105.8
Casino Fishing Reef	13326.3	47116.0
Liberty ship Fishing Reef	13305.2	47103.1
Santa Rosa barge Reef	13271.0	47108.3

Reprinted, in part, from Atlas of Artificial Reefs in Florida (MAP-30), *published by Florida Sea Grant College Program, University of Florida, Gainesville, Fl. 32611. MAP-30 provides additional details including latitude, longitude, reef materials, depth, distance from shore, and, in some cases, additional coordinates. Additional points for Fort Myers, Sarasota, Dry Tortugas, and vicinity courtesy of Norma Stoppelbein of the Florida League of Anglers and Southwest Anglers Club.*

Offshore Charter Boats

Tradewinds Charters	Fernandina Beach	904-261-9486
Amelia Angler	Fernandina Beach	904-261-6161
Monty's Marina	Mayport	904-246-7575
Allbritten Charters	Jacksonville	904-247-1150
Cap't Bob's Charters	Jacksonville	904-721-7696
Casa Mia Charters	Jacksonville	904-384-0154
Executive Charters	Jacksonville	904-725-0300
The Haifam	Jacksonville	904-641-4597
Road Runner	Jacksonville	904-353-0320
Moby Dick Charters	Jacksonville	904-733-4131
Critter Fleet	Daytona Beach	904-767-7676
Cindy Jay	Daytona Beach	904-759-2344
Dandy	Daytona Beach	904-767-7935
Don Al II	Daytona Beach	904-761-7789
Inlet Cove Marina	Daytona Beach	904-788-1224
Inlet Harbor Charters	Daytona Beach	904-767-3266

Joe-Ree	Daytona Beach	904-677-0761
Lunker Hole	Daytona Beach	904-775-9554
Marianne Fishing Boats	Daytona Beach	904-767-3406
Sea Love Marina	Daytona Beach	904-767-3406
Snow White Boats	Daytona Beach	904-767-6000
Sure Thing	Daytona Beach	904-788-3474
Dat-Sun-Of-A-Gun	Homosassa	904-628-2474
Cloud Nine	Hobe Sound	305-283-4112
Blue Jay	Palm Beach	305-844-1724
Warrior	Palm Beach	305-844-1724
Marker 32	Palm Beach	305-844-1724
Cowboy	Palm Beach	305-845-2052
Sea Datsun	Palm Beach	305-863-5299
Reel Fun	Palm Beach	305-844-9963
Oh Gee	Palm Beach	305-844-6994
Tropic Lightning	Palm Beach	305-842-9073
Corgello	Palm Beach	305-848-9405
Capri	West Palm Beach	305-655-6461
Blue Seas Fleet	Fort Pierce	305-464-4793
Flyer	Fort Pierce	305-465-9397
Breakwater	Fort Pierce	305-464-6243
Tantalizer	Fort Pierce	305-465-5823
Temptress	Fort Pierce	305-465-4638
Hooker Fleet	Fort Pierce	305-465-2101
Skipper II	Stuart	305-283-0449
Gannett II	Stuart	305-287-4339
Do Stay	Jupiter	305-746-6713
Lady Stuart	Port Salerno	305-286-1860
Capt. Sveling	Sebastian	305-589-4868
Big Time Charter	Pompano Beach	305-785-7327
Miss Jan II	Pompano Beach	305-946-1307
Fish City Fleet	Pompano Beach	305-943-8222
Helen S	Pompano Beach	305-941-3209
Hillsboro Inlet Fleet	Pompano Beach	305-941-6263
Sands Harbor Fleet	Pompano Beach	305-941-4529
Sir Fish-A-Lot	Pompano Beach	305-942-3177
Tomcat	Pompano Beach	305-946-2628
Flyin Fish	Boynton Beach	305-736-2270
Little Geno II	Boynton Beach	305-732-6006
R&R	Riviera Beach	305-842-6316
Real Estate	Coral Gables	305-446-4233
Majestic Fleet	Key Largo	305-451-2220
Snapdragon	Key Largo	305-852-5095
Keowee	Key Largo	305-852-5095
High Roller	Key Largo	305-451-3054
Dolphin III	Key Largo	305-451-4508
Oceanside Marina	Stock Island	305-294-2310
Scandia-Tomi	Summerland Key	305-745-3692
Pretty Patti	Loxahatchee	305-793-4187
Key Colony Marina	Marathon	305-289-1310
Nancy B	Marathon	305-743-3080
Rainbow Bend	Marathon	305-289-1505
Kacy-K	Marathon	305-289-1505
Unchained	Marathon	305-743-2324
Fascinating Lady	Marathon	305-743-5662
Jeni Lyn	Marathon	305-743-5807
Bounty Hunter	Marathon	305-743-2446
Suture Fancy	Marathon	305-289-0222
Challenger	Islamorada	305-664-8493
Genesis	Islamorada	305-247-2793
Catch 22	Islamorada	305-664-9314
Sump-N'-Special	Islamorada	305-852-9615
Duxspray	Islamorada	305-852-2438
Otter	Islamorada	305-664-9314
Reef Runner Also	Islamorada	305-852-3660
Winterhawk	Lower Matecumbe	305-664-4455
Sumptin Else	Lower Matecumbe	305-664-4455
Swash Buckler	Plantation Key	305-852-4581
Bel-Espirit	Plantation Key	305-852-9665
Hopa Long	Tavernier	305-852-9905
Kathy-Did-II	Tavernier	305-852-9115
Reef Runner	Key West	305-294-2282
Key West Charter Co.	Key West	305-294-3737
Amorous	Key West	305-296-5375
Anne-Marie	Key West	305-296-2803
Black Bean	Key West	305-294-2192
Sunday	Key West	305-294-7052
Billfisher	Key West	305-296-9969
Billfisher II	Key West	305-296-9969
Cyn-Bad	Key West	305-294-4206
Floalong	Key West	305-294-0454
Grandslam	Key West	305-296-8380
Linda D III	Key West	305-296-9798
Lookout III	Key West	305-294-4290
Lucky Strike	Key West	305-294-7988
Ramerezi	Key West	305-294-0803
Sandpiper	Key West	305-294-1604
Seabreeze	Key West	305-294-6027
Seadreamer	Key West	305-296-4558
Shark II	Key West	305-296-9798
Tenacious Too	Key West	305-296-4417
Why-Not	Key West	305-294-6098
Getaway Marina	Fort Myers	813-466-3600
Turkey Too	Fort Myers	813-463-6931
Native Star	Fort Myers	813-463-0390
Dat'Sa Ma Boat IV	Fort Myers	813-481-8201
Miss Renee II	Fort Myers	813-466-6513
Shady Lady II	Fort Myers	813-992-3488
Chipper II	Goodland	813-394-3584
Miss Jo Ann	Goodland	813-394-5513
Dee-Jay	Holmes Beach	813-778-1725
Johnny J	Isles of Capri	813-394-3452
White Horse	Isles of Capri	813-394-3452
Sable III	Longboat Key	813-371-4553
Makai	Madeira Beach	813-393-0407
Carole Ann II	Marco Island	813-394-9495
Sea Roach	Marco Island	813-394-3101
Endeavor	Marco Island	813-394-9388

Rosewall	Marco Island	813-394-2285
Bikini Manor	Sanibel	813-542-1521
Sanibel Marina	Sanibel	813-472-2531
Capt. Jim Burnsed	Sanibel	813-472-1779
Gone Fishing IV	Sanibel	813-466-6300
Miss Denise	Sanibel	813-542-6406
Gulf Star Marina	Sanibel	813-463-2219
King Fisher Charters	Punta Gorda	813-639-0969
Lehman's Charters	Bokeelia	813-283-2217
Betty G	Bonita Springs	813-992-6077
Malfunction II	Bonita Springs	813-992-5861
Gulf Diver	Bradenton	813-792-7266
Bay Fisher	Bradenton	813-792-5835
Magic	Bradenton	813-778-4755
The-Partner-Ship	Naples	813-775-3590
Sundowner	Naples	813-598-1805
Sur Thing	Naples	813-793-1551
Cuda	Naples	813-775-7787
A&B	Naples	813-775-4394
Lucky Strike	Naples	813-774-0339
Gee Gee	Naples	813-261-3164
Tarpon Hunter	Naples	813-775-5368
Big Al	Naples	813-775-2220
Southern Star	Clearwater	813-446-8962
Arete	Clearwater	813-447-8021
Primadonna II	Cortez	813-778-3005
Hydeaway	Englewood	813-474-7079
Escapade	Englewood	813-697-5212
Reel Pleasure	Anna Maria	813-778-9311
Sunrise Sunset	Anna Maria	813-778-7171
Apollo	Crystal River	904-795-3757
Capt. Anderson Fleet	Panama City	904-234-3435
Angler	Panama City	904-234-2334
Zodiac Fleet	Panama City	904-235-2628
Calypso	Panama City	904-235-0303
The Happy Hooker	Panama City	904-234-1308
Fu-Lin-U-II	Panama City	904-234-3634
Nick Nack	Panama City	904-234-7604
Pixie P	Panama City	904-235-1653
Sea Eagle	Panama City	904-235-2866
Treasure Island Boat	Panama City	904-234-8944
Capt. Sandy Ware	Panama City	904-234-3610
Capt. Buck	Panama City	904-785-7330
Capt. Bill Gorman	Panama City	904-785-4878
Capt. Dave Wells	Panama City	904-235-3339
Lazy River Gal	Panama City	904-234-7560
Sundowner	Panama City	904-235-0526
Capt. Duke's Charters	Panama City	904-235-4262
Capt. Tiny	Panama City	904-234-6740
Miss Penny	Panama City	904-871-9066
Capt. Marion Raffield	Panama City	904-769-8173
Capt. Bill Raffield	Panama City	904-763-2402
Raffield Charters	Panama City	904-769-0947
Gay Louise	Panama City	904-234-6216

Aquarian	Panama City	904-763-0699
Sirena	Panama City	904-234-7621
Dixie Grey	Panama City	904-234-6718
Best Bet	Panama City	904-234-0891
Duchess	Panama City	904-234-3063
Gotta Believe	Panama City	904-234-9409
Dynamic	Panama City	904-769-0175
Gulf Charter Service	Panama City	904-235-2809
Poseidon	Panama City	904-234-6122
A.R. Holley	Lynn Haven	904-265-2618
Sugarfoot	Fort Walton Beach	904-243-9045
Peggy Lee	Santa Rosa Beach	904-267-2159
Miss Suzette	Hernando Beach	904-596-4206
The Misty Bea	Mexico Beach	904-648-8900
Charisma	Mexico Beach	904-648-8211
El Sea Weed	Gulf Breeze	904-932-0022
Entertainer	Gulf Breeze	904-932-4166
Stacy Lee II	Gulf Breeze	904-932-4286
Finestkind	Destin	904-837-2343
Ole Salt	Destin	904-837-2343
Gotcha	Destin	904-837-6637
Miss Angie	Destin	904-837-2343
Seacatch	Destin	904-837-2343
Backdown	Destin	904-837-9551
Scamp	Destin	904-837-7633
Breakaway	Destin	904-837-2343
Jay Jay	Pensacola	904-492-0192
Wet Dream	Pensacola	904-433-4319

Headboats

Critter Fleet	Daytona Beach	904-767-7676
Capt. Anderson	Panama City	904-234-3435
Capt. Duke's Charters	Panama City	904-235-4262
King Neptune	Mayport	904-249-9732
Blue Seas V	Fort Pierce	305-464-4793
Miss Cape Canaveral	Port Canaveral	305-783-7284
Lady Stuart	Stuart	305-286-1860
Sea Mist III	Boynton Beach	305-732-9974
Fish City	Pompano Beach	305-781-1211
Garnsey's	Deerfield Beach	305-421-4842
Shamrock	Riviera Beach	305-842-4850
Sea Legs III	Hollywood	305-923-2109
Dragon	Fort Lauderdale	305-522-3474
M/V Tiki	Miami Beach	305-945-8571
Mucho - K	Miami Shores	305-947-3525
New Popeye	Miami Shores	305-947-3525
Hurricane	Miami Shores	305-947-3525
Mystery	Miami Shores	305-947-3525
Caloosa	Tavernier	305-664-5411

Viking Starship	Stock Island	305-294-2310
Majestic Fleet	Key Largo	305-451-2220
Marathon Lady IV	Marathon Shores	305-743-5580
Winner Party Boats	Marathon Shores	305-743-6969
Captain's Lady	Islamorada	305-664-4196
Caloosa	Islamorada	305-852-3200
Capt. Winner II	Islamorada	305-664-4196
Yankee Capt.	Key West	305-294-7009
Yankee Freedom	Key West	305-294-7009
Tortugas Unlimited	Key West	305-296-0111
Gulfstream III	Key West	305-296-8494
Greyhound V	Key West	305-296-5139
Miss Barnegat Light	Fort Myers Beach	813-466-8155
Getaway Marina	Fort Myers Beach	813-466-3600
Getaway I	Fort Myers Beach	813-463-0390
Class Act	Fort Myers Beach	813-463-7800
Double Eagle II	Clearwater Beach	813-446-1653
Double Eagle III	Clearwater Beach	813-446-1653
Let's Go Fishing	Sarasota	813-366-2159
Fish Hawk	Sarasota	813-346-0824
Divers Too	Englewood	813-474-9024
Capt. Gene Luciano	Naples	813-262-4545
Miss Pass A Grille	Passagrill Beach	813-360-2082
Kingfisher I	Punta Gorda	813-639-0969
Kingfisher II	Punta Gorda	813-639-0969
Folly VII	Punta Gorda	813-639-7758
Blue Seas II	Venice	813-484-5788
Funny Feelin	Venice	813-484-9044
Spider	Venice	813-497-3304

Sources of Information

Bay County Chamber of Commerce
P.O. Box 1850
Panama City, Fl. 32402-1850

Florida Department of Natural Resources
3900 Commonwealth Boulevard
Tallahassee, Fl. 32303

Florida DNR Marine Research Laboratory
100 Eighth Avenue, SE
St. Petersburg, Fl. 33701
813-896-8626

Florida Keys Visitors Bureau
P.O. Box 1147
Key West, Fl. 33041
1-800-FLA-KEYS

Florida Sea Grant
(*Map-30* and other publications)
McCarty Hall
University of Florida
Gainesville, Fl. 32611
904-393-1771

Lee County Tourist Development Council
(*Tarpon Times* and other information)
2106 First Street
Fort Myers, Fl. 33902
800-237-6444
813-335-2631

Marathon Chamber of Commerce
3330 Overseas Highway
Marathon, Fl. 33050
305-743-5417

Pompano Beach Chamber of Commerce
2200 East Atlantic Boulevard
Pompano Beach, Fl. 33062-5284

St. Lucie County Chamber of Commerce
2200 Virginia Avenue
Fort Pierce, Fl. 33450

Fishing Clubs

Florida League of Anglers (FLA)
Norma Stoppelbein
P.O. Box 1109
Sanibel, Fl. 33957

Lee-Collier Fishing Club
H.A. Stanley
Route 2, Box 540
Bonito Springs, Fl. 33923

Florida Sport Fishing Association, Inc.
P.O. Box 1216
Cape Canaveral, Fl. 32920

Tropical Anglers Club
Dr. Elliot Fox
1550 North Dixie Highway
Coral Gables, Fl. 33146

Fort Walton Beach Sailfish Club
Roy Gonzales
P.O. Box 164
Fort Walton Beach, Fl. 32548

Cape Coral Tarpon Hunters Club
Tom Swift
P.O. Box 842
Cape Coral, Fl. 33904

Fort Myers Beach Tarpon Hunters Club
George Gibbons
P.O. Box 2420
Fort Myers Beach, Fl. 33931

Islamorada Sportfishing Club
Rich Eyerdam
Islamorada, Fl. 33036

Northeast Florida Marlin Association
Frank Houpt
P.O. Box 24007
Jacksonville, Fl. 32241

Jacksonville Offshore Sportfishing Club
P.O. Box 16794
Jacksonville, Fl. 32216

South Florida Sportfishing Club
Allen Herman
9100 SW 124 Street
Miami, Fl. 33176

Miami Rod and Reel Club, Inc.
Dr. Fred Poppe
401 Coral Way
Miami, Fl. 33134

Sportfishermen of Broward
Stan Bauer
111 SE 6th Court
Pompano Beach, Fl. 33060

Southwest Anglers Club
Fritz Stoppelbein
534 North Yachtsman Drive
Sanibel, Fl. 33957

Suncoast Tarpon Club
Don Crawford
718 41st Avenue North
St. Petersburg, Fl. 33703

Stuart Sailfish Club
P.O. Box 2005
Stuart, Fl. 33495

Tampa Bay Sharkers
Bob Lastra
3006 West Broad Street
Tampa, Fl. 33614

Golden Triangle Sportfishing Club
Phil Woods
P.O. Box 13912
Tampa, Fl. 33681

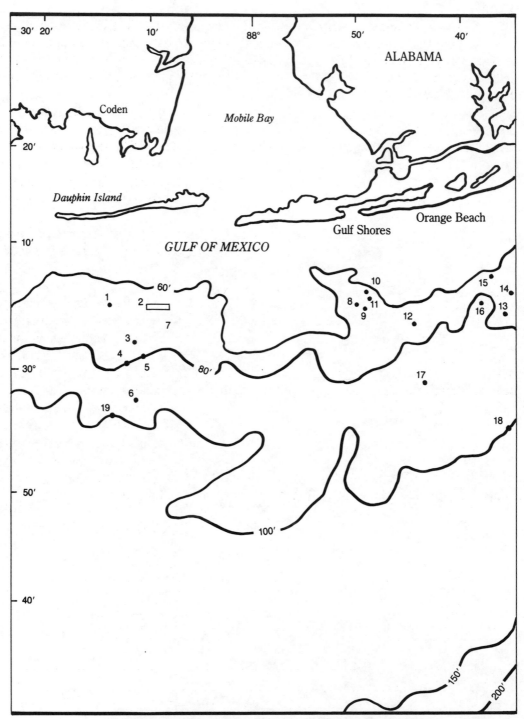

Approximate Locations of Existing Reefs off Alabama

From MASGP-86-021, p.704

Alabama

ood blue water runs up close to the beaches near the Florida line on some days, but that's not typical of Alabama's shoreline. Coastal Alabama is dominated by Mobile Bay, emptying point for the Alabama and Tombigbee rivers, which produce the fourth largest discharge in the United States. As a result, the salinity of the bay and near shore coastal waters varies considerably with statewide rainfall.

Eastern Alabama ends in two spits or peninsulas. In the center, facing the Gulf of Mexico, is Gulf Shores, 50 miles southeast of Mobile. The eastward peninsula protects small, shallow (about eight feet deep) Perdido Bay and Orange Beach, the principal offshore charter boat port. The western spit is Fort Morgan Peninsula, which juts into Mobile Bay. Directly west of the peninsula, and a 30-mile drive south of Mobile, is Dauphin Island. Inside the bay, just north of Dauphin Island, are extensive clamshell plantings known as Portersville Bay, Kings Bayou, Buoy, Sand, and Cedar Point reefs.

The Mobile and Perdido bay estuaries are well developed, due to the gentle slope of the land both onshore and offshore, heavy runoff of water and sediments, and minimal once-a-day tides of about 1.1 foot of amplitude. They are extremely productive for shrimp, crabs, spotted scatrout, red drum, croaker, and other estuarine-dependent species.

Offshore, the bottom is a shallow, featureless shelf with a gradual slope of about 3.2 feet per mile. The principal offshore fishing grounds are the numerous artificial reefs, constructed of culverts, cars, boats, Liberty ships, and the old Lillian Bridge. The DeSoto Canyon is too far east for most boats.

Coastal Alabama is largely the province of the inshore sportfisherman. Its waters are rich in seatrout, red drum, flounder, and, at hard bottom areas, sheepshead and black drum. The major offshore fishes taken by the small charter boat fleet are amberjack, snappers (red, vermilion, gray, and lane), king and Spanish mackerel, and little tunny. Only two important headboats service the Alabama coastal angler, and their distance and depth offshore is often determined by the weather. The principal sport fish taken by private boats are king and Spanish mackerel, bluefish, shark, croaker, red snapper, red drum, spotted and sand seatrout, crevalle jack, cobia, flounder, sea catfish, sheepshead, and kingfish (ground mullet).

NOAA Charts

11382	Pensacola Bay and Approaches
11376	Mobile Bay, Mobile Ship Channel
11360	Cape St. George to Mississippi Passes
11006	Gulf Coast—Key West to Mississippi River

NOAA Bathymetric Maps

NH 16-4	Mobile. Coastal west.
NH 16-5	Pensacola. Coastal east.
NH 16-7	Breton Sound. Inshore west.
NH 16-8	Destin Dome. Inshore east.
NH 16-10	Mississippi Canyon. Offshore west.
NH 16-11	DeSoto Canyon. Offshore east.
NG 16-1	Atwater. Far offshore west.
NG 16-2	Lloyd. Far offshore east.

Hangs, Rocks, Wrecks, and Reefs*

Hang		12652.2	47064.0
Hang		12652.5	47051.2
Hang		12654.9	47012.3
Hang		12655.0	47049.6
Hang		12655.0	47071.0
Southwest Rock/Banks (66 feet)	1**	12655.4	47050.4
Hang		12657.3	47063.5
Hang		12657.5	47052.9
Hang in 10 fathoms		12660.0	47042.0
Moved E. Lynn		12662.0	47064.5
Hang		12665.0	47001.9
Hang miles from beach		12666.5	47068.2
Hang		12666.6	47013.0
Hang		12669.5	47013.6
Hang		12670.6	47049.8
Hang		12676.0	47016.3
E & W Ship		12678.1	47012.1
Hang		12684.2	47063.7
Hang		12684.2	47067.9
Hang		12684.3	47069.9
7-fathom Boat		12685.3	47067.8
Hang		12688.8	47043.8
5.5-mile hang		12690.0	47060.0
Hang		12691.2	47049.7
Bridge rubble		12691.8	47049.9
Hang		12691.9	47050.0
Hang		12692.2	47059.8
Hang		12697.3	47063.5
Hang		12697.9	47051.7
Bridge rubble		12697.9	47054.7
Bridge rubble		12698.0	47051.8
Hang		12698.8	47051.8
Hang		12702.4	47068.0
Hang		12703.6	47046.9
Bridge rubble		12703.7	47046.9
Bridge rubble		12704.0	47046.9
Bridge rubble		12704.5	47046.9
Hang		12704.5	47071.4
Dry Dock		12704.6	47028.7
Hang		12704.9	47050.6
Hang		12705.7	47047.2
NW Buoy Dauphin Island Bridge	2	12706.0	47035.0
Hang		12707.5	47071.7
Bridge rubble		12708.7	47050.5
Bridge rubble		12708.9	47050.6
Hang		12709.7	47038.7
Bridge rubble		12709.7	47038.8
Bridge rubble		12709.9	47038.7
Hang		12709.9	47038.8
Dauphin Island Bridge	2	12735.0	47035.0
Tulsa Wreck	4	12711.9	47027.4
Hang		12711.8	47039.4
Hang		12712.2	47068.0
Bridge rubble		12713.0	47041.4
Hang		12713.6	47046.6
Hang		12713.7	47042.2
Bridge rubble		12715.2	47035.7
Hang		12716.4	47069.7
Bridge rubble		12716.7	47036.7
Hang		12716.7	47066.3
Bridge rubble		12716.9	47036.5
Bridge rubble		12717.0	47040.5
Bridge rubble		12719.2	47034.5
Bridge rubble		12720.4	47038.4
Bridge rubble		12720.5	47035.5
Hang		12722.1	47069.4
Hang		12722.9	47060.5
Bridge rubble		12723.7	47036.5
Bridge rubble		12724.8	47035.1
Airplane		12724.5	47064.6
Sunken Boat		12710.3	47027.2
SSA Trolling Alley (from)		12708.0	47030.0
SSA Trolling Alley (to)		12725.0	47030.0
Hang		12725.3	47069.6
West of Buoy		12725.5	47069.6
Southeast Channel		12726.0	47045.0
Southeast Channel		12728.6	47045.9
Bridge rubble		12726.2	47039.2
Bridge rubble		12726.7	47035.0
31-foot hang		12727.2	47070.1
Bridge rubble		12728.3	47035.6
Bridge rubble		12730.2	47035.3
Anderson Liberty ship	5	12733.4	47018.6
1.25 mile SW of Buoy		12734.3	47059.4
Bridge rubble		12735.3	47035.3
Hang		12737.4	47062.9
Hang		12741.3	47003.0
.25 mile ENE of Sea Buoy		12741.7	47058.5
Hang		12742.0	47044.0
Hang		12745.0	47050.4
Hang		12746.0	47058.0
Hang		12749.1	47050.2
Hang		12752.1	47049.1
Edwards Liberty ship, 84 feet	6	12709.4	47013.6
East of Bar Ella Lee hit		12756.2	47062.1
East of Bar Ella Lee hit		12756.2	47063.1
South of Buoy		12757.9	47048.2
.5 mile N of Buoy		12762.1	47063.0
1.75 miles from Buoy		12766.2	47063.2
Southeast of Channel		12770.9	47047.7
Pipe		12773.5	47060.2
Hang		12775.5	47017.0
Southeast Banks, 90 feet		12787.1	47025.9
Hang		12795.0	47073.0
Hang		12796.0	47068.8
Hang		12808.0	47074.7

Southeast Banks, 75 feet	7	12808.3	47027.0
2.75 miles from beach		12813.0	47071.7
Hang		12833.1	47045.8
Buffalo Barge II, 66 feet	8	12876.8	47044.3
Fort Morgan pipes	9	12883.1	47040.0
Hang		12882.7	47047.1
Buffalo Barge I, 54 feet	10	12881.9	47045.5
Lipscomb Tug	11	12900.9	47045.0
105-foot Tug	12	12957.8	47039.9
GCCA Trolling Alley (from)		13051.6	47052.4
GCCA Trolling Alley (to)		13059.2	47054.9
Lillian Bridge II	13	13059.2	47054.9
Allen Liberty ship	14	13069.2	47059.0
Kelley pipes & Lillian Bridge I	15	13046.7	47062.8
Wallace Liberty ship	16	13038.0	47046.0
Sparkman Liberty ship	17	12948.1	47020.2
Trysler Ground	18	13100.0	46990.0
Trysler Ground	18	13060.0	47000.0
Mail Ship	19	12678.1	47012.3

Most of the data herein presented are reprinted, with permission, from Underwater Obstructions in the North Central Gulf of Mexico, Perdido Pass to Biloxi. *The complete publication and a series of charts are available from Alabama Sea Grant Extension Service, 3940 Government Boulevard, Mobile, Al. 36609.*
**denotes map location.

Offshore Charter Boats

Area Code (205)

My Joy	Dauphin Island	861-6154
Terolyn II	Dauphin Island	861-4313
Lady Ann	Dauphin Island	861-5302
Dauphin Island Marina	Dauphin Island	861-5302
Four Winds	Mobile	666-5943
Hollywood	Gulf Shores	948-7459
Mystery	Gulf Shores	981-4621
Orange Beach Marina	Orange Beach	981-4510
Alabama Fishing Charters	Orange Beach	981-4850
Castle I	Orange Beach	981-4235
Fat Pat	Orange Beach	981-6227
Seahawk	Orange Beach	981-6507
Sea Reaper	Orange Beach	981-4444
Summer Wind	Orange Beach	981-4135
Riptide	Orange Beach	981-4729

Headboats

| Alabama's Island Lady | Orange Beach | 981-4510 |
| Moreno Queen | Gulf Shores | 981-8499 |

Sources of Information

Alabama Marine Resources Laboratory
Dauphin Island, Al. 36528
205-861-2882

Alabama Sea Grant Extension Service
3940 Government Boulevard
Mobile, Al. 36609

Mississippi-Alabama Sea Grant Consortium
Caylor Building
Gulf Coast Research Laboratory
Ocean Springs, Ms. 39564
601-875-9341

Mobile Area Chamber of Commerce
P.O. Box 2187
Mobile, Al. 36652
205-433-6951

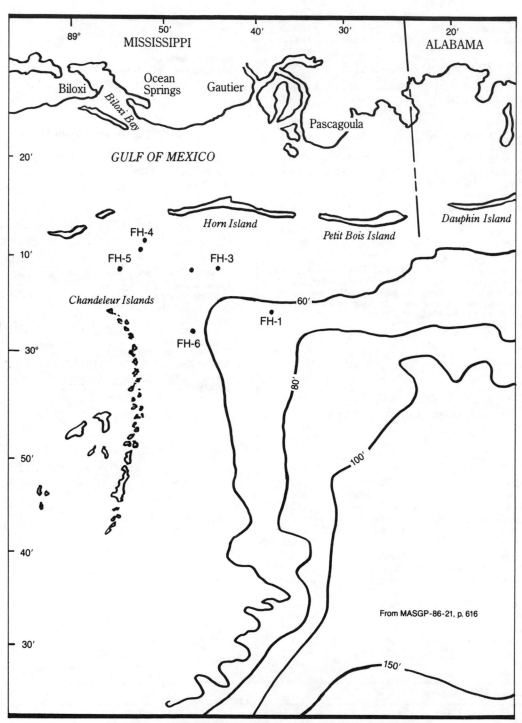

**Location of Existing and Permitted Reef Sites and
Unidentified Obstructions/Fish Havens Off Mississippi**

Mississippi

Mississippi is dominated by the freshwater runoff of the Mississippi River and the particles that form the deposits making up the Delta, filling the shallow continental shelf with mud, sand, or silt. Offshore, relief is rare and the bottom is a vast underwater plain of blue mud.

The Mississippi River influences circulation within the Gulf, dividing it into eastern and western zones. Because Gulf water generally circulates clockwise, the silt is generally washed eastward. A portion of the western Gulf of Mexico has an offshore area of high relief washed by silt-free, blue-black water (the Flower Gardens), but nothing like that exists off Mississippi.

The major ports, from east to west, are Pascagoula, Biloxi, Gulfport, Pass Christian, and Bay St. Louis. Offshore, a series of barrier islands parallels the coast, the largest ones directly off Pascagoula. This northern coastal region is dominated by Mississippi Sound. To the west, the Mississippi Delta extends far southward into the northern Gulf of Mexico. An important series of many small islands and one large one, known as the Chandeleur Islands, parallels the Delta from north to south and defines Chandeleur Sound to the west, which in turn contains smaller, inshore Breton Sound, named for the Breton Islands.

The best-known fishing grounds of the Mississippi coast are around the Chandeleur Islands. Here, seatrout, red drum, flounder, crevalle jack, sea catfish, tripletail, small bluefish, and croaker are taken by fishermen in small boats. Offshore, there are several clusters of oil and gas rigs. One cluster is in Breton Sound in the depth range of 30 to 50 feet. Another is in 20 to 40 feet of water just off Pass à Loutre on the Mississippi River Delta. The densest cluster is called the East Bay Rigs, located on the west side of the Delta, between South Pass and Southwest Pass in 20 to 100 feet of water.

The offshore outcrops support a small charter boat fleet. The artificial reefs and gas and oil rigs offer easily located structures within a reasonable ride off the Mississippi coast. Red and vermilion snappers, king and Spanish mackerel, amberjack, cobia, and grouper prowl these structures.

Billfishing is not well developed because of the long run to the Mississippi Canyon.

NOAA Charts

11360	Cape St. George to Mississippi Passes
11006	Gulf Coast—Key West to Mississippi River
11373	Mississippi Sound and Approaches
11363	Chandeleur and Breton Sounds
11361	Mississippi River Delta

NOAA Bathymetric Maps

NH 16-14	Mobile. Coastal.
NH 16-7	Breton Sound. Inshore.
NH 16-10	Mississippi Canyon. Offshore.
NG 16-1	Atwater. Far offshore.
NG 16-4	Lund. Extreme offshore.

Another valuable map is the Lower Mississippi Delta Open File Report 83-01, *Marine Recreational Fishing Map, U.S. Dept. of the Interior/Minerals Management Service. Order from Public Records, Minerals Management, P.O. Box 7944, Metairie, La. 70010.*

Rocks, Wrecks, and Reefs

FH-1 Barge A, bow	12405.8	47037.1
FH-1 Barge A, stern	12406.4	47037.3
FH-1 Barge B, bow	12407.7	47038.4
FH-1 Barge B, stern	12407.8	47038.3
FH-1 Barge C, bow	12405.9	47035.6
FH-1 Barge C, stern	12405.5	47035.6
FH-3 Liberty ship A, bow	12319.8	47061.6
FH-3 Liberty ship A, stern	12319.9	47061.3
FH-3 Liberty ship B, bow	12319.6	47061.5
FH-3 Liberty ship B, stern	12319.0	47061.6
FH-4 Barge A, port bow	12227.5	47061.3
FH-4 Barge A, starboard stern	12227.2	47061.3
FH-5 Barge A, port bow	12264.0	47063.1
FH-5 Barge A, starboard stern	12264.3	47063.2
FH-6 Ship A, bow	12356.1	47030.7
FH-6 Ship A, stern	12356.1	47031.0
FH-6 Ship B1, starboard midship	12355.9	47030.8
FH-6 Ship B1, port midship	12356.0	47030.8
FH-6 Ship B2, bow	12355.5	47030.5
FH-6 Ship B2, port midship	12355.8	47030.7
FH-6 Ship B2, starboard midship	12355.8	47030.6
FH-6 Ship C1, bow	12356.1	47030.4
FH-6 Ship C1, port midship	12355.6	47030.4
FH-6 Ship C1, starboard midship	12355.6	47030.6
FH-6 Ship C2, starboard midship	12355.1	47030.1
FH-6 Ship C2, port midship	12355.2	47030.2
FH-6 Ship C2, stern	12354.9	47030.3

Charter Boats

(Area Code 601)

Seven G's	Ocean Springs	875-5458
Outrageous Fiesta	Ocean Springs	875-9462
Fiesta	Ocean Springs	875-9462
Shearwater	Ocean Springs	875-3511
Peggy C	Gautier	457-2501
Ventura III	Gulfport	896-3469
Deep Sea Fishing Rodeo	Gulfport	896-2320
Bally-Hoo II	Gulfport	868-1009
Bounty Hunter	Gulfport	863-5324
Sand Dollar	Gulfport	432-2486
Sea Surey	Gulfport	896-3469
Snow Digger	Gulfport	863-5324
P.J.	Gulfport	863-2362
Lady Karen	Gulfport	863-2020
Riptide	Gulfport	864-5032
Absertion	Gulfport	863-6146
Man-Jo-Ann	Gulfport	863-6146
Seabestes	Gulfport	435-5336
Charter Boats, Inc.	Gulfport	863-7711
Charter Boat Association	Biloxi	432-5780
Bounty	Biloxi	432-7787
Pitch-N-Woo	Biloxi	392-1542
Big Red	Biloxi	875-2598
Baja 31	Biloxi	392-1520
Blue Bayou	Biloxi	392-4731
Sunchaser	Biloxi	392-1520
Sundown	Biloxi	432-2197
Miss Oscie	Biloxi	392-1737
Southern Belle	Biloxi	435-6570
Beachcomber	Biloxi	388-1151
High Times	Biloxi	392-5335
Hide-A-Way	Biloxi	875-9642
Skipper	Biloxi	392-2817
Belvedere	Biloxi	436-3700
Mr. Champ	Biloxi	432-0172
Silver Dollar	Biloxi	388-2209
Caine Mutiny	Biloxi	436-3757
Moby Dick	Biloxi	388-5535
Captain Tan	Biloxi	435-2306
Happy Hooker	Biloxi	388-5766
Sea Hooker	Biloxi	436-3690
Sea Queen	Biloxi	432-1029

Sea Rider	Biloxi	432-2224
Minx	Biloxi	432-1455
Renegade	Biloxi	374-1723
Ron Jon	Biloxi	432-8798

Headboats

Becuna	Biloxi	432-1215
Miss Hospitality	Biloxi	435-1592
Gay Jay	Biloxi	436-4108
Quick Silver	Biloxi	432-1215
Tiger Shark	Biloxi	388-5535
Skipper	Biloxi	392-2817
Blue Runner	Biloxi	374-3176
Hide-A-Way	Biloxi	875-9462
Sundown Two	Biloxi	432-2197

Sources of Information

Mississippi-Alabama Sea Grant Consortium
Caylor Building
Gulf Coast Research Laboratory
Ocean Springs, Ms. 39564
601-875-9341

Mississippi Gulf Fishing Banks, Inc.
(nonprofit artificial reef club)
P.O. Box 223
Biloxi, Ms. 39533
601-388-4710

Mississippi Sea Grant Advisory Service
(free newsletter, tide tables, fishing guides)
4646 West Beach Boulevard, Suite 1-E
Biloxi, Ms. 39531
601-388-4710

Coastal Conservation Association
Biloxi-Gulfport Chapter
764 Cove Drive
Biloxi, Ms. 39531
601-388-2209

Coastal Conservation Association
Pascagoula Chapter and State Office
1007 Wade Avenue
Pascagoula, Ms. 39507

Louisiana Coastline

LOUISIANA

T he principal ports of Louisiana, from east to west, are Grand Isle and Bayou Fourchon on the western side of the Mississippi Delta, Cocodrie south of Houma on Terrebonne Bay in southeast Louisiana, and Cameron and Grand Chenier south of Lake Charles. The ports front on vast areas of marshes rich in red drum (redfish) and spotted seatrout (speckled trout), with Cocodrie called one of the best inshore fishing areas on the entire Gulf Coast. The Isles Dernieres are big barrier islands, but many other islets punctuate the irregular coastline, making it a maze for those who might attempt to navigate by memory and eye. Guides are essential for novices, and some regulars never outgrow them. Blue water is very far offshore.

Strongly affected by the Mississippi and Atchafalaya rivers, Louisiana's brown inshore waters extend some 10 to 20 miles seaward, the bottom a mixture of sand and mud. Far offshore, the bottom abruptly drops and becomes studded with innumerable coral rocks, banks, and ledges. These are the Flower Gardens of the western Gulf of Mexico, a region extending from west of the Mississippi Delta all the way to Texas. The offshore water is less turbid, cleaner, and warmer. It circulates in a western loop. Beyond this isolated Eden, the bottom once more becomes the same sticky blue mud found off Alabama, the two blue mud zones separated by a vast plain of globigerina ooze. If barren, relief-free mud and ooze plains weren't bad enough, the bottom is also disturbed by major oil seeps.

The Flower Gardens are concentrated beween 91 and 95 degrees longitude, 25 to 100 miles offshore, and 75 to 400 feet deep. The near shore eastern outcrops are periodically bathed by cold coastal water, but, offshore, river influences end and the sea takes on tropical temperatures and full ocean salinities, producing extensive coral reef development on the rocky bottom. Here live snappers, groupers, angelfish, butterflyfish, wrasses, and other tropical species usually associated with Caribbean reefs. The Flower Gardens have been an isolated oasis for many tens of thousands of years, and the fish here seem to differ a bit from their relatives in the Bahamas.

Thousands of gas and oil platforms pepper the Gulf, providing hard structure high up into the water column and well away from the mud or sandy silt bottom. These platforms attract cobia, grouper, red and gray snapper, Spanish and king mackerel, amberjack, crevalle jack, and offshore pelagics like wahoo to otherwise barren bottom regions.

Louisiana offers three kinds of fishing. Most popular is inshore, weir, channel, grass bed, oyster bed, and island fishing for red drum (redfish) and spotted seatrout (speckled trout). Many skippers offer guide and charter services for trout and redfish throughout the coastal zone. Those charters could run as much as $450 a day for a party of six, plus gas.

Offshore charters for blue water fishing (same base cost, but more for gas) are also available. Dolphin, small tuna, wahoo and king mackerel are more frequent catches than white marlin and sailfish, and weather and seas often prevent runs to the very deepest offshore waters likely to hold blue marlin or giant yellowfins.

Headboats are numerous and vary from those holding a dozen people to those carrying close to a hundred. Many of the smaller boats fish near shore bottoms for flounder, sea bass, trout, croaker, and sheepshead. Other, usually much larger, boats specialize in red snapper fishing on the rocks and around platforms. As always, it pays to telephone ahead and find out which boats specialize in the different kinds of fishing. Be at the docks when they come in if you can.

NOAA Charts

11361	Mississippi River Delta
11358	Barataria Bay and Approaches
11359	Loop Deepwater Port (Offshore 11358)
11357	Timbalier and Terrebonne Bays
11356	Isles Derniers to Point au Fer
11351	Point au Fer to Marsh Island
11349	Vermilion Bay and Approaches
11344	Rollover Bayou to Calcasieu Pass
11341	Calcasieu Pass to Sabine Pass

NOAA Bathymetric Maps

NH 16-10	Mississippi Canyon. Offshore.
NG 16-1	Atwater. Far offshore.
NG 16-4	Lund. Extremely far offshore.
NH 15-12	Ewing Bank. Offshore.
NG 15-3	Green Canyon. Far offshore.
NG 15-6	Walker Ridge. Extremely far offshore.
F 89	Ewing Bank, NE (fishing bathymetric map).
F 90	Ewing Bank, NW (fishing bathymetric map).

Reefs, Wrecks, and Rocks*

18-fathom hang	26406.0	46814.0
11-fathom hang	26425.5	46879.7
11-fathom hang	26436.0	46889.4
14-fathom hang	26438.2	11126.8
18-fathom hang	26443.5	46815.1
22-fathom hang	26440.0	46793.9
25-fathom hang	26446.6	11192.7
25-fathom hang	26453.3	11190.3
26-fathom coral	26465.7	11206.5
13-fathom rocks	26498.8	46874.5
28-fathom coral	26488.3	11222.6
28-fathom coral	26481.1	11221.4
27-fathom coral	26507.0	11215.6
30-fathom rock and coral	26541.2	11247.4
30-fathom rock and coral	26582.2	11239.8
14-fathom pipeline	26580.6	11035.6
Jackman's 18-fathom Hole	26593.8	11196.5
40-fathom ridge	26587.1	11280.9
Oil Boat	26605.1	46960.3
30-fathom hang	26609.7	11241.3
30-fathom hang	26641.1	11244.7
23-fathom hang	26642.7	46789.9
20-fathom hang	26676.0	46793.0
Sunken Boat	26695.3	11179.8
28-fathom rocks	26698.4	11250.0
28-fathom rocks	26710.1	11249.2
31-fathom rocks	26695.1	11254.3
31-fathom rocks	26707.2	11255.4
Coral	26758.1	11169.6
Coral	26758.5	11173.0
Big pipe	26766.6	11241.3
Buoy	26777.2	46773.9
Candy Mountain	26787.7	11285.3
Golden Dawn	26797.4	11215.0
Wreck	26798.0	11237.1
Rocks	26798.4	11249.0
13-fathom hang	26800.0	46870.4
19-fathom hang	26800.3	11214.2
Rocks	26814.5	11323.0
25-fathom hang	26831.5	46774.2
Rocks	26880.3	11268.8
Rocks	26898.4	11268.1
Tony's Rock	26913.4	11299.8
Coral	26959.4	11193.4
Coral	26971.7	11302.5
Scattered coral at 40 fathoms	26979.0	11375.9
Scattered coral at 40 fathoms	27010.6	11385.0

Rocks	27024.1	11339.9
Coral	27030.4	11353.8
Jim's Rock at 200 feet	27052.4	11360.6
Rock at 200 feet	27068.0	46722.4
Jeane's Rock at 200 feet	27077.1	11355.6
Capped well	27072.9	46748.2
Pipeline at 22 fathoms	27084.0	46787.0
Wreck at 72 feet	27165.4	46848.0
Valve at 23 fathoms	27177.5	11327.1
Capped well	27190.0	46766.0
Deep rocks	27201.4	11424.6
Deep rocks	27222.6	11431.5
Deep rocks	27218.0	46697.5
Deep rocks	27235.0	46694.8
Capped well	27245.0	46730.2
29-fathom hang	27321.5	46732.7
Wreck	27342.9	46731.2
Well	27390.5	46788.5
Coral at 33 fathoms	27403.5	11459.0
High voltage cable	27432.7	46735.7
Well	27430.6	46729.6
Pipeline	27487.0	46728.5
Anchor	27485.5	46714.5
Anchor Buoy	27503.0	46740.6
Sunken Boat	27634.7	46795.3
Rig	27637.8	46697.0
Boat	27697.5	46683.2
Deep rocks	27721.1	46668.6
25-fathom hang	27835.0	46688.0
20-fathom hang	27927.0	46708.0
Wreck	27961.2	46766.4
Coral	27965.0	46692.0
Coral	27967.0	16000.0
Rocks	28115.0	46745.5
Rocks	28112.0	46744.0
Rocks	28170.5	46724.0
Wreck	28255.0	46802.5
24-fathom hang	28330.2	46743.4
24-fathom hang	28362.2	46740.2
Boat	28407.7	46769.9
Buoy	28464.7	46814.6
Dog Key	28485.4	46765.9
20-fathom hang	28534.3	46792.9
Boat	28636.5	46818.2
Alton	28666.3	46798.6
Alton	28660.3	46798.3

Selected data taken from Hangs and Bottom Obstructions of the Texas/Louisiana Coast, Loran C, by Gary L. Graham, Texas A & M University Sea Grant College Program, June 1983, with permission. For a copy of the complete publication, order TAMU-SG-81-501 from Marine Information Service, Texas A & M University, College Station, Tx. 77843, and enclose $5.00.

CHARTER BOATS

Logie Joe	Hopedale	504-887-7469
Nicole Marie	Hopedale	504-887-7469
Salt, Inc.	Chauvin	504-594-7581
Sportsman's Paradise	Chauvin	504-594-2414
Fantastic Island	Chauvin	504-594-4181
Coco Marina	Chauvin	504-594-6626
Sportsman I-VI	Chauvin	504-594-2414
Pat-Al	Harvey	504-368-3268
Angela Rose	Intracoastal City	504-234-4269
Yama 3	Intracoastal City	504-893-6952
Celeste Marie	Intracoastal City	504-232-9140
Battistella's Marina	Empire	504-523-6068
Bluewater I	Empire	504-454-2208
Capt. Don	Empire	504-436-4420
Capt. Bob	Empire	504-885-9945
Ditch Digger	Empire	504-657-5214
Deep Sea Lady	Empire	504-657-7206
Early Bird	Empire	504-361-9086
Miss Mississippi	Empire	504-657-9228
Sandy	Empire	504-561-8778
Superfish	Empire	504-393-0044
Superfish Marina	Empire	504-657-5370
The Insanity	Empire	504-833-8668
Taj 2	Buras	504-271-4062
Miss Kelly	Buras	504-271-4062
Silkie	Bayou Fourchon	504-396-2442
Swordfish	Bayou Fourchon	504-396-2442
Sailfish	Bayou Fourchon	504-396-2442
Miss Iris	Bayou Fourchon	504-396-2442
Star Fish	Bayou Fourchon	504-396-2442
Flying Fish II	Bayou Fourchon	504-396-2442
Aw Heck	Venice	504-656-2304
Pompano	Venice	504-272-5904
Hercules	Houma	504-851-0455
Mr. Todd	Houma	504-851-0455
Martin's Marina	Grand Isle	504-632-3448
Magnum	Grand Isle	504-787-9308
La Lunette	Grand Isle	504-787-9308
Lana Dave	Grand Isle	504-787-9308
Miss Alison	Grand Isle	504-787-2553
Wahoo	Grand Isle	504-787-2740
Shark	Grand Isle	504-787-2794
X-Rated	Grand Isle	504-787-2212
Bayou Charters	Grand Isle	504-888-4882
Sausage Time	Grand Isle	504-888-4882
Chandeleur Marina	Chalmette	504-277-8676
Kitty G	Cameron	504-433-4931
Pirate 2	Cameron	504-433-6773
Blue Water Charters	Metairie	504-454-2208
Fishing Boat Information	New Orleans	504-282-8111

Motor Vessel Fish	New Orleans	504-277-9216
Cypremort Point Supply	Weeks Island	504-867-4360
Franklin Marina	Baldwin	504-923-4486
Queen of Hearts	Abbeville	318-893-0868
Sandy B	New Iberia	318-356-6756
Southwind	New Iberia	318-364-7625
The Flying Greek	Pecan Island	318-276-6166
Acadiana Marina	Pecan Island	318-737-9358
Southern Sun	Grand Chenier	318-538-2197
Betty C	Grand Chenier	318-478-1777
Invader	Lake Charles	318-436-6686

Inshore Charter Boats

Bear's Guide Service	Houma	504-876-7028
Leon St. Martin	Houma	504-868-0536
Schouest Charter Service	Houma	504-879-1017
Sportsman's Paradise	Chauvin	504-594-2414
Reach Out Landing	Dulac	504-563-2590
Chandeleur Island Tours	New Iberia	318-364-2752
Cajun Fishing Tours	New Iberia	318-364-7141
Bayou Jack Marina	New Iberia	318-364-4729
Terry P. Shaughnessy	Hackberry	318-762-3391
Cameron Wildlife	Lake Charles	318-474-6598

Headboats

Bell Pass Marina	Leeville	504-396-2442
Capt. Don	Empire	504-436-4420
Cougar	Empire	504-656-2487
Early Bird	Empire	504-361-9086
Miss Mississippi	Empire	504-282-8111
Pat Al	Empire	504-466-1860
George Anthony	Venice	504-534-7684
Pirate's Cove Marina	Grand Isle	504-687-9560
Bogalee	Grand Isle	504-787-2122
Miss Iris	Grand Isle	504-787-2550
Sea Hawk	Grand Isle	504-787-3207
Kelty-O	Grand Isle	504-878-2240
Sea Hawk	Grand Isle	504-787-2750
Blue Jay	Grand Isle	504-888-4882
Flying Fish Too	Bayou Fourchon	504-396-2442
Starfish	Bayou Fourchon	504-396-2442
Swordfish	Bayou Fourchon	504-396-2442
Bayou Rose	Grand Chenier	504-478-0752
Thedmar	Grand Chenier	504-538-2411
Sunrise II	Grand Chenier	504-538-2063
Gulf Queen	Cameron	504-477-5310
Capt. Terry	Cocodrie	504-594-4181

Sources of Information

Grand Isle Tourist Commission
P.O. Box 776
Grand Isle, La. 70358

Louisiana Department of Wildlife and Fisheries
P.O. Box 44095
Capitol Station
Baton Rouge, La. 70804

Louisiana Office of Tourism
666 North Foster Drive
Baton Rouge, La. 70806

Louisiana Sea Grant
Center for Wetland Studies
Louisiana State University
Baton Rouge, La. 70803
504-388-6449

Fishing Clubs

Coastal Conservation Association (CCA)
11764 Haymarket
Baton Rouge, La. 70816
504-292-0290

CCA - Houma
106 John Street
Houma, La. 70605

CCA - New Orleans
4820 Bradley Drive
Jefferson, La. 70121
504-733-1981

CCA - Lafayette
313 Titan Drive
Lafayette, La. 70508

CCA - Morgan City
P.O. Box 630
Morgan City, La. 70381
504-385-1480

CCA - Bayou
P.O. Box 41
Thibodeaux, La. 70301
504-447-4245

CCA - Lake Charles
4901 Orleans
Lake Charles, La. 70605
318-478-4652

Golden Meadow Big Game Fishing Club
Marco Picciola
P.O. Box 567
Golden Meadow, La. 70357

New Orleans Big Game Fishing Club
Maumus Claverie
830 Union Street
New Orleans, La. 70112
504-524-5416

Greater New Orleans Tarpon Club
Lloyd van Geffen
1311 Cherokee Avenue
Metairie, La. 70005

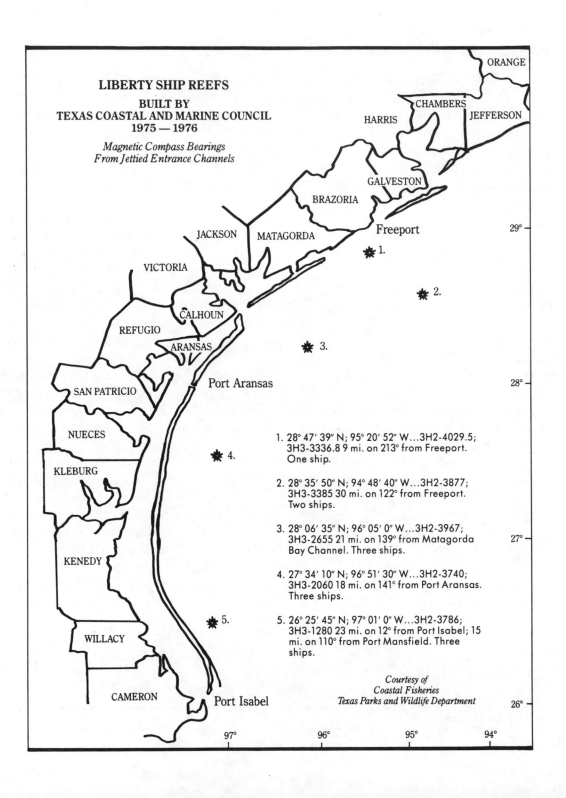

LIBERTY SHIP REEFS

BUILT BY
TEXAS COASTAL AND MARINE COUNCIL
1975 — 1976

Magnetic Compass Bearings
From Jettied Entrance Channels

ORANGE

CHAMBERS

HARRIS

JEFFERSON

GALVESTON

BRAZORIA

JACKSON

MATAGORDA

Freeport

29°

❋ 1.

❋ 2.

VICTORIA

CALHOUN

REFUGIO

ARANSAS

❋ 3.

SAN PATRICIO

Port Aransas

28°

NUECES

❋ 4.

KLEBURG

1. 28° 47' 39" N; 95° 20' 52" W...3H2-4029.5;
   3H3-3336.8 9 mi. on 213° from Freeport.
   One ship.

2. 28° 35' 50" N; 94° 48' 40" W...3H2-3877;
   3H3-3385 30 mi. on 122° from Freeport.
   Two ships.

3. 28° 06' 35" N; 96° 05' 0" W...3H2-3967;
   3H3-2655 21 mi. on 139° from Matagorda
   Bay Channel. Three ships.

27°

KENEDY

4. 27° 34' 10" N; 96° 51' 30" W...3H2-3740;
   3H3-2060 18 mi. on 141° from Port Aransas.
   Three ships.

❋ 5.

5. 26° 25' 45" N; 97° 01' 0" W...3H2-3786;
   3H3-1280 23 mi. on 12° from Port Isabel; 15
   mi. on 110° from Port Mansfield. Three
   ships.

WILLACY

Courtesy of
Coastal Fisheries
Texas Parks and Wildlife Department

CAMERON

Port Isabel

26°

97°　　　　96°　　　　95°　　　　94°

TEXAS

T he Texas coast is better than ever. The advances are mostly due to organizing, lobbying, and funding efforts of the powerful Coastal Conservation Association (formerly the Gulf Coast Conservation Association), which started in Texas, and cooperation from the Texas Department of Parks and Wildlife. Today, hatchery-produced red drum are stocked in many places, including hard-water lakes, and work is proceeding on the rearing and stocking of flounder, black drum, and black-red drum hybrids. The entire coast is rich in cobia and tarpon, tripletail off the beaches, and king mackerel and red snapper offshore at the moderate-depth oil and gas rigs.

Rocky outcrops are uncommon close to shore, but old wrecks, broken bottoms, coral outcrops, ledges, and holes are abundant, if scattered, offshore, and you need Loran to locate them. Texas has 402 oil and gas platforms and underwater sites, with 181 within state territorial waters. There are 68 artificial reef areas and 2,200 unintentional artificial reefs (rigs, shell pads, spoil disposal areas, piers, and docks) and fourteen jetties. Two drilling rigs and fourteen ships were sunk just between 1975 and 1983, and that has continued unabated. A list of artificial reef sites (Management Data Series Number 98, 1986) is available from the Texas Parks and Wildlife Department. It includes all the petroleum platforms constructed through 1981 by block number, with locations given in latitude and longitude.

Headboat fishing for red snapper is popular at Galveston, but charter fishing is coastwide. Big game fishermen work both the deep drop-offs and the deepwater, offshore oil rig platforms, which attract marlin and tuna in addition to king mackerel, snapper, and grouper. Sharks are abundant on the Texas coast, and occur in huge aggregations close to the beaches in the spring. In April of 1987, a teenager lost an arm to a shark while swimming in chest-deep water at Port Aransas. Attacks are rare, but are most likely from bull sharks feeding on stingrays and other fish in murky water. Bull sharks also drop their pups (calves? Tough for a bull!) in shoal water during the summer.

From north to south, the principal ports are Port Arthur (including Beaumont and Sabine) on the Louisiana line, Galveston (including Port Bolivar and Galveston Bay), Freeport, Port O'Conner, Port Aransas (including Aransas Pass, Corpus Christi, and Portland), Port Mansfield, which separates Padre Island from South Padre Island, and Port Isabel, near Brownsville and Harlingen just above the Mexican border. The ports are separated by peninsulas or barrier islands. The most beautiful stretch of barrier island is Padre Island National Seashore, between Corpus Christi and Port Mansfield.

Tom Wade (*Sport Fishing*, June/July 1987) recommended the best offshore fishing spots from all the main ports in Texas. At Galveston, the 100-fathom curve is 100 miles offshore. Rigs are closer and get more attention. Freeport anglers are 70 miles from the curve, and head for the

Little Sister, a 45-fathom hump on a 100-fathom bottom, where yellowfin and marlin are found. Other hot spots are the Cervesa and Tequila platforms, German Charley, the 32's, and Liberty ships. From Port O'Conner, the 100-fathom curve is only 50 miles offshore. Best spots here are the East Break, Pocket of Breaks, and the 500-Fathom Hump. From Port Aransas, look for snapper and grouper at the 40-Fathom Break about 40 miles offshore, and billfish beyond. Best bets are the Aransas Banks, East Breaks, Southern, and the Hospital. Other good spots are the Dumping Grounds, Dutra's Rock, and East Break. The 100-fathom curve is only 40 miles off South Padre Island, and here the hot spots are Big 56, Colt 45, Small Hole, Camel's Head, and South Spounge. Many of these distant offshore locations can be found on the appropriate NOAA bathymetric maps.

NOAA Charts

11332	Sabine Bank
11323	Approaches to Galveston Bay
11321	San Luis Pass to Matagorda Bay
11316	Matagorda Bay and Approaches
11313	Matagorda Light to Aransas Pass
11307	Aransas Pass to Baffin Bay
11304	Northern Part of Laguna Madre
11301	Southern Part of Laguna Madre

NOAA Bathymetric Maps

NH 15-8	Port Arthur. Inshore northeast.
NH 15-11	Bouma Bank. Offshore northeast.
NG 15-2	Garden Banks. Far offshore northeast.
NG 15-5	Keathley Canyon. Extreme offshore central.
NH 15-10	Bay City. Inshore north central.
NG 15-1	East Breaks. Offshore central.
NG 15-4	Alaminos Canyon. Extreme offshore south.
NG 14-3	Inshore. South.
NG 14-6	Inshore. Extreme south.

Wrecks, Rocks, and Reefs*

East Bank, south side	11207.9	23654.9
Rocky area	11201.1	23606.4
Rocky area	11198.8	23580.0
East Bank, north side	11196.9	23572.2
78-foot hang	11190.4	23493.9
180-foot hang	11181.1	23761.0

78-foot hang	11180.8	23468.5
Miss Ginger	11178.2	23746.2
150-foot hang	11173.6	23702.1
Floyd's Rock	11167.5	23817.4
Floyd's Rock	11163.1	23791.0
Wreck	11163.3	23678.9
39-fathom Bank	11154.0	23742.0
39-fathom Bank	11152.0	23752.0
114-foot hang	11152.4	23527.4
Toe Head	11146.4	23532.4
Three B's	11145.3	23512.5
Rock	11143.2	23528.7
Blackfish Ridge	11144.3	23761.8
Small Adam	11134.3	23725.9
Big Adam	11135.1	23743.6
Rock	11132.0	23534.0
Ranzell's Rock	11132.4	23838.8
Ranzell's Rock	11132.2	23833.3
120-foot hang	11124.4	23594.5
100-foot hang	11120.0	23586.0
Four Leaf Clover	11109.9	23596.4
Valley Dawn	11096.1	23690.1
84-foot hang	11093.8	23822.4
84-foot hang	11091.6	23819.4
84-foot hang	11090.7	23856.0
56-foot hang	11081.8	23875.4
Wreck	11085.6	23890.9
Wreck	11073.4	24000.3
Wreck	11079.5	24000.7
Big Southern	11111.8	24079.6
Big Southern	11110.2	24082.9
Wreck	11080.4	24118.3
Lyon L. Hudson (maybe)	11066.8	24126.0
Hospital	11102.6	24135.4
Aransas Bank	11110.4	24165.5
Rocks	11103.5	24178.0

100-foot hang	11081.7	24223.0	Outlook Wreck	11085.0	25186.6
100-foot hang	11081.1	24233.7	Wreck	11082.9	25186.1
115-foot hang	11082.3	24278.0	Gulf Wind	11046.4	25200.3
115-foot hang	11083.4	24270.0	Coral	11121.1	25208.4
Obstructions	11076.0	24345.0	Little Campeche	11132.8	25209.2
Obstructions	11076.8	24343.1	Little Campeche	11132.4	25215.1
Oil Rig on bottom	11088.9	24360.7	Doc's Hole	11123.7	25249.3
Rocky area	11098.3	24347.6	18's Rocks	11079.2	25251.9
Rocky area	11099.3	24362.2	18's Rocks	11086.9	25252.7
Rough bottom	11068.3	24376.0	Salvador Ridge	11124.4	25282.2
Rough bottom	11075.7	24375.7	Salvador Ridge	11122.4	25292.4
Big Dunn Bar	11097.8	24425.5	West Bank	11052.1	25204.4
Little Dunn Bar	11097.6	24440.1	Middle Bank	11053.6	25228.9
Rocks	11097.0	24424.0	Middle Bank	11056.0	25228.4
Rocks	11098.0	24420.0	East Bank	11054.0	25255.1
Miss Aransas	11101.0	24513.3	Platform	11070.3	25267.0
Buoy	11061.1	24561.7	Platform	11071.2	25260.2
Liberty ship	11078.6	24576.0	East 27's	11107.9	25307.5
Liberty ship	11078.9	24577.0	East 27's	11111.9	25321.9
Outrigger	11081.9	24588.5	Middle 27's	11117.0	25334.8
Wreck	11114.0	24638.0	Middle 27's	11115.0	25331.7
Moveable obstruction	11096.4	24651.0	Easterly 21's	11097.0	25388.2
Drop	11076.0	24684.4	Wreck	11102.1	25387.0
Wreck	11100.2	24689.9	Wreck	11056.9	25397.6
Coral	11109.1	24670.3	East 29's	11125.5	25428.3
East Break	11119.0	24650.0	East 29's	11124.2	25424.5
Wreck	11113.3	24679.3	Wreck	11122.5	25476.0
Under Wreck	11121.0	24766.4	Wreck	11110.5	25548.6
Dutra's Rock	11131.4	24501.7	Doc's Hole	11124.5	25549.5
Dumping Ground, SE corner	11155.0	24350.0	Slab Rock	46831.5	25615.1
Dumping Ground, NW corner	11135.0	24350.0	Wreck	46807.2	25622.9
Junk	11057.8	24805.0	Wreck	46830.0	25724.1
Sunken Rig	11059.2	24802.0	Wreck	46795.3	25746.2
Cherokee	11099.7	24804.5	Coral	11138.1	25761.2
Pipeline	11082.8	24876.3	Rock	11165.0	25783.7
Pipeline	11083.0	24877.0	Coral patch	11090.5	25799.9
Slab	11094.6	24902.8	Coral patch	11087.6	25802.6
Slab	11094.0	24928.8	Rocks	11128.2	25797.2
Michael Linnood	11103.1	24936.1	Picayune Hole	11084.7	25831.0
30-fathom Rock (the 32's)	11112.6	24918.9	Rocks	11145.4	25910.5
30-fathom Rock	11108.1	24938.1	Rough bottom	11149.8	25870.6
West 24's	11099.6	25033.2	Rough bottom	11158.0	25886.1
Coral Hole	11087.6	25041.7	Coral	11170.6	25926.9
Wreck	11078.6	25066.0	Coral	11169.4	25946.6
Snake Pit	11102.6	25087.7	Rocks	11132.5	25988.6
West 27's	11103.2	25085.0	Rocks	11126.4	26055.2
West 27's	11106.2	25116.1	Jean's Hole	11214.7	26000.9
East 30-fathom Rock	11112.1	25111.8	Slab	11130.2	26087.9
East 30-fathom Rock	11114.3	25111.8	Rock	46703.7	26087.0
Lady Ann (maybe)	11092.3	25133.5	Rock	46700.9	26081.4
Broken bottom	11057.0	25132.0	Coral	11167.9	26119.3
Inside Charlie Hole	11086.0	25164.6	Carol's Rock	11209.4	26109.8
West German Charlie	11090.6	25176.7	Carol's Rock	11207.8	26107.4
Wreck	11064.2	25175.3	Wreck	11085.9	26187.6

19-fathom Rock		11160.8	26263.8
Broken bottom		11086.7	26371.5
Coral		11192.6	26373.4
Coral		11187.7	26382.0
Slab		11226.0	26392.8

Selected data taken from Hangs and Bottom Obstructions of the Texas/Louisiana Coast, Loran C, by Gary L. Graham, Texas A & M University Sea Grant College Program, June 1983, with permission. For a copy of the complete publication, order TAMU-SG-81-501 from Marine Information Service, Texas A & M University, College Station, Tx. 77843, and enclose $5.00.

CHARTER BOATS

Mickey Nash	Beaumont	409-832-8553
Sea Hawk	Port Arthur	409-982-9643
Tom Johnston	Port Arthur	409-983-5563
Pleasure Pier Marina	Port Arthur	409-983-9100
George Swanson	Port Arthur	409-985-7488
Capt. Craig's Charters	Port Arthur	409-962-4173
Scorpion Fishing Charters	Port Arthur	409-899-2600
Rainbow Boat Charters	Port Arthur	409-962-0876
Rainbow Marina	Port Arthur	409-962-9004
Lady Sandpiper	Port Arthur	409-786-2922
Joel Singleton	Port Arthur	409-962-9604
Big Mama	Port Arthur	409-971-2444
Lucky Lady	Gilchrist	409-684-3070
Cherokee	Clute	409-265-0999
Lee Marie	Clute	409-265-0999
James R	Clute	409-265-0999
Billy K	Freeport	409-233-2364
Ruby K	Freeport	409-233-2364
African Queen	Freeport	409-233-1649
Deep Blue Charters	Port O'Conner	512-983-4232
Kalie	Port O'Conner	512-983-2832
Snapper Snatcher	Port O'Conner	512-983-4447
Miss Lottie Q	Port O'Conner	512-983-4609
Bait Skip	Port O'Conner	512-983-4609
Fisherman's Wharf	Port Aransas	512-749-5448
Robin	Port Aransas	512-949-8378
Nellie Belle	Port Aransas	512-749-6991
King Fisher	Port Aransas	512-749-5597
Pelican	Port Aransas	512-749-5597
Scat Cat	Port Aransas	512-749-5448
Wharf Cat	Port Aransas	512-749-5760
Wildcatter	Port Aransas	512-749-5942
Barbara D	Port Aransas	512-749-5924
Diablo	Port Aransas	512-749-4598
Susie T II	Port Aransas	512-749-5691

My Toy	Port Aransas	512-749-6633
Dolphin Dock	Port Aransas	512-749-6624
Island Moorings Marina	Port Aransas	512-749-4983
Deep Sea Headquarters	Port Aransas	512-749-5597
Woody's Sport Center	Port Aransas	512-749-5252
Fin & Feather Marina	Aransas Pass	512-758-5521
Redfish Bay Terminal	Aransas Pass	512-758-7671
Capt. Salyer's	Rockport	512-992-0631
CJC	Rockport	512-729-0400
Happy Day	Rockport	512-729-2472
Advantage Charters	Corpus Christi	512-241-3993
BG's Marina	Corpus Christi	512-937-3589
Buckshot	Corpus Christi	512-949-8378
Touche	Corpus Christi	512-992-0855
Sea Serpent Boats	Corpus Christi	512-937-3589
Miss Polly	Corpus Christi	512-949-8445
Charter Boat Association	Corpus Christi	512-881-8503
Jimmy's Marina	Padre Island	512-943-9700
White Sands Marine	Padre Island	512-943-6161
Chingadera	Port Mansfield	512-944-2678
Lil' Mako	Port Mansfield	512-944-2302
Fisherman's Wharf	South Padre I.	512-943-2412
Austin Fishing Service	South Padre I.	512-943-6282
Capt. Murphy's Charters	South Padre I.	512-943-2764
Jim's Pier	South Padre I.	512-943-2865
Capt. Summerlin	South Padre I.	512-943-2865
Capt. Adams	South Padre I.	512-943-2550
Capt. Bryan's Charters	South Padre I.	512-943-6301
Sea Ranch Marina	South Padre I.	512-943-2601
Capt. Stockton's Charters	Port Isabel	512-943-1621
Capt. Glick's Charters	Port Isabel	512-761-6060
Charter Fishing Service	Port Isabel	512-943-3332
Charter Captains Associates	Port Isabel	512-943-8029
Sea Ranch Marina	Port Isabel	512-943-2623
Wells Sportfishing Charters	Port Isabel	512-761-1628
Bee Jay	Port Isabel	512-943-6161
Defense Rests	Port Isabel	512-943-6161
La Paloma	Port Isabel	512-943-6161
Betty K	Port Isabel	512-943-8480
Sally 4th	Port Isabel	512-943-5878
The Raven	Port Isabel	512-943-3332
The TICD	Port Isabel	512-943-3332

HEADBOATS

New Buccaneer	Galveston	409-763-5423
Buccaneer	Galveston	409-763-5423
Dixie Green	Galveston	409-763-5423
Cavalier	Galveston	409-763-5423
Cobia	Freeport	409-233-1811
Capt. Casey	Freeport	409-233-1811
Bear Cat	Freeport	409-233-1811

Foxy K	Freeport	409-233-2264
Capt. Clark	Portland	512-884-4346
Thunderbird III	Port Isabel	512-943-2764
Miss Hospitality	Port Isabel	512-943-1621

Sources of Information

Corpus Christi Tourist Bureau
512-882-5603

Port Aransas Chamber of Commerce
512-749-5919

Port Arthur Visitor's Bureau
409-985-7822

Texas Chamber of Commerce
512-477-7030

Texas Parks and Wildlife Department
4200 Smith School Road
Austin, Texas 78744
512-479-4848

Texas Sea Grant College Program
Texas A & M University
College Station, Texas 77843-4115
409-845-7524

Fishing Clubs

Coastal Conservation Association (CCA)
Texas State Office
4801 Woodway, Suite 220-W
Houston, Texas 77056
713-626-4222

CCA-Austin
P.O. Box 17333
Austin, Texas 78764

CCA-Golden Triangle
745 Rankin
Beaumont, Texas 77706

CCA-Corpus Christi
206 Guaranty Bank Plaza
Corpus Christi, Texas 78475

CCA-Dallas
2601 N. Beckley
Dallas, Texas 75208

CCA-Brazoria County
P.O. Box 2502-B
Freeport, Texas 77541

CCA-Galveston
53 Lakeside Drive
Hitchcock, Texas 77563

CCA-Redfish Bay
P.O. Box 1438
Port Aransas, Texas 78373

CCA-Southwest
P.O. Box 8-C
San Antonio, Texas 78286

Illustration Credits

LITTLE TUNNY *Euthynnus alletteratus* p. 99,
SKIPJACK *Euthynnus pelamis* p. 101,
ATLANTIC BONITO *Sarda sarda* p. 101,
ALBACORE *Thunnus alalunga* p. 126,
YELLOWFIN TUNA *Thunnus albacares* p. 116,
BLACKFIN TUNA *Thunnus atlanticus* p. 125,
BIGEYE TUNA *Thunnus obesus* p. 119,
BLUEFIN TUNA *Thunnus thynnus* p. 102,
CHUB MACKEREL *Scomber japonicus* p. 95,
ATLANTIC MACKEREL *Scomber scombrus* p. 94,
SPANISH MACKEREL *Scomberomorus maculatus* p. 95,
CERO *Scomberomorus regalis* p. 97,
KING MACKEREL *Scomberomorus cavalla* p. 88, and
WAHOO *Acanthocybium solandri* p. 131.
Reprinted, by permission, from B. B. Collette and C. E. Nauen, 1983, *Scombrids of the World*.
FAO Fisheries Synopsis No. 125, Vol. 2, 137 pages.

ATLANTIC SAILFISH *Istiophorus albicans* p. 143,
WHITE MARLIN *Tetrapterus albidus* p. 146,
ATLANTIC BLUE MARLIN *Makaira nigricans* p. 148,
LONGBILL SPEARFISH *Tetrapterus pfluegeri* p. 151, and
SWORDFISH *Xiphias gladius* p. 152.
Reprinted, by permission, from I. Nakamura, 1985, *Billfishes of the World*. FAO Fisheries
Synopsis No. 125, Vol. 5, 65 pages.

DOLPHIN *Coryphaena hippurus* p. 128 and
PAMPANO DOLPHIN *Coryphaena equiselis* p. 131.
Reprinted, by permission, from B. J. Palko, G. L. Beardsley and W. J. Richards, 1982, *Synopsis of the Biological Data on Dolphin-fishes*. NOAA Technical Reports and Circulars 443, FAO Fisheries Synopsis No. 130, 28 pages.

TONGUEFISHES *Symphurus urospilus* p. 31.
Reprinted, by permission, from R. W. Topp and F. H. Hoff, Jr., Flatfishes. *Memoirs of the Hourglass Cruises*, Marine Research Laboratory, Florida Department of Natural Resources, 1972.

GULF FLOUNDER *Paralichthys albigutta* p. 32,
SOUTHERN FLOUNDER *Paralichthys lethostigma* p. 32,
BROAD FLOUNDER *Paralichthys squamilentis* p. 32,
PEACOCK (BLUERING) FLOUNDER *Bothus lunatus* p. 32, and
EYED FLOUNDER *Bothus ocellatus* p.33.
Reprinted, by permission, from E. J. Gutherz, *Field Guild to the Flatfishes of the Family Bothidae in the Western North Atlantic*. U.S.D.I. Fish & Wildlife Service, Bureau of Commercial Fisheries, Circular 263, 1967.

Index

Evermann, B. W. 97
Eyed flounder. *See* Flounder

F

False albacore 99
Fat albert 99
Fathom-Master 22
FDA 156
Fenwick 17
Fishes of North Carolina 97
Fish-finder (sonar) 9-11
Fish-Seeker 21
Flathead 118
Flatline 13
Flat-nose 118
Florida shoulder harness 78
Flounder 31-36
   blackback 35
   bluering 32
   broad 32
   eyed 33
   Gulf 32
   peacock 32
   southern 31
   summer 31
   winter 35, 36
Fluke (fish) 32
Fluke (parasite) 137
Fugu 61, 62
Furuno 8

G

Gag. *See* Grouper
Gall bladder 71
Gambierdiscus toxicus 167, 168
Garcia 16
Genetron 8
Geographic north 4
Glass ribbon larva 60
Global Positioning System (GPS) 7

Gloiopotes hygomianus 139
Glycogen 40
Golden tilefish 177
Goode & Bean 109
Gotcha 39, 45
Graham, G. L. 7
Grammatorcynus 134
Grander 149
Grangeville, Louisiana 5
Grass porgy 174
Grass shad 89
Gray grouper. *See* Grouper
Graysby. *See* Grouper
Gray seatrout. *See* Seatrout
Gray snapper 179
Gray triggerfish. *See* Triggerfish, gray
Green fish 51
Green machine 118
Grouper 159-166
   black 166
   coney 163
   dusky perch 166
   gag 165
   gray 165
   graysby 163
   hind(s) 163, 164
   jewfish 163
   Nassau 164
   red 165
   red hind 163
   rock hind 164
   scamp 165
   snowy 166
   speckled hind 164
   Warsaw 165
   wreckfish 164
   yellowfin 166
   yellowmouth 166
Group Repetition Interval (GRI) 5
Guide to Loran C 6
Gulf flounder. *See* Flounder
Gulf kingfish. *See* Kingfish, Gulf

H

Hammerhead shark 86, 87
Hangs and Bottom Obstructions of the Texas/Louisiana Coast, Loran C 7
Hangs and Obstructions to Trawl Fishing, Atlantic Coast of the United States 7
Hardtail 58, 89
Harness 78
Heat exchanger 108
c4-Heptenol 180
Hind(s). *See* Grouper
Hirudinella ventricosa 137
Hogarth, Bill 134
Hogchoker 34
Hopkins lure 39, 45, 96
Horse mackerel. *See* Bluefin tuna
Humminbird 8
Hypoxanthine 93

I

ICW 56
Inosine 93
International Commission for the Conservation of Atlantic Tunas (ICCAT) 102
International Marine 8
Istiophoridae 154

J

Jack crevalle. *See* Crevalle jack
Jellyball 72
Jellyfish (as bait) 71, 72
Jewfish. *See* Grouper
Jerk Jigger 39, 45
Jigmaster 14
Jolthead porgy 174, 175
Jupiter, Florida 5

K

Key to the identification of tunas 104
Kingfish, Gulf 43
Kingfish, southern 43
King mackerel 88-93
King whiting 43
Kirby, Captain 177
Kite 13, 24, 26, 27, 145
K meter, -value 93
Knobbed porgy 174, 175
Kona-type plug 149
Kunnan 17

L

Ladyfish 56, 57
Lane snapper 171
Leech 34, 137
Leger 41
Lemonfish 46
Lemon shark 85
Leptocephalus larva 53, 57, 58, 60
Light stick 153
Lines of position (LOPS) 5
Ling 46
Liquid-crystal display (LCD) 10
Listing of Offshore Oil, Gas, Mineral and Related Structures Including Sub-sea Installations in the Eighth Coast Guard District 7
Little tunny 99, 100
Live-bait well 24
Live bottom 158
Longbill spearfish 151, 152
Longfin snapper 170
Longspine porgy 175
Lookdown 59
Loran 5, 9, 159, 167
Loran C navigation 5, 6, 67
Loran C overlays 181
Loran C Users Handbook 6
Louvar 154
Luvaridae 154

M

Mackerel tree 95
Magnetic anti-backlash 15
Magnetic disturbances 4
Magnetic north 4
Mahi-mahi 128
Mahogany snapper 171
Mako shark 81
Malone, Florida 5
Marazine 140
Marine radio 8
Markell 4
Mass mortality 159, 178
Master transmitting station 5
Maxwell, Walter 84
McGee, J. A. 7
Menhaden oil 92
Mercury 123, 156
Mingo snapper 171
MirrOlure 39
Mishcuppauog 75
Mold 23
Moonfish 59
Moray eel 60
Mr. Twister 35, 39
Mundus, Frank 83
Mustad 160
Mutton snapper 171
Myoglobin 45

N

Nassau grouper. *See* Grouper
National Marine Electronics Association 6
Nautical mile 4
Newell 16, 22
New York ground shark 87
Night snapper 171
NOAA 153, 181
Nok-Out 19

t2,c6-Nonadienal 180
Northstar 8
Notch filters 6

O

Oceanic bonito 101
Office of Naval Research 140
Olive oil 180
Outrigger 13, 18, 19, 118

P

Pale-spotted eel 60
Parasite 34, 137, 138
Peacock flounder. *See* Flounder
Peanut oil 180
Penco Tackle 21
Penn 14, 15, 18, 20, 22
Pennella 139
Permit (jack) 59
Phillips Wiggle Jig 57
Pigfish 176
Piloting 4
Pinfish 75
Pink porgy 173
Planer 20, 21, 135
Pompano 59
Pompano dolphin 131
Porcupinefish 61
Porgy. *See* Scup
Portugese man-of-war 72
Power Squadron 3
Prairie-dog town 178
Protozoan 34
Psychobead 118
Puffer 61-63
Puppy drum 39

Q

Queen triggerfish. *See* Triggerfish, queen

White grunt 175, 176
White marlin 146-148
White pointer 83
White seatrout. *See* Seatrout
White shark 83, 84
Winter flounder. *See* Flounder
Wire line 20
Witch doctor 62
Wreckfish. *See* Grouper
Wristlets 142

X

Xiphiidae 154

Y

Yellowbellies 43
Yellow-eye snapper 170
Yellowfin grouper. *See* Grouper
Yellowfin tuna 116-119
Yellowmouth grouper. *See* Grouper
Yellow snapper 170
Yellowtail amberjack 172
Yellowtail snapper 172

Z

Zombie 61, 62

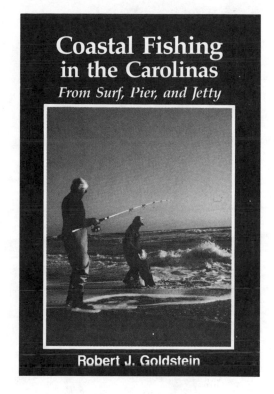

M